Heribert Rau

Mozart

A biographical romance

Heribert Rau

Mozart
A biographical romance

ISBN/EAN: 9783742879073

Manufactured in Europe, USA, Canada, Australia, Japa

Cover: Foto ©Thomas Meinert / pixelio.de

Manufactured and distributed by brebook publishing software
(www.brebook.com)

Heribert Rau

Mozart

MOZART

A BIOGRAPHICAL ROMANCE

FROM THE GERMAN OF

HERIBERT RAU

BY

E. R. SILL

———◄•●•►———

BOSTON:
OLIVER DITSON COMPANY.

NEW YORK:	CHICAGO:	PHILA:	BOSTON:
C. H. Ditson & Co.	Lyon & Healy.	J. E. Ditson & Co.	John C. Haynes & Co.

AUTHOR'S PREFACE.

" Low at his feet with loving heart I bow,
    And bring these leaves to crown the Master's brow."

THESE words of the great Goethe express the feeling which was the principal occasion of this book. It arose out of reverence, out of sincerest enthusiasm for Mozart, that beautiful soul, that exalted master of the Tone-art.

Not that worthy memorials of this noble spirit have not already been given a place in German literature. We have had, not long since, "The Life of Mozart," by Alexander Oulibicheff, and the excellent work of the same title by the Herr Professor, Dr. Jahn. Yet good as these works are, and especially the latter one, they have evidently a wholly different purpose from the present book. Both are, in a literal sense, " musical works," devoted to an analysis of Mozart's creations. They appeal only to those readers who are themselves musicians; their purpose lies, therefore, purely in the sphere of art and science.

The object of the present book is different. Its unpretending aim is, by means of the familiar and confidential style of a romance, to bring closer to the heart of the German people one of its noblest sons; and so to newly awaken a love, veneration, and enthusiasm for Mozart and for his creations. In behalf of those who may desire to go deeper into musical analysis, reference is continually made to the works of Oulibicheff and Jahn.

At the same time, the higher task of the historical romance has never been lost sight of; and pains have been taken to unroll before the reader's eyes a true picture of the history and social circumstances of the epoch which it represents.

Such is the object of this book, and the task it has set before it. Perhaps it will a little touch the conscience of the German people, which so gladly raises monuments to its heroes, when once it has allowed them to perish.

And so may right many turn over these leaves and listen with loving pleasure to what they shall tell them, for,

> " On heights of olden story
> Fair beckoning spirits stand,
> Who hint the golden glory
> Hidden in wonder-land."

And this wonder-land is the kingdom of the Tone-world, and Mozart wore its crown.

HERIBERT RAU.

TRANSLATOR'S NOTICE.

Some liberties, mainly of omission, have been taken with the German original of this book. It was thought that some portions of the work, which would have swelled the volume to an undesirable size, were of exclusively foreign interest, and would not increase its value for American readers. A few changes were made from other consider ations. E. R. S.

CONTENTS

PART I.

THE WONDERFUL CHILD.

PART II.

MOZART'S YOUTH—IN ITALY.

PART III.

ILLUSIONS.

PART IV.

KING AND SLAVE.

PART V.

NOONDAY.

PART VI.

EVENING AND NIGHT.

MOZART:

A BIOGRAPHICAL ROMANCE.

PART I.

THE WONDERFUL CHILD.

CHAPTER I.

A BIRTHDAY—DECEMBER 14, 1759.[1]

"WHAT a sight you are, Wolferl!" cried Frau Vice-Capellmeister Mozart to her little three-years-old son, as with motherly care she brushed the dust from his clothes, and set to rights the rumpled kerchief which let the child's open breast be seen. "How in the world did all this sand get in your hair? Your sister had brushed it so nicely, and to-day is father's birthday!"

"Yes, Mamma, I and Andreas have been turning summersaults!" said Wolfgang earnestly, and looked up with such a frank and winning smile in his beaming blue eyes, that the light folds gathering on the high brow of Frau Mozart quickly disappeared.

"Summersaults!" answered the mother, hardly repressing a smile, as she gave the little rogue a gentle tap on his cheek; "people can't turn summersaults with their Sunday clothes on. Don't you know that these cost the father a great deal of money, and that the money cost him so much hard work?"

"Yes, Mamma," cried the boy; and his great eyes grew moist as his tender heart took in the thought that he had troubled his dear father and mother. "But 'twas only my head got into the dirt; the legs were all the time in the air!"

---

[1] Leopold Mozart was born December 14, 1719. His son, Wolfgang Amadeus, the great musician, was born at Salzburg, January 27, 1756.

" And that's the reason your hair is full of sand, and youɪ clothes all dust from top to bottom."

" Please, then, get the sand out of my hair, and it shan'ɪ get in again.   And"—he added coaxingly, as he leaned his brown head against the full, but still beautiful form of his mother — "you won't be angry with me, will you, Mamachen ?" [1]

" No, indeed, dear child, when you are good," answered Frau Mozart, as she pressed a kiss on the childish lips. Then Wolfgang ran out, and called to his little friend Andreas Schachtner, [2] who had remained in the outer room.

" What shall we do next ?" he asked ; " for we can't turn any more summersaults."

" Then," replied Andreas, " let us play school."

" Good !" Wolfgang responded ; " but let us go into the other room.   It's warmer there.   I'm schoolmaster, and you shall go to school to me.   You take the little bench, and I'll take the table and the piece of chalk."

Andreas obeyed.   But when he was starting to go into the other room, Wolfgang seized him fast by the arm, and cried :

" That's not the way !   Put yourself behind me !   So— and now we must march first all around the room, while I sing the music."

Then the little fellow, with sparkling eyes, sang, in his childish tones, a march that he had learned, while the four little shoes stamped on the floor in time to the tune, till the dust flew about the room in clouds. [3]

Now it happened that his mother was at this moment busy in the kitchen, where Nannerl, his seven-years-old sister, was helping her ; for this was the father's birthday, and an exception must be made in their usually strict and economical housekeeping.   Already the roast upon the spit was filling the house with its savory fragrance, and a notable loaf of cake was in the oven, browning its rich crust into perfection.

While these luxurious preparations were going on, the two youngsters had established themselves in the warm room. Andreas sat on the floor, with a footstool placed over his outstretched legs, on which his slate lay.   But Wolfgang, in the capacity of schoolmaster, had applied the chalk to floor,

---

[1] The terminations *chen, erl,* etc., are diminutive.   The Germans use the diminutive as a sort of vocal caress.
[2] Afterward a good musician, and a poet.
[3] Historical.—Nissen, p. 17.   Jahn, Part I., p. 29.

walls, and furniture, covering them with white scribblings, apparently the alphabet of some unknown tongue which the elf had learned from the fairies. In his zeal he was just on the point of using the old leather-covered sofa as a basis for his mystic hieroglyphics, when his sister, with the dinner-things on her arm, entered the room. But knives, and forks, and linen were like to have fallen from her hands at her first glance. She stood a second as if dumbfounded, and then cried—

"What in the world have you been about, Wolfgang?"

Her brother looked at her in surprise, and asked in perfect innocence—

"Why, what is it, Nannerl?"

"The chalk, child!"

"I'm the schoolmaster," answered the urchin, with comical dignity; "and so I must set copies, and cipher."

"But not on the floor and the walls!" cried his sister in dismay. "Mamma and I sat up half the night to make everything neat and beautiful, and now—"

"Then I'll wipe it all out," said Wolfgang; but his sister threw the whole table furniture in a heap on the sofa, and sprang forward, for the little schoolmaster was just about to wipe off the chairs with the elbow of his Sunday jacket. Fortunately Nannerl anticipated the motion, and shoved him aside, while with her apron and a sponge she destroyed the works of the small philosopher.

Meanwhile Wolfgang, who now for the first time began to reflect on what he had done, stood ashamed, and looked at his sister in silence. It was an additional grief to him that he had troubled Nannerl, and put her to double labor.

When at last she had finished with her cleansing operations he went softly up to her, pulled at her dress, and asked, as he was wont to do at least twenty times in the day—

"Nannerl, do you love me?"

But his sister was really angry, and said:

"No, when you do such naughty things, I don't love you!"

This was too much for the tender little heart. Turning around quickly, that the tears which swam in his eyes might not be seen, he sat down in a corner of the room, and looked in mournful silence straight before him. At that moment the roof of clouds, which till then had darkened the wintry sky, was rent asunder. A sunbeam fell into the little room, and as it struck the cage of a golden-winged canary hanging before the window, the bird turned his little head up in delight, hopped a few times from one perch to the other, and then began to warble and trill a song that was bright and joyous as the blue sky.

But what is this? Why brightens up little Wolfgang's face at once so wondrously? His eyes are beaming, and his cheeks grow ruddy; a rapt and passionate expression, far beyond his years, gives to the childish face a strange—one might almost say, an unearthly—look.

Wolfgang—the little three-years-old Wolfgang—is now all ear. He listens to the ringing trills of his feathered darling, and forgotten is his small trouble, forgotten are sister and playmate; to him the world contains but one existence, and that a song.

It is a child, who is listening here to those sweet tones; but the soul of this child is so wondrously organized, that music touches every fibre of nerve and brain with thrills of ecstasy, till his soul itself seems to throb on in musical pulsation,—the shadowy, vanishing presage of an immortal harmony, which one day will ring throughout the world.

Little Wolfgang understands not what music is; only, wherever and however it strikes his ear, he is thrilled as by electric waves. He must sing himself a march, as he bears his playthings to another room; he is ravished with delight, if his canary answers a sudden sunbeam with a song.

The bird had long since ceased his singing; the little playmate, Andreas, had slipped away home; but Wolfgang still sits motionless in his corner, seeing and hearing nothing about him; waking-dreams are passing across his mind. Fancies like fairy-tales set to music are weaving within him; like the stories which the mother tells him, before bed-time, in the twilight. He dreams that he is a king; and imagination builds him strange inhabitants for his realm—grotesque creatures, cities and castles by mountain lakes, to which he gives fantastic names. On his head a crown sits, and from it shines a splendid light, far out into the distance of the world.

Long dreams the boy in this manner,—and long would he have gone on dreaming, had not a kiss startled him awake. He looks up in astonishment. It is his sister, bending down her dear affectionate face above him. Swiftly his little arms clasp tight about her neck, and his first question is, "Do you love me, Nannerl?"

"Indeed I do!" she answers heartily, as they hold each other fast in their arms.

It was a pretty group; but the little restless creature, so sensitively organized to catch every impression from without, had already noticed something else besides his sister's caress. It was comical to see the small head lift itself suddenly up from her embrace, and the wide-open nostrils testify that Wolfgang had discovered, through the sense of smell, the gastronomic preparations of his mother. His face beamed, and not with more triumphant joy did the sea-worn mariners of Columbus raise the cry of "Land-ho!" than the little Mozart now cried out, "There's the dinner!"

"Yes," said his sister, "and a birthday dinner, too; for you know to-day Papa is forty years old." Then the two went racing into the other room, where an appetizing repast was smoking on the table, and the father and mother already awaited them.

The Vice-Capellmeister was a fine-looking man, not of great size, but well proportioned. His dress was exceedingly plain— one might almost call it poor; yet was there a stateliness in his presence, which was increased by the noble earnestness of his fine face, with its small, delicately cut mouth, thoughtful eyes, and the high full brow, which at once betrayed the musician. The genuine stamp of a true man was not to be mistaken in him. His wife, too, bore the traces of great beauty, and prided herself a good deal, still, on the fact that they had been formerly reputed to be the handsomest pair ever married in Salzburg. It is true that sorrows, many and severe, had ploughed furrows in both their faces, but love at least, founded as it was on mutual respect, had in no wise yielded to their assaults. On the contrary, it had been doubly tempered and strengthened in the fire of fate, growing ever more and more heartfelt through the many anxious seasons which they had battled through together.

Therefore, in the festivities of this birthday, quietly and simply as it was celebrated, there was no pretence. They sprang out of the heart, and they went to the heart as well. Herr Leopold Mozart was wont to say that these little family-feasts were as necessary to the household life as the Sundays and holidays are to the public life, giving it color, light, and warmth.

With evident emotion, therefore, the usually cold and practical man received the good wishes of his household.

Before the dinner Wolfgang was mounted on a footstool, where he recited a little poem in honor of his father. The strange *oldness* in the child's face, and his mature appreciation of what he was saying, might have moved his parents' hearts with a painful anxiety, had it not been accompanied by the boy's childlike and roguish utterance.

When the poem had been recited, he stood there on the stool, reached his little arms around his father's neck, and said slowly, "Papachen, I love you so very, very much! And do you know? after God, next comes my Papa!" [1]

The father embraced him, but could answer nothing, except, "Keep both in your heart, and all will go well with you!"

At this moment two of the Court-musicians, Adlgasser and Lipp, both good friends of Father Mozart, entered the room. They had been bidden to dinner, and since it was not an ordinary thing for the Mozart family to entertain guests, their presence was so much the greater addition to the common cheerfulness. They jested, and told stories, and talked of this thing and that, and at last came upon the subject of their common poverty. It was probably no laughing matter for any one of them, but they treated it so, and discussed the slender incomes which music yielded them, as though it were the most comical of all occurrences.

"Yes," said Adlgasser, "we all have to pinch; but Father Mozart has at least the comfort of having done something extraordinary, nevertheless."

"Something extraordinary?" returned the Capellmeister. "I'm sure I didn't know of it."

"Oh, oh, how modest!" cried the other. "Isn't it anything, then, to gain fame and honor?"

"And how have I deserved that?" asked Leopold Mozart, brimming his friend's glass with red wine. "Do you mean the violin lessons?"

"No!" replied Adlgasser. "Those have brought you honor, indeed; but it is the 'School for the Violin,' I meant, which has attracted so much notice." [2]

"And has already been translated into French and Dutch," added Lipp.

"Well," returned Mozart, rubbing his hands and looking pleased, "I confess the result of that undertaking has given

---

[1] The child's own words.—Nissen and Jahn.
[2] Historical.—Jahn and Marpurg.

me a great deal of pleasure. I give thanks to my Maker
every day right heartily that He has given me so much taste
for music. And as for my violin, that stands first with me,
after wife and children. The soul of music, the celestial
comforter, speaks itself best and purest from the tone of a
solo instrument; for this tone, disdaining all admixture with
alien sounds, is the serenest expression of the spirit. Yes,
my friends! when I am happy, then it is the violin that best
rings out my joy: if I would pray from my innermost heart,
it is in the bell-tones of the violin that the prayer must be
expressed; if sadness weighs me down to the earth, it is the
violin that weeps with me, or comforts me like an angel sent
from God. Is not music, indeed, the mystical language of
God, moving the heart of every mortal, who will but receive
its message, with wondrous might? Is it not the chosen
language, in which the eternal Divine Spirit yearns out of
nature toward us all—when the spring-time rejoices, or the
storm howls, when the lark trills his song, or the raging
ocean thunders out its sublime harmonies?"

"Yes, yes," cried Adlgasser with flashing eyes; "there
lies a wondrous magic in it. Orpheus' lyre opened the gates
of the nether world:—what a deep significance lurks in that
charming Grecian story!"

"There lies hidden in it," said Lipp, "this exalted and
blessed truth—that music opens to men an undiscovered
realm, a world which has nothing in common with the outer
world of sense."

"Yea!" cried Adlgasser, "a world of noblest desire, of
holiest love, of purest pain, of divinest passion."

"Let us, then, empty one glass to the honor of *Musica*, the
ravishing goddess!" broke in Father Mozart. "Happy is he
to whom God has given a taste and susceptibility for her
charms. Though he be a poor devil, as we all are, yet there
are hours in which, through the grace of this divine one, he
dreams himself a Crœsus and a king. So, *vivat Musica!*"
and the glasses clinked, and a joyous "*Vivat!*" rang out, in
which little Wolfgang joined with the rest, although he did
not comprehend what the conversation had been about, and
the good things of the dinner had claimed his undivided
attention. But the gaze of his father rested with contentment and tenderness on him and his sister.

"You two," he said, almost sadly, "are all that th Lord
has left me of seven. I wonder whether any little drop

of musical taste will overflow upon you, from my own life?"

"Wherefore not?" responded the mother. "Nannerl has a great fancy for it already. Let it be tested at once. You long ago promised to commence piano-lessons with her."

"Ah yes, Papachen," begged the child; "let me at last learn to play. I am seven years old now, and I promise to try very hard."

"Good, then!" said the father. "You shall all see that I am grateful for the love you have brought me to-day, for I will commence Nannerl's lessons this very night."

"And me, too?" cried Wolfgang. "Mayn't I learn music too?"

They all laughed, and the father said: "You, little man, must grow some inches before you will be able to reach the keys. But would you really become a musician?"

"Yes!" cried the little one, "and I can play some now!"

"Indeed you can," said the mother—"summersaults with Andreas!"

"No," cried Wolfgang, with heat, for his sensitive pride was touched, "I played a march for him this morning!"

A great laugh followed this childish declaration, as the company rose from the table, and separated—the musicians to go into the city till evening, Nannerl and her mother to pursue their household avocations, while the little Mozart betook himself to his favorite high seat by the window, and watched the clouds with his great sad eyes, till the clattering dishes set the canary to singing its song, which wound him in a woof of childish dreams.

It was a dark December day, and night already had closed about the earth when the Mozart family gathered at the tea-table. The wind made its weird music without, but a warm fire burned in the grate, around which the chairs were drawn after tea, and they sat in contented silence in the glow of the fire, and listened to the wind in the chimney, fluttering as if invisible wings were descending it, and then roaring and rumbling like the bass-notes of a huge-throated organ-pipe. Nannerl gazed into the red coals, and built crumbling castles there, splendid as transitory, and seemed to see her future in the shifting tracery of the flame. The old people watched instead the flitting shadows cast upon the walls, and in those fading and glimmering cartoons they saw only pictures of the past. But little Wolfgang's quiet blue eyes took in the whole scene—the shine and the shadows, the old hearts and the young—and melted it all in love unto a soft, unspoken, unspeakable music, deep down in his childish soul.

When the candles were brought in, Father Mozart, true to his promise, opened the piano and called Nannerl to take her first lesson.

The little girl showed, from the beginning, a patient deter· mination, and a brightness of apprehension, which promised well for her progress. Wolfgang planted himself, with his hands behind his back, close at the side of his sister, still as a statue, watching every motion of her fingers. He was a charming sight, as he stood there, with the light of the candles from the piano falling on his brown hair and beautiful elfin figure. The open breast, only half concealed by the white folds of the kerchief, the tender face, with its delicate features, lighting up more and more as the lesson went on, formed a lovely little figure, on which the mother's eyes hung in still ravishment.

In this way an hour passed by, in which the boy, usually so restless and bent on childish play, had not moved for an instant from his place. New ideas were crowding upon the sensitive brain. Many a time had he heard his father bring finest music from those glistening keys, without its calling his attention from his sport; but now those first gropings of his sister among them fastened him with magical power. The father's skilful playing had lain too far beyond the boy's comprehension; the intricate harmonies had gone sweeping high over his head. But now for the first time the thought flashed through him, " Thou, too, canst do this !"

His eyes, therefore, never left Nannerl's fingers, as they crept hesitatingly among the white and the black keys, his ear easily grasping the simple relations of the different tones; and when his father had finished the lesson, and Nannerl left the piano, he slipped softly into her place, and began with his little hands to seek out thirds.[1] When he found the notes which harmonized, how his face beamed with rapture ! Little did he know what significance of prophecy lay in those first touches upon the " cold keys;" it was the first tread of the royal child over the boundary to take possession of his k'ng-lom.

Father Mozart had lit his pipe and taken up the news

---

[1] Historical.—Oulibicheff, Part I., p. 7; Nissen, p. 15

paper, and at first gave no heed to these earliest experiments of his little son. By and by his wife plucked him by the sleeve, and pointed at Wolfgang: slowly he let the newspaper sink at his side, and then the pipe also. More and more joyful grew his look, greater and greater was the astonishment gathering in his face; but he could scarcely trust his ears and eyes when Wolfgang, the little three-years-old creature, repeated faultlessly with his bits of fingers the simple exercise which had been given to his sister. The newspaper now lay on the floor; the pipe had gone out; the tall smoking-cap, which his left hand had unconsciously pushed back from his forehead in his amazement, hung now on the back of his venerable head, while his eyes were brimmed full of happy tears. At last he found motion and speech. Hastening to the piano, he caught up his little son stormily, and, with an expression of indescribable delight, cried out—

"Wolferl! little Star-beam! Yes, you too will be a musician!"

Father and mother both kissed the wondering child, and, wiping the tears from his eyes, Father Mozart said, slowly and solemnly, looking upward, "Lord, I thank Thee for this gift! I think that Thy goodness has granted to me a wondrous blossom, and in gratitude I would devote my whole life and being to Thy service, forever!"

Then he took the child, and, as he was wont to do every evening before he went to rest, placed him on a footstool before him, folded his small hands together, and repeated before him his simple evening prayer. But this time the father's voice trembled, as with the deepest feeling he said these words:

"Dear Heavenly Father, I thank Thee for Thy goodness—"

And the little Wolfgang repeated after him with his childish voice:

"Dear Heavenly Father, I thank thee for Thy goodness:"
"Thou hast bestowed upon me a precious gift"—
"Thou hast bestowed upon me a precious gift:"
"Grant me Thy blessing, that I may use it aright"—
"Grant me Thy blessing, that I may use it aright:"
"For Thy glory, and for my best good"—
"For Thy glory, and for my best good:"
"Amen!"
"Amen!"

But the last words were repeated slowly and wearily, for sleep began to claim its rights over the boy, and the mother had scarcely made the little form ready for bed, when he was fast asleep.

And now fluttered a flock of white-winged dreams about his soul, hovering nearer and nearer, till—he seemed to be standing in a summer meadow. Thousands of blossoms clustered about his feet, and nestled by the side of mossy stones, and printed their starry shadows on other and smaller blossoms; the sky was swept pure by the round white clouds, and out of its blue depths the sun streamed warm and clear. How the child's heart leaped to hear the singing of the birds, and the humming of the bees! And now he sprang forward to pluck a pearl-white lily,—but lo! as soon as he touched the flower, it began to breathe forth beautiful tones; another and another he touched, and always they began to sing the loveliest melodies, that mingled with each other in rare sweet music, which swelled and swelled, deeper and louder, and the flowers grew with it in his hands, higher and higher, till the sound was the tumbling billows of the sea, and the blossoms had become stars. There in the sky they were burning and flashing,—but now the heavens were no longer blue and bright, but shadowy sombre. Then the child wept for grief; but as the tears rolled down his cheeks, the beautiful tones swept over him again, and the stars had become mightiest harmonies, whose rushing majesty bore him away with it, up and up, till there was no longer any earth, nor anything but the still rapture of his own infantile, fathomless soul.

CHAPTER II.

PROPHETIC INK-BLOTS.

THE winter was over; spring had taken away the shroud of snow, replacing it with her green and blossom-broidered robe, and greeted the resurrection of the living earth with jubilant bird-songs. Summer was already changing the green of the harvest-fields into gold. Bees were contentedly humming among the flowers, and the afternoon sunbeams were bright and still over all the land. Father Mozart was walking home from Hellebrunn to Salzburg, and that sedate, courtly man accompanying him was Count Herberstein, his friend. The conversation had turned upon the family of the Vice-Capellmeister, who had found his favorite topic in expatiating on the marvellous performances of his little Wolfgang, who was now four years old.

"You should see him," cried the father, with an enthusiasm very different from his usual steady manner, "when he sits at the piano on his little stool, scarce able to reach the keys, and practises his exercises! Would you believe it, that the child already plays quite skilfully?"

"Impossible!"

"It is even so," continued Mozart, "and he invariably remembers all the most brilliant airs which he hears.[1] It takes him scarcely a half-hour to learn a whole minuet; and for longer pieces, an hour is all that is necessary."

"And the child really plays them afterward?"

"Yes, with perfect accuracy, and a firm confident touch.[2] He even has taken a fancy for composing, and if I did not think it best to hold him back, rather than push him, I should already be teaching him the rules for musical composition."

"But, my dear friend," cried the count, standing still in his astonishment, "that's a miracle! The child must be bewitched. Won't you take me home with you? I must set eyes on this new marvel."

"With the greatest pleasure," replied the Vice-Capellmeister; and as soon as they reached Salzburg, the two hastened toward his humble dwelling.

While they had been on the road from Hellebrunn, a curious scene had been preparing for them at the Mozart house.

The afternoon sun laid its level beams of gold into the clean and tidy room, where the little Wolfgang had seated himself at his father's writing-table. His mother and sister were busy in the next room, and all was quiet and peaceful about him; only the trill of the canary was now and then to be heard, as he sang good-night to the setting sun.

Was it only the glow of the sunbeams, or was it an inward exaltation which made the boy's face so radiant? Kneeling on a high stool, with one elbow propped on his father's desk,

[1] Historica.—Nissen, p. 15.   [2] Historical.—Oulibicheff, Part I., p. 8.

and his little chin upon his hand, he gazes straight before him, as if in deepest thought. It must be a daring idea which is engaging the small creature's brain, for his deep blue eyes, now flashing out, and then drawing back into themselves, give evidence of an intense inner activity. At the same time the lips softly move, and from time to time the murmuring childish voice seems to express a search after vanishing melodies, that tempt and elude the longing imagination of the boy.

All at once his whole countenance lights up like an electric flash. Swiftly he seizes a sheet of paper that lies near him, grasps a pen, plunges it into the ink, and commences to write.

But, O luckless elf! in his sacred fury he had thrust the pen-point down against the bottom of the inkstand, and at the third note a mighty blot suddenly descends upon the paper, and drowns the surrounding tract in a dismal flood.

Little did the boy mind this. Without letting himself be delayed, he wipes the blot off with the palm of his hand, streaking the ink away from it in a curve, like a dingy comet. Still his ideas are not at all disturbed. Note after note soon covers the paper; and as the boy's zeal increases, blot after blot accompanies them, all of which, like their first-born brother, are wiped out with the already ink-soaked palm, till one can imagine what a looking sheet was there. It could very well represent, figuratively, the Black Sea, with all its bays and promontories.

And still the little composer dashes down the notes, weeping bitterly now with anger at the blots, but in no wise letting himself be. disturbed. The salty drops mingle with the inky ones, and both together are wiped out with the inexorable little dingy palm; and still the notes follow each other thicker and faster, half of them next to illegible, but yet written, and—the door opens, and in walks the Vice-Capellmeister, and with him Count Herberstein.

The small creature hears them not; he hums half aloud a melody; he goes on writing—crossing out—writing again—makes new blots—wipes them out—writes again—and now, a cry of exultation, as he flings the pen out of his inky fingers.

Then he hears a wondering voice:

"What in the name of Heaven are you doing, Wolferl?'
Wolfgang looked around, and seeing his father standing

.here with a pleasant-faced stranger, he spreads his soaked
fingers wide apart, and cries gleefully—

"O Papa! A piano sonata; the first part is already done!"

Father Mozart and the count looked at each other with a
smile, and Mozart called out, jestingly—

"Let us see it; it must be something fine!"

But the youngster held back the sheet, and cried warmly—

"No, no! 'tisn't ready yet!" But at his father's bidding he delivered it up reluctantly, and then the two old
musicians laughed till their sides ached; for the sonata, with
its variegated embellishments of splashes, and blots, and
spider-tracks, was a wonderful sight to see.

But what is this? Why looks' the father with sudden surprise at the notes, and why do his eyes fill slowly with tears
of wondering pleasure?

"Look you here! Only look, dear count!" he cries, holding the paper trembling in his hand; "do you see how it is
all written correctly, and according to rule? Only, one could
never play it; it is so intricate and difficult."

"But it's a sonata, Papachen!" cried Wolfgang; "one
must practise it first, of course; but this is the way it should
go." And he sprang to the piano and commenced to play.
The harder parts he could not bring out, but the small and
stumbling fingers gave enough of it to show to his audience,
which now was increased by his mother and sister, what was
his idea.

The piece was written correctly, and arranged with all
the parts.[1]

They all stood speechless for astonishment, till Father
Mozart, catching the child to his breast, and kissing him,
cried: "Wolfgang! you will become a great man!"

And the count added, "Yes, and all Germany shall one
day be proud of you, dear child!" Then turning to the
father, he said, with a smile, "Who now is the richer, you or
the king?"

And Father Mozart answered, with beaming eyes, "I would
not give this hour for all the kingdoms of the earth!"

---

[1] Historical.—Nissen, p. 18; Oulibicheff and Jahn.

CHAPTER III.

THE LITTLE VIRTUOSO.

THE father's prophecy appeared to commence its fulfil ment with wonderful speed. Wolfgang made extraor-dinary progress, and in his fifth year would constantly com-pose little pieces for his father, many of which have been preserved and may be examined by whosoever will.[1]

The father had the clearness of sight to see at once that he had no common powers to direct in the boy, and soon gave up all other employment for the education of his son. Not alone in music did he show a strange quickness and power; in all his studies, and particularly in mathematics, which has such mysterious connections with music, he showed marvel-lous ability. No one knew what to think of the child. He wandered about among the common persons who surrounded him, like a being of another race. No matter what was taught him, his spirit seemed to have had a previous intima-tion of it—some dim remembrances which needed only to be recalled by least hints and suggestions. Looking deep down into the wise childish eyes, and watching the beautiful mouth, in whose expression all sweet experiences seemed already to have clustered, one could not but feel that this strange life had been lived before, in some purer country, where wisdom was a natural birthright, and music was the common speech of souls.

Two years passed swiftly by, and Wolfgang was six years old, and now the great world was opening to the boy. In company with his father, he left Salzburg, and started upon a long course of travel.

To genius,—at least when it is as yet untarnished by the common uses of the world—when its wings, still moist with the dew of the dawn, are mighty to soar,—to young genius the finite is infinite. The eye takes in the distance, the height, the depth, but not the boundaries and limitations. The blue sky and the blue ocean seem alike fathomless; the

---

[1] *Vide* Nissen, p. 14.

momentary woe appears an eternity, and joy and beauty are immortal.

Salzburg had been a world to the little Mozart; its streets had been to him endless vistas, reaching—he knew not whence nor whither; save that here was home—the centre, and there was the world, and life—the circumference. If already the little experiences and sight of the small city had become transmuted into music in the child's dreaming heart, what now did mountains, forests, rivers, multitudes of living men, and the unbounded sea, give to him? Every new landscape, each scene that unrolled its fresh pictures before the childish eyes, as they journeyed from day to day, had for his heart a message. Out of them all a voice seemed to call to him for expression. Nature and Life—the two dumb, enchanted genii—seemed to stretch out imploring arms to him, and beg for the voice of his music to express their infinite sorrow, their immortal and triumphant joy.

Everywhere they went, the fame of the little Mozart preceded them. At every court he must show his marvellous skill. But it was not at court that the boy most delighted to prove his power. Here and there in quiet places, in some solitary chapel, it was his greatest pleasure to fill the silence with fantastic melodies, or with joyous strains.

His first experience of a large organ was in the monastery of a little town on the bank of the Danube. All day long they had been sailing down that majestic river, past crumbling ruins, frowning castles, cloisters hidden away among the crags, towering cliffs, quiet villages nestled in sunny valleys, and here and there a deep gorge that opened back from the gliding river, its hollow distance blue with fathomless shadow, and its loneliness and stillness awing the boy's heart like some dim and vast cathedral.

The company of monks with whom they had been travelling that day, were at supper in the refectory of the cloister, when Father Mozart took Wolfgang into the chapel to see the organ. The boy had been since morning more than commonly reserved and thoughtful; but now, as he gazed with something of awe upon the great instrument, looming up in the shadows of the empty church, he seemed to come out of his moodiness, and become his bright and cheery self. His face was lit up with serene satisfaction, and yet every motion and attitude of the little figure which stood gazing up at the organ, expressed a wondering reverence. What tones must even now be slumbering in those mighty pipes! Tones, which, if once awakened, could give utterance to all that voiceless beauty which the day's scenes had showed him— Life and Death; Present and Past; the peaceful river, and the deserted ruin; the sunshine unfailing, and the unfailing shadow at its side.

"Father," said the boy, "explain to me those pedals at the organ's feet, and let me play!"

Well-pleased, the father complied. Then Wolfgang pushed aside the stool, and when Father Mozart had filled the great bellows, the elfin organist stood upon the pedals, and trod them as though he had never needed to have their management explained.[1]

How the deep tones woke the sombre stillness of the old church! The organ seemed some great uncouth creature, roaring for very joy at the caresses of the marvellous child.

The monks, eating their supper in the refectory, heard the tones, and dropped knife and fork in astonishment. The organist of the brotherhood was among them; but never had he played with such power and freedom. They listened and listened: some grew pale; others crossed themselves; till the Prior rose up, summoned all his courage, and hastened into the chapel. The others followed, but when they looked up into the organ-loft, lo! there was no sign of any organist to be seen, though the deep tones still massed themselves in new harmonies, and made the stone arches thrill with their power.

"It is the Devil himself," cried the last one of the monks, drawing closer to his companions, and giving a scared look over his shoulder into the darkness of the aisle.

"It is a miracle!" said others. But when the boldest of their number mounted the stairs to the organ front, they stood as if petrified with amazement.

There stood the tiny figure, treading from pedal to pedal, and at the same time clutching the keys above with his little hands, gathering handfuls of those wonderful chords as if they were violets, and flinging them out into the solemn gloom behind him. He heard nothing, saw nothing, besides; his eyes beamed like stars, and his whole face lightened with impassioned joy. Louder and fuller rose the harmonies, and

[1] Historical.—Nissen, pp. 22–37; Jahn, Part I., p. 35.

streamed forth in swelling billows, till at last they seemed to reach a sunny shore, on which they broke; and then a whispering ripple of faintest melody lingered a moment in the air like the last murmur of a wind-harp, and all was still.

CHAPTER IV.

THE COURT OF VIENNA.

THE first triumph of the little Mozart, in a worldly sense, was at Vienna. Here he played before the Archduke Joseph, and created at once quite an excitement among the nobility. It was one round of invitations to great dinners and parties, at which the small virtuoso was the crowning feature. Soon came an invitation to play before the Empress Maria Theresa and her court.

It was with mingled feelings of pride, anxiety, and excitement that Father Mozart and the two children waited in the anteroom, till they should be bidden to the presence of the great empress.

At last the door was thrown open. It was a splendid apartment into which they entered—an octagon, of whose eight sides, four were covered with immense gold-frame Venetian mirrors. Two of the others showed great windows, half-covered with drooping folds of heavy silk; while the remaining two sides led through folding-doors to the ante-chamber and the inner rooms. A large chandelier of massive silver, laid with gold, whose eight arms were carved in curious intricacies of design, hung from the frescoed ceiling by a heavy chain of the same metal. The walls were covered with tapestry of white silk, on which bunches of many-colored flowers were embroidered, and the furniture was upholstered with the same rich material, and its carven wood-work inlaid throughout with gold. The inlaid floor was smooth and shining as glare ice, and answered the bright colors of the frescoes above by the reflection from silk and gold below. Two richly ornamented Augsburg pianos completed the splendor of the apartment; which was imposing in its simple richness, at the same time that it breathed an air of cheerful goodness of heart.

In the centre of this room sat Maria Theresa, on a raised seat, over which glittered a golden crown. Around her were grouped the princes and ladies of her court, while her consort, Francis I., leaned upon one of the instruments.

It was a group which might well attract and delight the eye. For the empress, though at this time forty-five years old, and of late grown quite stout, was still exceedingly handsome. The slightly curved nose, the delicately chiselled, lips, the large blue eyes beneath the fearless brows and lofty forehead, gave her face an expression of nobleness and quiet dignity; while the glance, and a certain look about the mouth, betrayed the tenderness and goodness of her character.

One must be attracted to her involuntarily, and it was easy now for the Vice-Capellmeister to understand how Maria Theresa's beauty and loveliness could bewitch and captivate the heart of Hungary.

To complete this charming group, several of the young archdukes and duchesses were clustered about their mother, among whom a child of seven years, with a face like an angel, laid her curly head against the arm of the empress. This was Marie Antoinette, afterwards the unhappy Queen of France. Who could have dreamed that the sweet darling, standing there in all the witching grace of innocent childhood, would, after so few summers, breathe out her life on the scaffold? God be praised for His mercy in veiling the future from mortal eyes!

The background of this interesting picture was made up of figures who would have been comical in any eyes but their own. They were the antiquated court-dames, with their stiff, proud faces and bejewelled robes, striving to make up in starch and glitter what they lacked in grace; and the ancient cavaliers, with mighty perukes adorning their gray heads, and their clothes so resplendent with inflexible gilt and stiffness, that they could with difficulty move at all.

Little Wolfgang, in the mean time, saw nothing of all this on entering, except the kind eyes of the empress resting upon him, and the curly head of Marie Antoinette, which pleased him more than any sight he had ever yet seen. He had small time to consider this, for Francis I. had already advanced to meet him, and led him to the empress, who stretched out both hands to him in a motherly way, with the words—

"So this is the little pianist of whom we have heard so many stories?"

"Yes, your Majesty!" answered Wolfgang, with as complete an absence of hesitation or embarrassment as if he were addressing his own mother. "I am little, that is true; but I can play on the piano, nevertheless, as I would gladly prove to you, lady Empress!"

At these unconstrained words of the child, a panic terror smote the whole imperial train, like an electric shock; and only the gigantic coiffures of the court-dames and the heavy perukes of the cavaliers prevented their most noble hair from standing straight up on end, at this outrageous invasion of court etiquette.

But the emperor and empress laughed good-humoredly; and the latter, who took an evident delight in the frank nature of the boy, asked—

"Are you, then, so confident of your powers? Behind us here are many gentlemen who understand music, and they will be sure to sharply criticise you."

At these words of the empress, Wolfgang turned to one side, and gazed at the group of courtiers with his great wise eyes; then he shook his head with a contemptuous look, and said—

"H'm! None of those people seem to me to know anything of music!"

"Why so?" asked Maria Theresa.

"I see it in their looks: they are a great deal too stiff!"

At this the empress could not but laugh aloud; and the whole court circle, little as they felt themselves flattered, felt obliged to laugh also, though the sweet-and-sour look on many of their high-mightiness' faces showed that the laughter was by no means hearty.

But Maria Theresa stroked the boy's cheeks, and, turning to her husband with that winning gentleness which she always showed in the circle of her family, said—

"Franzerl, here is a sprite who bids fair to make a statesman, if not a courtier. He has sharp eyes, at least!"

"And is certainly not lacking in courage," answered the emperor, laughing.

"Then let us keep him here!" broke in the little Marie Antoinette, lifting her curly head, and looking up with bright eyes into her mother's face; "I like him, too!"

" That were not so bad a plan," replied the mother. " You would all at least have a good example in him, to make you practise on the piano."

" Does he play so well, then ?"

" Finely, every one says."

" Then shall he let us hear him now ?"

Wolfgang's small face was in a glow with the strange feelings which these words of the charming little archduchess awakened. His pride was aroused, and, it may be, the presage of another and a deeper emotion also, which hereafter would so often touch his tender heart. Quickly he turned to the instrument, determined to do his best, that the little imperial lady might see he had not been too highly praised. But the emperor stopped him with the words—

" Hold, little man ! If you do not deem those lords and dames your equals in the art, nor think them capable of criticising your playing, who then shall we have for judge of it ?"

The boy bethought himself a moment—

" Is not Herr Wagenseil[1] here ?" cried he, so loud that all could hear him. " He must come, for he understands it !'

The emperor, more and more delighted with the boy's *naïveté,* gave a sign that Wagenseil should be summoned. Meanwhile Wolfgang had pulled his sister forward, and presented her to the empress without any ceremony, only saying—

" This is Nannerl, my sister, who plays, as well as I !"

Maria Theresa was greatly amused at this straightforward introduction. Beckoning to Father Mozart, she conversed with him for some time in a friendly manner concerning the two children and their wonderful gift.

In the mean time the archduchesses had approached Nannerl, and Marie Antoinette plied Wolfgang with friendly questions, till his cheeks were all on fire again.

Soon the empress took notice of this conversation, and when Wolfgang, greatly to her delight, praised his sister's playing, without the least shade of envy, she asked him—

" Do you, then, love Nannerl so much ?"

" Yes, indeed," cried the boy, looking at the empress with beaming eyes, and taking her two outstretched

---

[1] An eminent composer of that time, and music-teacher to the empress.

hands.   " And I love you also, for you please me ever so
much!" [1]

" Most flattering!" said the empress pleasantly.   " And
how will you prove that to me?"

" With a kiss!" cried the boy; and before the court-dames
had time to think of fainting away at this unheard-of boldness, and while the prim gentlemen knew not whether to
draw their swords or sink into the floor, little Wolfgang had
sprung into the empress's lap, clasped his small arms about
her neck, and given her a hearty kiss. [2]

Maria Theresa, the emperor, and the older archduchesses
laughed at this exploit, till they had to wipe the tears out of
their eyes; and when the rest of the company heard this,
they recovered from their righteous indignation as fast as
possible, and joined in the merriment.

Meantime Wagenseil had made his appearance, and, quick
as a flash, Wolfgang was seated at the piano.   Then, turning
to the empress's *maestro*, he said—

" I'm right glad you have come, Herr Wagenseil.   I'm
going to play a concerto of yours, and you must turn over
the leaves for me." [3]

Now the small fingers commenced to fly over the keys
with a swiftness and strength which astonished everybody.
As he played on and on, the silence in the room became
more and more profound, till one could hear the heaving of
a sigh.

The boy's playing took them by storm, especially when he
went on improvising, taking the melody of Wagenseil's concerto as a theme.   When he had finished, every voice cried,
" Bravo! bravo!" and endless applause greeted him; but
what he most cared for was the light clapping of Marie
Antoinette's small palms, and her bright face, which seemed
to give him a thousand thanks in its delighted expression.

Nannerl's playing also pleased them; but her brother's
age, as well as his extraordinary apprehension and execution,
threw her performance comparatively into the shade.

The empress congratulated Father Mozart on his good fortune in having two such children.   " May they," said she,
" find every happiness in life.   The dear God has bestowed
upon you a great gift, but with it He lays upon you heavy

[1] The boy's own language.—Oulibicheff, Part I., p. 12.
Historical.—Nissen, p. 24.   [3] His own words.—Jahn, Part I., p. 38.

responsibilities; for it were a crime not to complete by edu
cation what Nature has already so wondrously begun."

"Your Majesty," answered Mozart, with unaffected humility, "I certainly feel this great mercy of God; I understand fully what should be my life's task; and should it please
Heaven to provide the necessary means to complete the education of these children, there shall be no failure on my
part."

"The means will not be wanting," said Maria Theresa;
"and were we not involved in this unhappy war with Prus-
sia, which claims all the financial resources of the land, we
would ourselves undertake the whole future education of the
children. Yet what is possible at present shall be done.
You remain some time in Vienna?"

"Already this gracious inquiry of your Imperial Majesty
would be to me a command, even if it were not in accordance
with our plans. This is the very city of musicians—the me-
tropolis of art. Where could the children better begin their
career than in Vienna?"

"That is true!" answered the empress; "and how are you
pleased with our nobility? It is to be hoped they interest
themselves in rising artists, like these of yours!"

"Certainly!" replied Father Mozart. But there played at
the same time such a peculiar smile about the mouth of the
Vice-Capellmeister, that Maria Theresa inquired its cause.

"Certainly," he answered, "we cannot complain of the
kindness of this reception; if only the Art is not lost sight
of in the wonder over the extraordinary child."

"I know," returned the empress; "but it is the same in all
great towns as it is here in Vienna. The world must have
its wonders, to rouse it out of its *ennui* by their remarkable-
ness. Everywhere can be found those who only cultivate
music because it is the fashion, or out of jealousy at some
one else's accomplishments; and with what owlish wisdom
they will discuss its principles, or the performances of its
professors! Yet, Herr Vice-Capellmeister, we may console
ourselves by knowing that the judgment of a few who understand, outweighs the chatter of these shallow pates a hundred-fold."

A sudden burst of laughter, from the side of the room
where the emperor was talking with Wolfgang, interrupted
the conversation at this point. Maria Theresa looked around
in surprise, and something like anger shone in her eyes. But

she herself had to smile when her husband approached her, and said that he had just asked the boy whom he considered the greatest musician of past times, and he had replied " The trumpeter who blew down the walls of Jericho !"

When the time had arrived for their departure, Maria Theresa raised the boy up and gave him a motherly kiss; then giving her hand to Nannerl, she bade them good-bye, and they separated. Wolfgang and Nannerl each held a beautiful diamond ring in their hands, and Father Mozart's countenance shone with satisfied pride.

CHAPTER V.

A SURPRISE.

ON Wolfgang's seventh birthday, the winter lay heavy and cold upon Salzburg; but in the heart of that city's " wonder-child" it was spring-time. No matter what snow and ice might lock up the earth as in a marble tomb, it was all sunshine and song in the boy's soul. More and more as the months went by, it became evident that music was with him no mere fancy, but the passion of his life. Wherever harmonious sounds were, there was his happiness; nothing but discords and jangling noises could cast a shadow over his always cheery face.[1]

When at last the May month had come upon the earth, with joy of larks and songs of nightingales, with hue and odor of early blossoms, and all the twigs were roughening, and every little bud was swelling, and million-fold new life was putting fortn on every side; then in the breast of the boy rose jubilant songs and streaming melodies of joy, and his quickening life put forth buds like the flower-stems ; a mighty impulse toward creative effort awoke in his soul, and

---

[1] An incident, related by Oulibicheff (Part I., p. 15) illustrates the exceeding sensitiveness of Mozart's organization. Up to his tenth year he retained an unconquerable aversion to the trumpet (his friend Schlachtner's favorite instrument). In order to overcome what seemed to his father a mere whim, he had a trumpet sounded suddenly once near the child's ear. The little frame shook like an aspen, and sank to the ground as though felled by a blow. Later in life Mozart conquered this repugnance, and no one knew better than he how to make the trumpets splendidly effective in orchestra

the whole world seemed to him too narrow and confined. *His* world was the realm of Music, and its boundaries must, before all other things, be widened and enlarged.

"The piano no longer pleases me!" said he one day; "I must learn the violin."

A few weeks afterward, the old friends Schlachtner, Adlgasser, and Lipp were assembled one day at the house of the Vice-Capellmeister.

It was a lovely spring afternoon. The sky lay sunken in a sea of deepest blue; the luminous green of the new vegetation seemed to smile upon mankind, fresh, and cool, and pure, as if it were the maidenly morning-greeting of the year—as bright, and as transient. For soon the mounting sun will bathe field and forest in deeper colors, even as the innocent laughter of childhood fades under the heat and passion of life, and gives place to a sadder earnestness.

But to-day there was no sadness in Nature's face; all was joy and laughter, youth and brimming life, trustfulness and hope!

In the little garden of the Vice-Capellmeister, also, there was bloom and odor, costly and rare. Tulips lifted their proud splendors along the borders, and creamy hyacinths breathed their delicious fragrance on every side, while thousands of bees hummed and buzzed about the great apple-tree, with its countless delicate blossoms, under which the little company was gathered.

Frau Mozart, busy about her housewifely affairs, had remained at home, but she had taken care to send out to her husband and his friends, who had met for a sort of musical picnic, a goodly supply of wine and cold viands, and had despatched little Nannerl to set the table, which now appeared decked in its snowy linen under the vine-shadows of the rustic summer-house. Just as Nannerl, having put the last touches to her handiwork, and received a kiss from her father for her wages, was taking her departure, Wolfgang entered with another of the Vice-Capellmeister's friends.

This was the violinist Wenzel, who had for some time been taking lessons of Father Mozart in composition, in order to complete his musical culture. He was a little natty man, nicely dressed, with uncommonly pretty hands and feet, and small eyes, black as juniper-berries, which rolled about continually, in a manner almost terrifying to behold. Yet, small and restless as they were, out of them shot fiery and soulful glances, and the thin face, nearly hidden under the peruke, bore an expression of great intelligence.

Father Mozart had an affection for this young man—young at least in comparison with his own years—because he took hold of the science of counterpoint with extraordinary quickness, and really showed a remarkable talent for composition. With joy, therefore, he stretched out both hands to the newcomer, and bade him welcome,—not noticing, meantime, how Wolfgang slipped into the summer-house, concealing something behind his back with his two hands.

"I am delighted, dear Wenzel," said the Capellmeister, "that you have come out to join us here in God's free world of nature. See how everything is luminous and fragrant; and this air—one feels like drinking it in in deep draughts; while in the city yonder it seems sultry, and thick, and smothering!"

"Oh yes, Herr Capellmeister," replied Wenzel, shaking hands heartily with his friend, and rolling his round black eyes over the group; "everything is beautiful here: what a rare spot to write a poem or a symphony!"

"Indeed is it!" answered Father Mozart, with a contented smile. "Whatever may be within a man, outside there it is all sweetest poetry and glorious music. Look you how the river draws on, gleaming like liquid silver, to the mill of the convent, over whose wheel it leaps in roaring foam. On beyond, behind those cool meadows and the blossoming orchard-trees, stretch out the rich farms and summer residences, up to the foot of the mountain, rising there in its bold majesty against the heavens. There, on the summit, frowns the castle, with its towers and turrets overlooking the park, just now putting on its green summer-robes. And over all, the precious pure blue sky. Tell me, is not that a poem, such as no son of man can write, and a symphony which only the Creator could compose?"

"Truly it is so," responded Wenzel, "and you yourself become a poet in gazing at it!"

"Well, my friend, one needs to be so," replied the Vice-Capellmeister. "If a man would not become utterly dried up in the world, plodding along its beaten paths day after day, he must have something which shall snatch him away from the clutches of business, now and then, as this little garden, with its charming prospect, does me."

"You chose the prettiest spot in the country for it," said Schlachtner.

"And it has cost money enough, too," sighed Fathei Mozart, rubbing his ear.

"Now, old stingy-pate," cried Lipp, laughing, "it can't have been such a mint of money!"

"Little you bachelors know about that," returned the Vice-Capellmeister. "Still, some wings a man must put to his life, or it will drag in the dirt. But this gossip has kept me from asking a question: What is it that has brought friend Wenzel to us to-day? for I am sure he has not come so far merely for the view or the visit—I know him too well for that! Methinks, too, I spy a roll of music under his arm. What will you bet he does not astonish us with a new composition?"

"By Jupiter, Herr Vice-Capellmeister, you can take the crown as the great imperial prince of guessers!" replied the little violinist, slightly coloring, with a pleased twinkle in his round black eyes; "for you have just hit it. I bring you a trifling effort of my humble powers. But it has at least given me pleasure in working at it, and has taken most of my leisure during your absence to Vienna."

"And what is it?" asked Father Mozart and Adlgasser in a breath.

"Six trios," answered Wenzel, "on which I would gladly hear my *maestro's* judgment; and if you have all brought your instruments with you, as I thought I could venture to predict, we can go over them together."

"That is just the thing," cried Father Mozart, as they all sprang up to get their instruments. "Wenzel shall play first violin, Schlachtner second, and I will undertake the bass with my viola."

At this moment Father Mozart felt himself softly touched on the elbow, and looking round, there stood little Wolfgang, holding a small violin, which had been given him in Vienna.

"Papa," whispered the boy, in a beseeching tone, "let me play second violin!"

"Oh certainly," replied his father, laughing, "in your head you may take that part; perhaps some day you can do it in earnest!"

"I *can* do it in earnest!" cried Wolfgang, and there beamed from his eyes that proud joy which is kindled only by the consciousness of innate power.

"Did you learn it in your sleep?" asked his father, jestingly.

"No, Papachen; only let me try once, and you will see!"

"At home you can, Wolferl," replied Father Mozart, in a comforting voice; "at home you shall play that first minuet of yours for me."

"Oh, minuet!" cried the boy, laughing proudly. "What minuet? Let me play Herr Wenzel's trio with you; that is something like!"

But the boy's persistence now was making his father angry, and in a harsh tone, which one rarely heard from his lips, he said: "There, there! Stop talking: you are a foolish child to think of it! Because you can play the piano so well, it does not follow that you can take a violin part, without ever learning the instrument. Leave us, and learn to be more modest in future!"

This was too much for the little fellow's heart. The severe words, all the harder from a man so kind as his father usually was, and the doubt of his ability, coming at the same time with the disappointment of his little plan of surprise, cut the child's heart so keenly that he began to weep bitterly, and turned away, sobbing, with his violin pressed tightly under his arm.

But already good Father Mozart repented of the harsh words; and when Schlachtner put in a plea that the boy might be permitted to play at least with him, the Vice-Capellmeister said, kindly—

"Come! only stop howling, and don't always be as soft as butter! For aught I care, come and play by the side of Herr Schlachtner; but, mind now, so softly, that none shall hear you!"

Like a flash, Wolfgang had brushed his sleeve across the wet eyes, shining now like the sunlight in dew, and taken his place beside the others. Then they put the notes before them, beat a measure, and began.

The trio was an excellent composition, but exceedingly difficult. At first Schlachtner gave himself up to the music, and played down the first page in entire forgetfulness that the little Mozart was accompanying him. Soon, however, he gave a start. What a beautiful pure tone was that! How cleanly the little violin was cutting out the notes! and how the face of the boy betrayed his complete absorption in his work! Softer and softer became Schlachtner's playing, till he stopped short in utter astonishment, letting bow and in-strument slowly sink down at his side.

And Father Mozart?—When Schlachtner, speechless with wonder, stopped playing, and looked over at him, he knew not whether to laugh or cry; for, without for a moment slackening his bow arm, or looking away from his notes, Father Mozart was standing there, with the big tears slowly rolling down his cheeks, for tenderness and joy.

As for Wolfgang, he neither had eyes nor ears for anything which was going on about him. He was music—nothing but music. His face absolutely shone with ravishment, as he played away with heart and soul, till the six trios were ended.

And then what a jubilation, as with joyful pride Father Mozart pressed his kisses on the child's cheek and mouth!

"And when—when, little Star-beam! did you learn it?" he cried.

"When you were at church, or giving lessons!" answered the boy, in triumph. "And now let me try the first violin once!"

They all smiled at this boldness of the young *maestro*, but for the amusement of the thing, were willing to try him; and all were abundantly astonished to find that he got over the extreme difficulties of the part, sometimes with incorrect and curious fingering, yet with excellent success.[1]

And now the happy afternoon drew to a close. The sinking sun sent his red beams streaming over the little party, paying back their waves of music with a tide of golden color; and as they lifted their glasses, ruddy with the pearling wine, in a *viva* to the new *maestro*, the last sunbeam mellowed their friendly faces; and the great bald mountain away yonder seemed to grow rosy-faced in sympathy, and the whole quiet, pleasant land lay spread out before them, like Paradise before the eyes of the Blessed.

[1] The whole incident is historical.—Jahn, Part I., p. 33.

CHAPTER VI.

AN EVENING AT THE COURT OF VERSAILLES.

THE Queen's apartments, in the palace at Versailles, were open. They formed a suite of fifteen rooms, each of which was a *salon* worthy of a royal occupant. Upon this evening, they were glittering in a flood of light, poured down from more than seven hundred wax-candles, which flamed in countless chandeliers, massive and splendid with gold and crystal, while the gleam and lustre of all the carven marble, the rich gildings, stuccoes, and paintings, and of the elegant clocks, vases, and statues, and costly tapestry, was flashed back in hundred-fold magical reduplications from the gigantic mirrors.

Yet these apartments of the queen were plain, in comparison with those which the Marquise de Pompadour occupied, or the great royal *salons* of Louis XIV. and Louis XV.

At this time, there was no royal residence in the world which could stand in comparison with that of Versailles. The earliest mention of Versailles is of about the year 1037, when it appears as an inconsiderable village, with one old feudal castle. In 1627, Louis XIII. built on one of its flanks a hunting-seat, which remained as the centre of the subsequent colossal additions, by means of which Louis XIV. built up Versailles, after Mansard's plan, to one of the most notable points in the history of European art and politics.

Strange was the life which now went on in this magnificent old palace. A life whose " splendid, rotten glory" was more like the fevered dream of a hasheesh-eater, than a real era of human existence; a life whose fearful motto was given by its crowning character, Madame Pompadour, in the famous words : *Après nous le déluge!*

Singing, revelling, exultant, that frenzied life went reeling on above the abyss which so soon was to yawn beneath the feet of Louis XVI. and the ill-fated Marie Antoinette.

But who now, on this festive evening, but dreamed of the possibility of such a catastrophe ? As the courtly assemblage in those royal apartments mingled the glitter of their jewels with the glare which flooded down from thousands of wax-lights upon gold and gorgeous adornments, what eye, dazzled by the splendor streaming out through those lofty windows defiantly into the night-shadows, could perceive how those shadows were gathering thicker and more sombre, closing in upon that brilliant company with inexorable doom?

The grouping of the persons who were present in the principal *salon*, was remarkable. The king had not yet appeared, having but just returned from a belated hunting-party, and the whole company had gathered in two groups, round two separate centres. One of these points was the *fauteuil* on which the queen reclined, surrounded by her nearest friends. But how small was the train which gathered about her and the princesses Madame Adelaide and Madame Victoire! how simple and modest appeared the queen herself; and with what quiet grace, overshadowed by a visible sadness, she guided the conversation into the channels of art and religion!

Far otherwise was it with the second group, which, almost at the other end of the *salon*, had collected about the Marquise de Pompadour. She, too, reclined upon a sofa, and made a fitting centre to the brilliant company who surrounded her. Her person sparkled with gems, which, on their background of rich black velvet, flashed and glittered with double splendor. Her brow bore a diadem, which resembled a crown. It was a gift from the king; its front formed a bouquet of diamonds, whose centre was a magnificent rose, surrounded on each side by seven smaller roses. Necklace, bracelets, and brooch corresponded to the diadem, and gave the marquise so much the appearance of a queen, that the design was only too apparent. Over her feet trailed the folds of a costly ermine, and from her negligent and haughty posture on the sofa, which she made a throne, she cast a disdainful, indifferent glance over the gossipping circles about her, which contained, besides the Dukes of Choiseul, Goutant, Aiguillon, Richelieu, and La Valette, the Abbé St. Cyr, the Chevalier de Montaigne, the Princes Soubise and Guiche, as well as the Count and Countess de Campan, and almost all the other nobility of the court.

Her position was so resplendent, and so agreeable to the insatiable ambition, the boundless *hauteur* of the marquise, that she could not but throw a proud and triumphant glance, now and then, in the direction of her royal rival. But the queen was too sadly accustomed to a constrained humility, and her spirit had too long ago been broken, to give back defiance for defiance to the haughty mistress of the king Even the slave at last grows wonted to the shackles, and in Maria of France the queen had long disappeared in the religious enthusiast, the saint, and the martyr. She was certainly gentle and pious, but the once regal spirit was become weak as water.

It was different with the princesses. Both of them felt their royal blood boil in its veins, at such moments as this; yet they were forced to submit themselves to the iron will of their lord and king, Louis XV.

The entrance of his majesty into the noisy and hilarious room was not altogether a joyful occurrence; since the whole court was forced to keep a disagreeable silence, during the quarter-hour which etiquette demanded that he should spend in conversation with the queen and her circle. This constrained quiet was especially unendurable to Madame Pompadour, since she perceived that the Princess Adelaide, whose lofty and intellectual countenance was now so animated, in conversation with the king, cast toward her now and then a look of proud and disdainful triumph. Even this temporary possession of the king's attention, sent the hot flush into the cheeks of the marquise, and, in defiance of etiquette, she turned suddenly to Prince Soubise, who stood near her, saying sharply, "Prince, you are more tiresome to-night than ever!"

Soubise and the whole court started in surprise, for all knew how great a stress the king laid on the rule of silence during his interview with his family. But the prince dared not refuse the challenge of the irritated marquise, whose single word might banish him from Versailles, and he replied—

"So fair a mouth as yours, Madame, need only command, and Soubise must obey its lightest wish."

"Then," replied the Pompadour, "I command that you be no longer tiresome, but tell us some spicy anecdote at once!"

The old courtier was never at a loss with tales of scandal, one of which he now commenced, while his wrinkled but courtly face lighted up with a smile compounded of sarcasm, levity, and lascivious wit. It was a story of amorous intrigue in the last reign, and the group about the marquise was soon in boisterous mirth over its dubious incidents, so spicily narrated by the unscrupulous old wit

It was but half finished, when the king broke oft his conversation with the queen with a cool nod, and approached
the group at the other end of the *salon*.

"Madame the Marquise," said he in a sharp tone, "seem₁
to enjoy her chat with these lively gentlemen extremely!"

"The banner of *ennui* bears for its coat of arms a pair of
yawning jaws; who would make so bold as to set it up by the
side of the lilies of France?" replied the Pompadour gayly
throwing all that witchery which she knew so well how to
wield into her soft voice, while her deep, passionate eyes
rested on the king with a look which thrilled his inmost soul
with pleasure.

In an instant his short anger at the breach of sacred etiquette
had vanished, and Louis XV. replied—

"Truly, there is no more horrible thing in the world than
ennui—that sickness of the soul—that scourge of mankind.
Life is but a quarantine for the port of Paradise; and anything which will give us side-looks out of our monotonous
imprisonment into that haven is a blessing. Long live
amusement! and therefore—bring us the cards at once!
Madame the Marquise, it is your deal!"

Meantime the queen's circle had been receiving visitors—
no less than our friend the Vice-Capellmeister, and the
"wonder-child," little Wolfgang Amadeus. Madame Victoire, the younger of the two princesses, had presented them
to her majesty, and after some kind conversation with the
boy, it was announced to the king that the famous musical
prodigy from Germany was present.

"*Eh bien!*" said his majesty, glancing up from his cards,
"we are curious to hear the little virtuoso!"

These words were a command. The richly carved and
inlaid piano was opened, and Wolfgang took his seat. He
began with a difficult and brilliant composition, which was
executed with surprising skill, and without the least appearance of effort or fatigue.

The king's play went on, meanwhile, without interruption.

At first no one of the Court except the queen herself, with
the Princess Victoire and Countess Tessé, took any notice of
the music. Fine as the execution of the piece was, they had
often heard good playing before. Court ladies and gentlemen were too much accustomed to having their taste in art
satisfied, to betray any especial pleasure in it; excellence was

commonplace to them, and they entirely foigot that the boy's age made such skill wonderful.

The Princess Victoire alone, therefore, expressed in warm words her satisfaction with the performance. The queen only nodded kindly, for the indifference of her husband had its effect upon her.

Little Wolfgang did not let the tears come at this coolness, as he would have done a year before, but, getting off the stool, he clapped the music-book together in indignation, and proudly stepping up to his father, he said—

" Come, Papa, let's go away; these people know nothing about music !"

" Well, if you choose, Wolferl," said his father, after vainly endeavoring to persuade the boy ; " but what will the world say when it hears that little Mozart, about whom such a noise was made, went to Versailles, and as good as failed. If I were in your place, I'd force the king and the whole court to pay attention, by playing twice as finely."

Wolfgang's blue eyes lit up at this as with a sudden sunbeam. His face glowed ; he felt as a general does who has just lost a skirmish, and now, sure of victory, orders a cavalry-charge.

Seating himself again at the piano, he began to play, softly at first, but with a smothered fire in the tones. Stronger and stronger grew his touch, as he went on improvising, expressing in music the impressions which had been thrown upon him ;—the splendid, frivolous, glancing company, the beautiful princess, the sad-eyed queen, the cold, proud hearts which had refused his music—all this, with an under-current of grief at the disappointment, anger at the slight, and a jubilant intimation of triumph to come.

The king had thrown down his cards, and the whole company were grouped together about the instrument, listening to the fiery, passionate strains which the little magician was calling forth. The king passed his hand over his forehead and eyes, as if to assure himself that it was neither a dream nor some trick of witchcraft. The queen's sorrowful eyes were brightening, as with beautiful dim starlight. All, even Prince Soubise and the Pompadour, were moved to their inmost souls. The invisible might of the noble, the pure, the beautiful, had laid hold upon them, and lifted them above the dust of triviality. They felt themselves, for the moment at least, other and better men.

Wonderful, wonderful is the inner reality of music: man cannot solve its secrets; he can but accept them, and listen in awe and delight. Science may analyze, explain, and prate glibly of the relations of its harmonies, and after the explanation, the marvellous thing is there, as it was before. The philosopher's mind coolly takes music to pieces, and gives the law for this result and that; and then, the man's heart bows down before it, and he only knows that the sense was there to receive, and the music is here to give, and both are inexplicable. Like a still, soft breath, it draws through his bosom; but this soft, still breath becomes now a resistless power, taking possession of his soul, and filling it with such a flood of blissful life, that the billows of it lift him high up above this poor existence, with its depressing cares and pain. Then awakens the man in him, like a giant—like an unbound Titan; divine power thrills through him, and unconsciously yielding himself to the everlasting Being that fills the universe, he hears and understands the language of the supreme Creator—yea, himself becomes a creator, and calls forth from fathomless deeps within his soul new worlds, full of ravishment and wonder.

So was it here, in the midst of the glittering Court of Versailles, at least for those few moments, in that carnival-time of frivolity and corruption. It was as though into that Sodom and Gomorrah of civilization had floated suddenly a soft breath of purer air, balmy with the enchanted-sweet blossom-odors of another world. For a moment, every bosom inhaled the balm-breath of the lost Paradise in deep draughts—drew it in with childlike rapturous delight; forgetting that, long since, this Eden was shut, for them—shut, and guarded by the angel of their own conscience—defended with the flaming sword of conscious guilt.

Wolfgang had finished. A loud "*Bravo!*" from the king was the signal for a storm of applause, sufficiently rare at the court of Versailles. But the Princess Victoire, the darling of Louis XV., hastening to the child-artist, caressed him and covered him with kisses.

And now, Madame Pompadour having expressed a desire to see the boy more closely, the king gave a sign to Monsieur Hebert, who acted as master of ceremonies on such occasions, and that polished gentleman, with a world of elaborate politeness, led Wolfgang at once to the marquise.

"A small bit of a creature," she exclaimed, jestingly, "but

indeed a great genius! Put him up before me on the table!"

The master of ceremonies having complied, with unwonted lack of gracefulness, being in some doubt as to the best manner of lifting the stately little fellow, she looked at him graciously, as she stood before him, when Wolfgang on a sudden bent forward to kiss her, in his German fashion. But fire and flame mounted to his face, when, at this motion, the proud dame drew herself back, and turned haughtily away.

"Ha!" cried he, angrily, " who is this, then, that she won't kiss me? Wasn't I kissed by the Empress?" [1]

Fortunately, these indiscreet words were spoken in German, which none of the bystanders understood, except the Princess Victoire, who was greatly amused at the occurrence.

The Princess Adelaide, to test the powers of the boy, now asked him if he could extemporize an accompaniment to a new song of hers. Without the least hesitation he sat down at the piano, and not only accompanied the song gracefully, but played a new and different accompaniment for each of the ten repetitions of the song, which the Princess gave in order to try his inventive skill.[2]

During the remainder of the evening, the Princess Victoire scarcely would let Wolfgang go out of her arms. She unfastened a diamond brooch from her breast, and put it upon the boy's bosom; while the queen could not sufficiently caress him, and give him motherly kisses.

A few weeks later, Father Mozart and the little Wolfgang took their leave of the French court at the royal country seat of Choisy-le-Roi. And if the boy had received costly presents from the queen and the princesses, it was now his turn to do them honor, little as they appreciated it then, by a precious gift. He had, during these weeks in France, composed his first two published works (and was yet only seven years old!) Each *opus* consisted of two piano sonatas, with

---

[1] Historical.—Oulibicheff, Part I., p. 20.
[2] Historical.—Grimm's letter to a German Prince. Nissen, p. 47; Oulibicheff Part I., p. 20; Jahn, Part I., p. 51.
[3]
　　　　　　Sonates pour le Clavecin,
qui peuvent se jouer avec l'accompagnement de Violon,
　　　　dédiées à Madame Victoire de France.
　Par J. G. W. Mozart de Salzbourg, âgé de sept ans.
　　　　　　Ouvre premier.

　　　　　　Sonates pour le Clavecin,
qui peuvent se jouer avec l'accompagnement de Violon.
　　　dédiées à Madame la Comtesse de Tessé, etc.
　Par J G. W. Mozart de Salzbourg, âgé de sept ans.
　　　　　　Ouvre II.

violin accompaniment; the first was dedicated to the Princess Victoire, the second to the Countess Tessé.

These two compositions little Mozart brought, and with his own hands presented to the ladies, who had so won his heart by their kindness and appreciation.

When the time came for his departure, after having played the sonatas for them with his usual power, and received their praises and thanks, the young princesses approached the boy to say adieu. But, suddenly turning his back, he leaped out of one of the long windows which opened on the terrace, and disappeared among the trees in the park. They stood in astonishment, and were almost ready to believe that success had turned the child's head, and bereft him of reason. But hark! There came in through the open window where little Mozart had disappeared, a strain of sweet music. It was the voice of the great organ in the park-chapel.

The boy had chosen his own manner of leave-taking. His heart had been too full for polite speeches; and his grief too sincere for words: music was his only language for farewell.

At first softly, almost sadly, breathed the strain, like a regretful adieu; then deeper and mightier it swelled forth, as though the pain of parting grew ever more mighty and deep; and then, in chords whose wailing minor bemoaned their very weakness to utter the ineffable woe, the sorrowful music wandered away into the distance, and sank to silence. Oh! that was no mere leave-taking from these human friends; it was the sobbing of farewells to a vanished Paradise—the lost Eden of Childhood, which to-day had ended, as l is work in the world began.

PART II.

MOZART'S YOUTH.—IN ITALY.

CHAPTER I.

EVENING-TWILIGHT AND MORNING-RED.

A BRIGHT March day of the year 1770 was flooding with its golden sunshine the famous old town of Bologna. The sky of Italy, from its deep blue eyes, seemed smiling down upon the city as upon its darling. But this loving glance of heaven was scarcely returned as tenderly; for Bologna lay beneath it, dark and stern, among its palaces, cloisters, and churches—lost in sombre thoughts upon long-departed centuries—as if it were the image of the Middle Ages, turned to stone.

The lofty buildings all exhibited the severe mediæval style of architecture; every house was built up with heavy porches, every pillar of these porches buttressed with its deep shadow, so that the streets had an expression almost of gloom.

Over the whole conduct and life of the people, too, there seemed to be an all-pervading breath of mediæval times; an appearance which was increased by the frequent companies of cowled monks and proud-looking priests passing silently along the streets and squares.

It was in the rich villas in the neighborhood of Bologna that the best evidence was to be seen of the real life and culture which existed in Italy at the time of which we write. At the gate of one of these villas, not far from the city, a noble and stately form paused for a moment before entering, to watch the full sunshine of noonday pour its splendor over the marble roofs and spires of Bologna, and the luxuriant groves and greenery of the country about its walls. His silvered hair, and something in the yet stately and commanding presence, betrayed the approach of age. His dress was rich, though severely simple; the deep and meditative still-ness of the dark eyes, the endless good feeling and friendli-ness in the lines of the handsome mouth, as well as the air of artistic culture about the whole man, had an effect upon you which seemed to harmonize exactly with the impression made by the appearance of the abode which he was about to enter.

The villa was not of great extent, but a noble and elegant taste had evidently reigned in its design. Cheerfully, airily, and lightly it lifted itself, like a crown, on the brow of a gently-ascending slope, the slender pillars bearing up the porticoes like flower-stems. Olive, chestnut, and pomegranate trees mingled their deep shadows with those of the pine, cypress, and laurel, in picturesque beauty. Between this rich leafage and the broad beds of flowers stood costly sculp-tures;—a Perseus of the famous Donatello, victorious with the awful head of Medusa in his hand; a daring Roman, half-fiercely, half-tenderly supporting on his sinewy arm a ravished Sabine, done by John of Bologna; with other of the great creations of the Italian masters.

It was a spot of rare beauty. One could not but perceive that here unusual wealth and refinement of taste had built themselves a chosen temple, and at the same time one saw that rest and peace had here their dwelling. Ah! and rest and peace—one has said—are found so seldom among man-kind, that even their mere outward aspect is felt to be a talisman, under whose protection we would gladly place all the wild desires, all the passionate conflicts of our own souls.

The stately form which now opened the vine-clambered gate of the garden was that of Signor Carlo Broschi, sur-named Farinelli, one of the most famous men of his century. He had been the greatest singer of his own or any preceding time. Gifted by nature with a marvellous voice and a genius for music, he had received all the culture which wealth and Italy could give him, and had stood for years without a rival. During a long residence at the court of Spain, he had re-ceived almost royal honor and favor; for all through the reign of the unfortunate Philip V., as well as through that of his successor, Ferdinand VI., upon whose life an equally terrible blight had settled, Farinelli had been more than a David to the stricken Saul. His music had been almost the only power which was able to rouse the bed-ridden monarch for some small portion of the day, to his duties as sovereign of Spain.[1]

Farinelli had returned to Italy, laden with honor and wealth, to spend his declining years in the culture of art and philosophy, and' had built this villa as a quiet refuge for the peaceful close of a brilliant and successful life.

The inner aspect of this new Tusculum was in harmony with its exterior. The entrance to the house was through a wide veranda, whose slender pillars were already clasped about by the young leafage of twining vines. Handsome and cosy armchairs and a quaintly carven desk betrayed that this was the favorite nook of the venerable philosopher and musician.

Through this veranda you entered a roomy hall, on both sides of which stood white marble busts of the greatest men of the Roman world. The furniture of the whole ground-floor was of the antique style, and its solid simplicity, and harmony with the architecture of the building, would have done honor to the abode of a Roman emperor.

Quite different was the upper story of the villa. If the apartments below were fitted for the reception of aristocratic visitors or royal guests, these chambers above were evidently meant to be a quiet and comfortable home, rich in noble associations of the past, for a true artist and philosopher.

Of the two spacious front rooms on each side of the richly ornamented hall, the one to the east contained the world-renowned musical library of Farinelli, the costly inheritance of the Queen of Spain; while the western room held the pianos and other musical instruments, also the gift of that same royal hand, in gratitude and veneration towards the benefactor of two kings. Each instrument bore the name of some one of the great Italian painters—Raphael, Correggio, Titian, Guido, etc. Besides these was the most rare and precious one of all—the famous violin, Farinelli's especial darling, named by him the *viola d'amour*, a masterpiece from the hand of Amati, at Cremona, in the sixteenth century.

The stately old musician was not wholly alone in his elegant mansion. One friend he had, who was more to him than wife or brother. This was the learned Franciscan, John Baptiste Martini, Italy's greatest master of musical science,

[1] *Vide* Bu... .., s Histoire de la Musique, Lamberg's Mémorial d'un Mondain, p. 97 Schlosser's History of the 18th and 19th centuries

the president of the renowned Philharmonic Academy of Bologna, and author of the great work, "Laggio Fondamentale Prattico di Contrapunto," on account of which, and in grateful acknowledgment of the service he had rendered to the world of art, Frederick the Great had sent him his likeness, set in jewels, accompanied by an autograph letter of friendly congratulation.[1]

The two old friends were at this time deeply engaged in a "History of Music," which was to be a most extensive and philosophical work. It was the especial undertaking of Martini, but his comrade contributed to the work the use of his immense library, as well as the results of his own life-long study.

When now (not being delayed as we have been by the foregoing long description) Farinelli entered his library, he found Father Martini bending over his writing-desk, which stood in the centre of the great room, half buried under a heap of folio tomes and rolls of parchment.

But, for some reason, the venerable Franciscan, as Farinelli could not but notice after the first cordial greeting, was not so cheerfully at work as usual. Something in his manner betrayed a restlessness most unusual in him. At last he put away the ink-stained quill and arose.

"It does not go at all to-day!" said he, as if his conscience a little disturbed him for his want of diligence. "I am too much excited and preoccupied."

"Is it so?" responded Farinelli with a smile, as he motioned to a white-haired old servitor who had entered behind him, and who now offered to each of them a sparkling glass of real *Lachrima Christi.* "I thought it was only myself who was so taken possession of by the concert last evening!"

"It is not so much the concert which has moved me," replied Father Martini, pushing back the black velvet cap from his high, white forehead, "but the thoughts which the appearance of this wonderful young *maestro* has awakened in me. He has captivated me, but yet I cannot but tremble for him. I fear lest, instead of being the great musical creator, whose prophetic possibility darkles in his deep blue eyes, he shall become a mere prodigy of superficial brightness—only a skilful and popular *performer*, as these prodigies usually turn out to be."

[1] *Vide* Wilhelm von Vallo—Antologia Romana.

"But, my dear friend and brother, remember that the whole history of the young Amadeus Mozart, so far, contradicts this fear. Think what they have written us about him, from Vienna, Paris, and London. In Vienna he wrote two operas, and now·this youth of fourteen years has engaged to furnish a new opera for the next carnival at Milan, as though it were the lightest undertaking in the world."

"Yes," returned Father Martini, sipping his *Lachrima Christi* with an anxious look; "but now he has entered Italy, and is brought face to face with music—not as a mere amusement, not as a mere field for the display of skill, but as a noble and mysterious art. If we could but bring him into the Philharmonic Academy, then, as a *cavaliere filarmonico*, his career would be -certain in Italy; but it is a terrible ordeal he would have to pass!"

"We will see what can be done," replied Farinelli. "One thing is certain—the young Mozart has spent the last years in most earnest study of the great masters. Stradella, Carissimi, Scarlatti, Leo, Hasse, Bach, and Handel have been his familiar spirits, as his father testifies; and I know that his perfect acquaintance with our language has made him at home with the Italian masters. Fear not, Martini! Where genius is, there is the finger of God to direct its course."

"It is a comfort to remember that," answered the Franciscan. "As for me, I feel that the young *maestro*, with his bright fair face, and those passionate eyes, as deep and blue as the sky above us, has stolen away my heart!"

"And, dear Martini," returned his friend, leaning forward in his earnestness, "let me make a confession. The appearance of this young musician has reminded me anew of something which a thousand times before has come to my mind, but never without painful thoughts."

"And that is— ?" asked the Franciscan.

"The departure, and the farewell so soon to be spoken! As I gazed into the great spiritual eyes of the young *maestro*, it was clear to me as sunlight that these were the morning stars which would usher in a new day for music. Around us, dear brother—around us lies the evening-twilight; but there, glows the morning-red!"

"What matters it?" asked Father Martini, while a smile full of rest and contentment played on his noble countenance· "the life of the individual and the life of the race, both exist only through eternal changes of light and shadow—

morning and evening—the dewy bud and the fallen flower."

"That know I well !" returned Farinelli; "think me not so childish that into the great All, and for the great All, I would not cheerfully go away. If only the separation—the farewell, were not there before me !"

"As for me," said the Franciscan, a little sadly, "I have said farewell to so many things, during my life, that it is a familiar sound to me !"

Farinelli seemed not to have heard these words, but appeared lost in recollection. After a moment he continued, as if clearing himself from a misunderstanding—

"Not that I complain of departing joys; but only that I must rend myself away—who knows how soon—from all these surroundings, among which I have felt myself so sheltered and at home; from all these circumstances and employments which have grown a part of my life. It is not the great matters, the supreme joys, which fasten upon the human heart with such force, but the small interests and pleasures—the unnoticeable violets—from which the departure is so painful. When some pitiless fate has grasped with iron hand the fortune of a whole life, a heroic will stands up in man's breast, and cries in calm defiance, 'Take it then; I can live my life without it !' and then a noble self-respect over-masters the pain of bereavement, and we stand firmly and proudly among the ruins of our hopes. But when fate seizes upon one great expectancy after another, takes one flower after another from our lives, and color after color fades out of the picture of our days, till at last it lies before us cold and gray—then a nameless sorrow comes upon the man, and he feels his heart shaken within him."

"But, oh, my friend !" returned the Franciscan, "what then is this life, with all its joys and sorrows ? We are standing, indeed, in the evening twilight, and all is disappearing about us. We also, as all things on this earth-ball, are passing by. The moment comes, and as it delights his heart, man says, 'Tarry with me !' but while he speaks it has vanished, and another is in its place. Yet, swift as the moments are, their image remains with us, and the echoes of the feelings which that image awakens in us, can bless us forever. See, my brother, this is the transfiguration of bereavement. The joys of life are not alone like the rainbow, in that they are formed of moments which incessantly fall

3

and aie replaced, but in this also, that they are most radiant when far away. And has not God blessed us above most men?—has He not given us a cheerful old age, the joy of noble labor and creation, a holy enthusiasm for divine art—has He not given us one another? Oh, my brother! I would not give the evening-twilight for any morning-red!"

"Yes!" said Farinelli, grasping his friend's hand with emotion, as his face lit up with a smile of good-will and gratitude, "I have to thank God for many happy hours—and, most of all, that these hours, like the years of childhood, leave no after-taste of bitterness behind."

"We may confess, too, at least to ourselves," added Father Martini with a smile, "that we possess the main conditions of quiet happiness in ourselves; I mean that thoughtfulness of the spirit, which receives life in its depth and purity, and, amid the stormy moments incessantly fleeting by, discerns the permanent and immortal; and also that cheerful seren-ity, which is disturbed by no Titan-battles of the passions, and dwells untouched by envy or undisciplined ambition. In these two blessings God has given us the telescope through which the inner eyes of man may discover the streaming constellations of the everlasting life. Only through it is dis-cerned, faintly and afar, out from the dim nebulæ of earthly virtue and beauty, the star-shine of other worlds, which show us, in the fathomless darkness of the future, the immortality of our being!"

At that moment the door of the library was opened, and the servitor announced—"Signor Amadeus Mozart!"

CHAPTER II.

IL CAVALIERE FILARMONICO.

THE enthusiasm of the Italians is lavish in its expression, because it comes from the heart. Nowhere found the young Mozart such a warm reception, such universal good-will, and so immediate a recognition as in Italy. Both among the nobility and the artists, and especially at Bologna, he found cordial friends and allies at once.

But greatly as Amadeus[1] was pleased with such a result, his spirit was too childlike and modest to be carried away by any popular homage. If in years and outward appearance he was but a boy, in musical development his soul was that of a full-grown man. In Bologna, his main thought was to be recognized at the incorruptible judgment-seat of the Philharmonic Academy—which was the leader of the musical world at that time—as a *maestro ;* and to win the approval of Father Martini, whom the Italians almost worshipped, and whose judgment in musical questions was decisive for all Europe.

To-day, therefore, in his visit to the *villa Farinelli,* Wolfgang approached the famous president of the Academy with the most profound respect, and with that sincere admiration which true genius so readily gives to true genius. If as a child he had said, "After God, comes my papa!" he might now have added, "And after papa, Father Martini!"

Mozart was in raptures over Farinelli's instruments, and was as pleased as a child at the famous names with which the old Italian had baptized them. He fixed upon the grand piano named "Raphael" as his favorite, and sitting down to the costly instrument, he improvised for a long time, weaving and unweaving his golden phantasies in beautiful tones, till Farinelli and the Franciscan were enthusiastic over his marvellous playing.

When they had spent some time in music and conversation, Father Martini brought to Wolfgang a theme, expressed in a few notes, and said—

"My son, let us hear you perform the fugue which I have hinted here."

Amadeus complied, and brought out the strong harmonies with a fire as unusual as was his audience. "Raphael" thrilled and trembled under his nervous fingers, as did the hearts of his hearers, with the majesty of the composition. When he had done, they both took him cordially by the hand, and Father Martini said, with the tears flashing in his dark eyes, to his friend—

"Evening-twilight and morning-red! How truly you said it, my brother! And this dawn foretells a glorious day!"

The time soon came when Amadeus was to be examined as a candidate for membership of the *Accademia Filarmonica.*

---

[1] The Italians always called Mozart *Amadeus,* because it suited their musical language better than *Wolfgang.*

It was an important day for him. A refusal would ruin h's prospect for life; an admission would establish his fame for ever. On the appointed afternoon the whole cultured and musical world of Bologna was in motion. On foot and in carriages, people were hastening to the imposing building in whose rooms the Academy held its sittings. At the scene of examination only the members might be present, but the announcement of admission, if the vote were favorable, was made in public. The candidate, Wolfgang Amadeus Mozart, made his appearance at four o'clock in the afternoon in the hall of the Academy. The members were already present, Father Martini and Farinelli among them, sitting in a wide circle, with the president and the censors, all of them distinguished composers, in their places, awaiting the candidate, whose age—only fourteen years—made the event an unprecedented one.

After the formalities of introduction, the president and censors arose, and Amadeus was presented with an *Antiphonia*, from the *Antiphonarium Romanum*,[1] which was to be arranged for four voices, in a closed room, in the space of three hours. Amadeus received the sheet with a respectful obeisance, and, with a quick and confident tread, followed the official, who showed him into a small writing-room, shutting the door behind him with a clang.

To arrange such an antiphony for four voices was a severe trial of musical knowledge and ability. Only a master could accomplish it; and already many a musician of celebrity had been wrecked on this rock, in his attempt to enter the Academy. Composers of ability had before now, in the same place where Amadeus was sitting, occupied the whole three hours in working out an antiphony of only three parts.

Who can describe the amazement of the whole Academy, when, at the expiration of only half an hour, the official entered, and, himself pale with astonishment, announced that the young composer had given the sign that his work was finished. A universal excitement now communicated itself throughout the assemblage. For more than a hundred years the Academy had existed, but there had never in all that time been such a case before. Was this boy of fourteen years a magician?

Father Martini and the censors arose, in evident excite-

---

[1] Antiph. ad Magnificat. Dom. XIV., post Pentecost et in festo Cajetani.

ment, and went to the writing-room. At the door the official received the key from the president's hand, threw back the bolt, and they entered. There stood Wolfgang, smiling good-humoredly, with the manuscript in his hand. On his frank, boyish face there shone an expression of great joy—a joy which was mingled with the pride of conscious power, but far removed from any arrogance or vanity; it was that radiant expression which Raphael delighted to depict upon the faces of the angels who bear up the Queen of Heaven on her throne of billowy clouds.

Father Martini's eyes beamed with pleasure, though he spoke no word; and it was with difficulty that he refrained from taking Wolfgang to his breast in a rapturous embrace.

But custom prescribed a second shutting up of the candidate, while his work was being examined by the assembled composers and judges. This occupied nearly an hour. At last it was concluded, and the president called for the vote. In profound silence a black and a white ball were distributed to each one of the circle. No word betrayed the intention of the voters, but the sparkling eyes of most told the tale. And now the box was emptied before the president, and the moment of decision had come—and it was favorable.

"All the balls white!" cried Father Martini; "the candidate is accepted!"

Then the doors were thrown open, and while the people streamed in at one side, Wolfgang entered at the other, and was greeted by the Academy with an enthusiastic clapping of hands, while the people thundered their *vivas* to the new *cavaliere filarmonico!*

CHAPTER III.

KISSING ST. PETER.

PASSION-WEEK is among all the Catholic people of Christendom the great epoch of the year. But nowhere is it so grandly celebrated as in that greatest temple of the world, the sublime St. Peter's Church, in Rome.

Early in the morning of Maundy-Thursday, crowds of people are already streaming in from all parts of the holy

city and the neighboring country; while for days beforehand
strangers have been gathering from north, south, east, and
west. Piety and zeal, curiosity and the search for excitement, penitence and worldly pleasure, jealousy, cupidity, and
every other human interest and passion, were at the bottom
of this gathering, which now filled the streets of Rome till
they were one swaying sea of people.

It would be difficult to find a finer sight than this joyous
throng of humanity, dressed for the most part in picturesque
costumes, crowding, laughing, bantering, scolding, along the
blocked-up streets leading to the church. Mountaineers in
their brigandish-looking garb, peasants clothed in sheep-skins,
noblemen in splendid robes, fiery-eyed women from the
country, haughty dames and voluptuous girls of the city—
all pressing on, without regard to rank or station, age or race,
toward the lofty dome of St. Peter's; where all—peasant-
girls and duchesses, princes and fishermen, rich and poor,
sick and sound—in a kind of fanatical insanity, crowd about
the seat of the Pope, who is to grant absolution to these souls
languishing in sin.

Yet let no one suppose that an earnest religious feeling
animated this moving mass of people. Oh, no! They jested
and laughed, told good stories and discussed pretty women
(for the proverb goes in Italy, *La mattina una messetta,
l'apodinar una basetta, la sera una donetta*). They sought
the Pope's chair, partly because it was the fashion, partly because they wanted to be on hand to see everybody else do it,
and partly because, to an Italian, a hundred days' absolution
in advance is always a pleasant and convenient thing to
have.

Let us follow the stream of humanity which, on this glorious sunny day, is entering the majestic porch of St. Peter's.
Above, the great dome glitters, at its giddy height, far away
toward the clouds. Below, this mass of living creatures,
moving slowly up the marble steps, seems like a swarm of
ants, in comparison with the vastness of the building. See,
on the right-hand side of the entrance stands an ancient
bronze statue of St. Peter. It was once worshipped by the
old Romans as Jupiter Olympus. How are the mighty fallen!
Every one who enters stops to kiss the foot of the statue—
almost worn out by the millions and millions of kisses it has
received.

Now the throng divides reverently to make way for a car

dinal and his train. He, too, leaves a holy kiss on the apostle's toes; but before his train can follow him in this pious act, a mass of people storms, and struggles, and quarrels as to who shall kiss first after the cardinal, as if that carried a special blessing in it. When the momentary turmoil is over, the servants of the great priest draw near; but they first reverently wipe the sacred toes with their handkerchiefs before they put their lips to them, and then they, too, pass on.

"Let's make haste!" said at this moment a beautiful young girl to her youthful companion—"let's make haste, Veronica, for the crowd is growing thicker every minute. If we don't get a place soon, we shall miss the feet-washing."

"But, Giuditta!" replied the other in astonishment, "shan't we get a blessing from the Holy Father at all?"

"Let that be till Easter," answered Giuditta; "the feet-washing is a great deal more interesting."

"But shan't we kiss St. Peter's foot, first?" asked the other, rather anxiously.

"For aught I care!" cried Giuditta, in a cheerful tone; "anything, so we go ahead."

And with these words she took her companion by the arm, and pulled her energetically toward the apostle's statue.

Giuditta was a girl of fourteen years, charming as a freshly-opening rose-bud. There was a certain peculiar appearance of natural vigor about her, and the graceful figure, slender yet fully developed, and with an air of voluptuous strength, was well matched by the frank face, with its brown Italian tint, and its fiery dark eyes. She was dressed in the picturesque garb of the Roman maiden, which seems made to show such young creatures in all the fulness of their beauty.

A frock of some soft material, blue as the sky of Italy, concealed the graceful form; and as the bodice only covered the waist, above it there was nothing but the snow-white chemise, gathered in light folds over the breast and back,—so that its pure white, together with that of the wide sleeves, made a rare contrast with the rich tint of neck and arms.

A high comb of silver confined her heavy black hair, while a long white veil covered her head, beneath the lace points of which the perfect oval of her blooming little face looked out, *naïve* and innocent.

It was a real pleasure to watch the two maidens, both dressed almost alike, and both brimming with youth and life. And this youthful overflow of life expressed itself in every·

thing about them—in the frank smile playing about the mouth, in the soft fire of the dusky eyes, and the suddenness and energy of gesture and movement. It was the true Italian blood! How it would, sooner or later, stormily awake in both those young hearts; what fierce passions were asleep there beneath that rosy dawn of girlhood, like the flames of Vesuvius under laughing vineyards and olive-groves!

It made a picture which Raphael's pencil would have loved to catch, when the two maidens knelt before the pedestal of the ancient bronze statue of the apostle, rising above their beautiful heads in its stern, grim antiquity. But Giuditta's attention seemed to be wandering while she prayed. The beads of her rosary were indeed slipping through her pretty fingers, and the ripe young lips were in motion, but her thoughts were evidently somewhere else, and those dark fixed eyes rested on a handsome boy, who, in company with an elderly man, was approaching the statue of St. Peter.

They must be strangers—that was evident from their garments, and from the look of wonder which their fine faces wore. The boy seemed to be some travelling prince, so easy and courtly were his manners and all his motions.

Giuditta had taken note of all this between the beads of her rosary; and during the *Paternoster* and *Ave Maria* she imparted her impressions to her friend.

"Cospetto di Bacco!" she whispered now; "the little prince pleases me. Only look at his blue eyes and fair forehead!"

"And the small mouth!" added Veronica.

"And how elegantly he is clothed!" continued Giuditta; "his cocked hat is fastened with a jewel which has all the colors of the rainbow."

"Do you suppose he is English?" whispered her friend.

Giuditta shook her little head, said an *Ave*, and replied—

"He must be German, his face is so pleasant; you know I ought to judge pretty well, for—*Deum de Deo, Lumen de Lumine*—father is a papal courier, and—*genitum non factum* —we have a roomy house—*consubstantialem Patri*—and see many guests of all sorts of countries; and to-morrow they are to arrive—*per quem omnia facta sunt*—two Germans; a gentleman with his son—*qui propter nos homines*—who is a magician."

"A magician?" whispered Veronica, aghast.

"Yes, but only in music," continued Giuditta. "Look!

there come the prince and his companion. How piously the older one kisses the holy foot!"

"And now the prince is going to, also."

"But see—he cannot reach above the pedestal, he is so small."

"And nobody helps him; his companion is praying, and pays no attention."

"Eh!" cried Giuditta, and her dusky eyes flashed fire. "Then I must help the prince myself!"

And before Veronica could hold her back, she had sprung up, caught the handsome boy in her arms, and lifted him up.'

The youngster, supposing of course that it was his companion who was doing him this friendly service, bent his head over the worn foot of the bronze saint, and pressed a kiss upon it. As he slipped gently down, it seemed to him that he felt a woman's garment and form behind him. Quickly turning his head, the red blood mounted to his cheeks, for he was looking into a beautiful girlish face that was blushing like his own. But it was only an instant. Scarcely had his feet touched the floor, when the angel had vanished, and a new crowd of people pushed Amadeus and his father into the church.

CHAPTER IV.

THE MISERERE.

THE evening of the day on which the incident related in the last chapter occurred, brought to Amadeus the hour to which he had been looking forward all his life—the hour for which he had longed with all the strength of his soul.

¹ Historical.—The following is the boy's own account of it, in a letter to his sister (Mozart's Letters, No. 9: N. Y., Leypoldt & Holt. 1867.)

ROME, *April* 14, 1770.

I am thankful to say that my stupid pen and I are all right, so we send a thousand kisses to you both. Papa has just told me that the loveliest flowers are being carried past at this moment. That I am no wiseacre is pretty well known. Oh! I have one annoyance—there is only a single bed in our lodgings, so mamma may easily imagine that I get no rest beside papa. I rejoice at the thoughts of a new lodging. I have just finished sketching St. Peter with his keys, St. Paul with his sword, and St. Luke with—my sister, etc., etc. *I had the honor of kissing St. Peter's foot at San Pietro, and as I have the misfortune to be so short, your good old'*
WOLFGANG MOZART
was lifted up '

That evening he was to be present at the performance of
Mass in the Sistine Chapel, and the young musician was in a
state of excitement and agitation which he had never experienced before.

The *Miserere* of Allegri is perhaps the most wonderful
composition which the world has ever seen. It is in some respects beyond all other music of human creation.[1] It is truly
an unearthly music, in its removal from all the expressions
of common human feelings or ideas. There is in it none of
that tremulous, expectant, and then exultant, resolution of
dissonances, which image our pain—hope—triumph—ever
momentary and vanishing. It has no rhythm, which follows
the flight of the wings of Time, and is measured by the
pulsations of human hearts; nothing which awakens a
worldly thought, or speaks the language of mortal passion.
It is a *sacred* music, more literally than any other that was
ever composed. *Holiness* is written upon its mysterious
tones. It is ancient, but its antiquity knows no growing old
—its beauty and its wonder are eternal.

Only a soul which lives wholly and entirely in music, as in
a separate world—a soul which carries music into all its works
and ways, into every meditation and aspiration, into thought
and feeling, effort and desire, as did Mozart—can imagine the
mood which possessed his spirit as he awaited the experience
of this evening. It was such as fills the unfolding rosebud,
over which, in the sultry summer night, the first breath of a
tempest blows; such as trembles through the maiden's heart
upon her bridal night, when the first kiss of her beloved is
pressed upon her lips.

That practical person, Father Mozart, enthusiastic lover of

---

[1] [H. Taine, writing from Rome, 1864, says of the *Miserere* of Palestrina and Allegri: " These two *Miserere* are above, and perhaps beyond, all music to which I ever
listened; previous to acquaintance with these, one could only imagine such sweetness and melancholy, such strangeness and sublimity. Three points are very striking—discords abound sometimes, so as to produce what, in ears like ours, accustomed to agreeable sensations, we call false notes. The parts are multiplied in an
extraordinary degree, so that the same chord contains three or four harmonies, and
two or three discords, all constautly decomposed and recomposed in its various portions; some voice at every instant is heard detaching itself through its own theme,
the aggregate number being so well distributed that the harmony seems an effect of
chance, like the low and intermittent concert of rural harmonies: the continuous
tone is that of a plaintive ecstatic prayer, ever persistent, or unweariedly recurring
without regard to symmetrical chant or ordinary rhythm; an indefatigable aspiration of the suffering heart which can and will find rest only in God—the ever-renewed
yearnings of captive spirits sinking to their native dust through their own burden—
the prolonged sighs of an infinite number of loving, tender, unhappy souls, never
discouraged in adoring and in worshipping."—TR.]

music as he was, could not resist an unwonted fever of ex
pectation to-night; yet he could not share the intensity of
Wolfgang's mood.   But he was too wise a man to check or
chide his son for an emotion, because he could not perfectly
sympathize with it.

At the appointed hour they entered the Sistine Chapel.
What a spectacle met their eyes !   The world has not another
similar one.   More than seven hundred burning wax-candles
lit up the vast and already crowded building.   The colossal
dome lifted itself above, like the arch of the blue heaven.
The walls were painted in gigantic frescoes; and on the opposite wall, as you entered, loomed up the sublime *Last Judgment* of Michael Angelo.

It smote upon the sensitive and imaginative spirit of
Amadeus with an irresistible awe.   He felt his limbs tremble,
and the blood gather at his heart.   But now—on a sudden—
all the countless lights were extinguished, as by magic, except fifteen, which twinkled above the altar; and the whole
Sistine Chapel lay in ghostly gloom.   And then began the
Matutino delle tenebre, from a choir of thirty-two voices,
without instrumental accompaniment.   This famous composition consists of fifteen psalms, and a number of prayers,
and concludes with the *Miserere.*

A stillness as of death reigned in the great building.   As
each psalm was ended, one of the fifteen candles was extinguished, and the gloom and silence throughout the church
became more profound and awful, and the singing grew sadder and deeper, till its tender pathos was as if a nightingale,
wounded to the death, were singing its pain;—and then it
deepened and swelled, till it was the woe of all humanity for
the wrongs of its noblest sons, going up before the throne of
the Eternal Spirit.

Then hot tears rushed from the hearts of the listeners, and
they forgot that they were children of the dust, in a dust-
born world.

And when now the fifteenth psalm was ended, and the last
light was extinguished, and the darkness of the grave reigned
over the whole chapel, then arose the *Miserere.*

The impression was indescribable.   Amadeus no longer
was a bodily existence; he neither felt, nor saw, nor breathed
in the flesh.

The *Miserere* had long been finished; but Amadeus stil,

stood motionless. A gigantic cross, brilliant with hundreds of blazing lights, was lowered from the centre of the dome, and flooded the darkness with a sudden sea of splendor. It was a magical effect: but Amadeus marked it not; he stood unmoved. The stream of thronging humanity had crowded by, and only a few loiterers remained in the empty chapel; but he knew not of it, and still stood motionless, as if stricken to a statue.

Then his father, almost in alarm, bent down, and said, with a voice full of affection, "Wolfgang! it is time for us to go!"

The boy started, as out of a dream, and stared with great eyes at his father. Then, passing his hand over brow and eyes, and looking about him, as though to recollect where he was, he nodded to his father, and silently followed him into the open air.

Not a word came from the boy's lips, as they walked homeward: father Mozart, too, was full of thought; and when they reached the house, he was glad to have his son hasten to their chamber, which they occupied together, and retire to rest. But scarcely had his father fallen asleep by his side, when Amadeus softly arose, lit the lamp, and made ready pen and music-paper. Then he quietly threw open one of the windows, and gazed out.

There it lay at his feet—the Eternal City—the tomb of so many centuries—the mausoleum of half the history of the world; and over its ruined glory that heavenly night had folded the moonlight like a shroud.

For a few minutes Amadeus gazed upon the impressive scene; then, with a glance at the splendid night-sky, he closed the window hastily, and seated himself before the music-paper at the table.

When the next morning's kindling sunrise greeted the earth, it threw its first rays over a beautiful boyish head that was resting on folded arms across the desk, fast asleep with weariness and toil; and it gilded the sheets of music-paper that lay beside the young sleeper, on whose closely-written pages appeared the *Miserere of Allegri*.

Wolfgang Amadeus Mozart, the boy of fourteen years, had performed what has ever since been considered almost a miracle—he had written out, incredible as it may seem, that wonderful masterpiece of composition, which the Romish

Church held so jealously guarded under pain of excommu·
nication to any one of its singers who should lend, show, or
copy a single note of it—written it out from memory, after
one hearing, and without an error ![1]

CHAPTER V.

GIUDITTA.

A MADEUS was a fully ripened and mature man, only
in music : in all other respects he was as boyish as need
be. It was, therefore, with the greatest delight that he accompanied his father, the next day, to their new quarters, at
the house of Signor Uslinghi. There was no trace left in
him of the last night's exaltation and mental strain ; except,
perhaps, the reaction from it, which expressed itself in all
manner of pranks and jollity, as they threaded the streets of
Rome to find their future abode. Father Mozart, too, was
pleased at the prospect of a change from their previous narrow lodgings, and especially so since he had learned that the
Italian gentleman, who was to be his host, was a papal
courier, and therefore that he would meet at his house none
but such people as he would desire to know.

The outer door of the house stood wide open, as they approached, and on entering they passed through a cool hall
into a still cooler court, surrounded by stone arches. Large
vines clasped the pillars in their sturdy embrace, and cling-
ing to the heavy arches, dropped a slender arm here and
there, with whose tendrils the wind lightly played ; while a
tossing fountain, which sprang up in the midst of the court,
from a crumbling antique marble basin, kept up a pleasant
murmur with its continual plashing.

Near the fountain sat a woman, dressed in the picturesque
Roman costume, whose white hands were busy at the spinning-wheel. As soon as she saw the two strangers, she rose
quickly, and hastening forward to meet them, as though
they were well known to her, she said, in a friendly tone—

[1] Historical.—*Vide* Oulibicheff ; and Jahn, Part I., p. 199. It was only of a piece
with other of Mozart's surprising feats.

"I am heartily glad to see you; for I am greatly mistaken
if you are not the Monsignore Mozart who was so warmly
commended to me with his son, the *maestro illustrissimo*, by
Signor Farinelli!"

"I am Capellmeister Mozart, certainly," replied the Ger
man, in his straightforward style, "and this is my son, the
musician; but we are neither princes, as has been reported
here, nor *Monsignore*, nor *illustrissimo*."

"Ah, well!" cried Signora Uslinghi, laughing, "'tis all
one! That's their fashion in Rome. The proverb says: 'Al
gato del papa si dice Monsignore!' (The pope's cat is called
Sir.) You find a touch of exaggeration everywhere. If
there is a crowd of a hundred men here, in the next street
they'll have it a thousand. If they talk to you, as a musician,
about a concert-room, it will be 'l'anticamera del Paradiso!'
Every house that has two windows more than its neighbor,
is called a palace; and every old stone has a miracle under
it. Oh! you will see a good many queer things in Rome: a
prince who is next door to beggary talks of his 'court;' and
many a *Donna*, in the greatest state, and with a servant
behind her, hasn't a garment to spare. Everything is put
under magnifying glasses here, my friend!"

"I admire your frankness, dear Madam!" replied Father
Mozart, in a lively tone; "I always get on best with plain-
spoken people. And now that you have guessed who we are,
allow me the same privilege. Are you not Madam Uslinghi,
wife of the papal courier?"

"I am," answered the lady, with some pride; "and as my
husband happens now to be in Portugal, on business for the
Holy Father, and only I and my little daughter are at home,
you, Monsignore, shall be master of the house, and we will
be at your service! And I am sure," she went on, with a
volubility which ever increased, like a mountain-torrent after
a storm, "you'll like it here with us. There's a good deal
of flourish and bombast, to be sure; but, after all's said and
done, Rome is the city of the world. For my part, I have
never been outside the Pope's dominions; but Uslinghi has
said to me a thousand times—and you know he has travelled
hither and yon—he has said to me, says he, 'Give me Rome
and Naples! Rome for art and life—Naples for nature. In
Naples you're in paradise: in Rome you're in heaven!"

Well, is it not almost as the good lady said, in her holy
zeal? Has not a great philosopher also testified—"In Rome

we live as the gods live?" A glass of ice-water and a crust
are nectar and ambrosia, with the Vatican to loiter in, and
Raphael's faces for company! The *blue* blue sky of Italy;
the inspiring atmosphere; the classic surroundings of art;
the luscious fruits and golden wine; the living models of
Raphael's Madonnas and Guido's Magdalens, with their passionate eyes and voluptuous forms; the ever-verdant oaks,
and plane-trees, and pines, with those symbols of the victo-
ries of heroes and martyrs, the tufted palms; all this glowing
Southern land, lapped by the azure sea; where else—O fortunate mortal, whose eyes have beheld Rome—where else
will you find all these?

In further lively talk, the worthy dame rattled on (or
rather rippled on, for the Italian tongue never rattles) without interruption, somewhat at the expense of her guests'
patience. At last she seemed to bethink herself, and cried,
spreading out her hands, "But, holy Maria! here I am chattering on, and leaving your Excellency standing in the courtyard. Come in—come in! I will show you and the young
maestro to your chambers."

In saying this, the kind dame showed such hearty hospi-
tality, that the slight impatience of the Mozarts gave place
immediately to a sense of being at home, such as they had
not experienced since they left Salzburg. This feeling was
increased when they saw the apartments to which Madame
Uslinghi conducted them. They had already become accustomed to expect untidiness in every Italian household, but
here all was clean and neat as at home. There was an air of
comfort and tasteful elegance in all the furniture and arrangement of the rooms; and in the windows stood slender vases
full of fresh flowers. Just as Father Mozart was turning to
ask whom he had to thank for this attention, the door opened,
and Giuditta entered, bearing in one hand, pressed against
her round bosom, another vase of blossoms. It had nearly
fallen, so surprised was she at the sight of the strangers; and
as she grasped it with her other quick hand, she uttered a
little cry, and the words, "Ha, the prince!" It would be
difficult to say whose cheeks burned with the rosiest blush,
hers or Wolfgang's, as they caught each other's eye.

This did not escape the mother's keen glance, who asked
Giuditta for an explanation; and now the whole story of
yesterday's occurrence at St. Peter's came out, and there was
talk and jest and banter about it, till they all four felt as well

acquainted as though they had been old friends. Father Mozart and the *Senora* were very well pleased with each other; and as for Giuditta and Amadeus, they were, before an hour had passed, one heart and one soul.

Before the expiration of a week, invitations began to come in from the highest nobility in Rome, at all whose houses Amadeus was received with great attention, and, as soon as opportunities for a display of his musical powers occurred, with enthusiastic welcome.

The musical world of Italy, at that time, formed a solid phalanx—a compact, united band, suffering no opposition, and overwhelming all resistance. Its apostles were sent all over the earth, and preached as those that had authority, for the Italian school held the monopoly and the power.

It was therefore indispensable to every European musician that he should go to Italy. There, all were sure of recognition from their common mother. Indeed, sometimes she gave the preference to foreigners, over her own most famous children, and adopted them with love, and took pride in their triumphs: only, however, on condition that they came to her to be taught, and not to teach; and that they, in turn, completely adopted the Italian style. Even Handel and Gluck had won their spurs in Italy, and given to their foster-parent their first tribute of *imitation*—that most flattering homage, which she so inexorably claimed. But woe to that musician who should dare to hold by the doctrines of any foreign school! He was sure, like poor Jomelli, to be hunted to death with hisses and anathemas.

Amadeus, however, won the caresses of this exacting Italy upon his first arrival. Perhaps the boy's excellent command of the language aided to this result. At all events, they looked upon him, in Rome, as a child of the soil. Foremost among his friends was Cardinal Pallavicini, who paid him every attention, and even introduced him to His Holiness the Pope. Vieing with the cardinal in kindness were the Neapolitan prince St. Angelo, Prince Ghigi, Princess Barbarini, the Duke of Braiciano, and others.

But it was not this favor and flattery which threw such a golden glow, for Amadeus, over his residence in Rome; nor was it the great city's wealth of historical associations and glorious art. True, he spent many a happy afternoon with his father, wandering among the ruined monuments of long-sunken centuries; many a memorable hour was devoted to the enjoyment of statues and paintings, the lavish treasures of the Eternal City. But Amadeus found in Rome another treasure: a pearl, which to him—who was, and ever remained, in the midst of his wondrous genius, so thoroughly and merely a man—was priceless then, and costly with consequences for his whole future. Years came and went—storms spent their fury upon his head—joys and woes, triumphs and disasters came to him—but always memory held in his heart one bright and happy spot, where lay the recollections of those days which were spent in the quiet abode of Uslinghi, and of the bliss which bloomed there for him, from a heart as glad and as freshly innocent as his own.

Whether his meeting with the passionate-eyed young maiden in the porch of St. Peter's, at the foot of the stern old statue, had been merely a freak of fortune; or his good genius had determined that the vigorous round arms and soft form of the Roman girl should help him to the holy kiss,—certain it is, that from this moment commenced an attraction between these two young hearts, which grew stronger with every hour of their intercourse. But this inclination took, in each, a form as different as were their two nationalities. Amadeus looked upon Giuditta as another Nannerl, and with the most unrestrained brotherly affection he clung to the joyous and bewitching girl, who made the few hours of each day which were passed at home the brightest portion of his life at Rome.

Always merry, as he was, and often running almost wild with mad pranks, he found in her an equal madcap with himself; but Wolfgang never stopped to suspect that the innocent wantonness of the young Roman had any different source from his own. In him was this curious mixture—full musical maturity in union with physical and spiritual boyhood. His body and mind had arisen upon earth like those of other mortals, and were growing in healthy and natural development toward manhood; but his musical being seemed to have lived a previous existence, and to find all earthly things only reminiscences of that former life. To such an extent, at least, the poet's words seemed to be verified in Mozart:

> "Our birth is but a sleep and a forgetting:
> The soul that rises with us, our life's star,
>   Hath had elsewhere its setting,
>   And cometh from afar.

> Not in entire forgetfulness,
> And not in utter nakedness,
> But trailing clouds of glory, do we come
> From God, who is our home."

Where music was in question, he was, as we know, man and master; but for all that, Nature gave not up her rights; the youthful flood of life broke through in the careless and romping boy. Nothing shows this more plainly than his own letters to his mother and sister, which, through all his residence in Italy, are brimful of boyish nonsense;—as that one which we have quoted, where he calls himself, apparently conscious of this boyishness, "no wiseacre." So that it was unfolding power, a demand for free expansion, an exuberant overflow of young animal spirits, which were the sources of his wild sportiveness. Quite otherwise was it with Giuditta. In her veins the hot southern blood was in motion. Physically, she was fully developed—she was a flower of the warm Italian sunshine. A girl of only fourteen summers it is true she was; but behind a form so fully and ripely rounded as was hers, and under eyes of such a dusky fieriness, lies already the possibility of passion; and when it has once awakened, it kindles, not as in the northern blood, slowly and smoulderingly—but, lit to-day, to-morrow it flames up in burning fire, and threatens to consume its own heart or another's.

When Giuditta, seized with a sudden impulse, had clasped her arms round the boy, and raised him up to kiss St. Peter's foot, she had been only a child, with the most quiet heart in the world. When, a minute later, Amadeus turned his beautiful, glowing face to hers, the gaze of those soulful eyes and the touch of his form thrilled her like a magnetic current, and her heart beat fast—its childish rest was broken forever. And now, since Wolfgang had come to live under the same roof, she loved him—not after the cool northern fashion, but in the Italian way—deeply, warmly, passionately. Yet she was herself too much a child to understand this passion, and its object was still more incapable of comprehending it. But there it was, blossoming and burning within her—and she hid it under playful wantonness and sport.

She could not whisper to her fair young friend what was going on within her; but when they were playing together, teasing each other, and what not, she could laughingly put her soft arms around his neck, and press herself to him, and give him little bites and kisses. In all this there was something, they knew not what, endlessly delightful to them both; and a wild, sweet glow made each more beautiful than ever. Amadeus called her his "little wild-cat!" and often would he lie down under the cool vine-trellis of the courtyard, and beckon her as one does a kitten, to come and bite him and be caressed.

With his violin, too, he often enticed her to his side; especially when some voluptuous Italian night hung over the earth, and the older people were walking up and down the garden. Then she would lay herself down at his feet, with her hands clasped under her head, and her gaze fixed on the starry night-sky, and listen in still ravishment to the tones which Amadeus conjured, like a magician, from the instrument. Hour after hour he would play, and she would listen. Not a word would be spoken, but her dusky eyes told the starlight what his ravishing melodies told the deep night; an old, old story—the most beautiful story upon earth; the innocent expression of that pure passion—which has no purpose but itself, not even pleasure—which is pure as dew, and pure as fire.

At the end, Amadeus would very likely sink upon one knee, and press a kiss on the full lips which had long been pouting up for it. And then would follow the sport between the boy and his "wild-cat."

When at last they sought their beds, Wolfgang would have a good laugh by himself over their frolic, and quickly be asleep. Not so with Giuditta. All the ice-water she would drink cooled her not; sleep would not come as it used to; and when it came, she tossed and murmured in strange dreams.

CHAPTER VI.

STRATEGY AGAINST STRATEGY.

THE beautiful Roman girl had one great sorrow, and one great rival, in her love for Amadeus. Her rival was music; and her sorrow was, that her friend forever slipped from her embrace, as it were, into another world whither she could not follow him. Together they would be sitting, hand in hand, and suddenly the soul of the young *maestro* would be far away in his own enchanted realm of music, and, like the maiden in the fairy-tale, she would hear the gate harshly clang behind her lost prince, and be left weeping by herself. She indeed loved music, and did not lack appreciative talent in the art; but as yet she could *do* nothing in it.

But now Amadeus discovered that she possessed a fine contralto voice, and at once determined to give her instruction in singing. This plan pleased his charming friend extremely; for it would be a splendid opportunity to have Amadeus all to herself, unrestrainedly, for several hours in the day. She was a most diligent pupil,—only, it had sometimes a strange effect on her teacher, when, in her zeal for the art which was to be learned, she would lay her soft arm about him, and, listening intently to every word and tone, with her pleading dark eyes would sink her very soul deep, deep down into the clear blue depths of his own. Then he would feel her warm hand tremble in his, till a glow would pass over him, and a feeling touch him, which was half pain and half joy, and made his heart beat stormily.

These two innocents had a wonderful similarity in their method of rewards to each other. If Giuditta had practised bravely, and learned her singing lesson well, then her teacher was wont to take his "little wild-cat" by the chin, turn her tempting face to his, and give her, in pay for her diligence, divers sound kisses. But then, of course, Giuditta, feeling that she did not deserve any reward, and that she could not sufficiently thank Amadeus for his painstaking with her, so dull a pupil, would press close to him, and imprint the most glowing kisses on his lips—kisses so burning and passionate, that the young teacher would grow rosy to his very ears, and be nearly dizzy. Then he would look at her with such affectionate pleasure, in return for her caresses, that the just soul felt obliged to repeat her repayment, over and over again.

Father Mozart, overcome by the languor of the southern climate, was accustomed to take his *siesta* at the hour when these lessons were in progress; and, after the first practising had begun, usually went sound asleep.

But nothing is immortal in this world—except mortality—and so the time which had been fixed for their residence in Rome drew near its close. The Capellmeister already was making preparations for their departure to Naples.

It is easy to imagine what grief the approaching separation
brought to these two young hearts. They had but one comfort, and that was the sure expectation of seeing each other
again after a few weeks. For Father Mozart had begun to
discover that Wolfgang felt something more than a brotherly
affection for the charming daughter of the house, and he was
so much the more determined to depart on the appointed day;
and he used so much strategy, as to lay great stress on the
hope of a speedy return to Uslinghi's hospitable mansion,
making very light of their departure, as for a mere pleasure-
trip to Naples. But the last afternoon of their stay, in order
to cut the leave-takings as short as possible, the astute Capellmeister suddenly announced that, on the advice of Cardinal
Pallavicini, they would join company with some White Friars
who would leave their convent for Marino at daybreak the
next morning; and in order not to delay their starting, it
would be best for them to spend the night at the convent.
The prudent man had already made the necessary preparations, and now the word was "mount and away!"

Father Mozart was uncommonly cheerful; he joked with
Madame Uslinghi, kissed Giuditta, and spoke only of a
speedy return to their pleasant quarters.

The jollier the father became, the more disconsolate grew
the young folks. Amadeus had a cheery and vivid imagination, which overleaped the few weeks of separation before
them, but there was a nameless something in his relations
with his beautiful friend, which made it seem impossible to
depart without her. Yet the father's will was a law with
the boy, and he must go.

Giuditta allowed none to see what she felt in her heart.
Was she too proud to show her pain? or was she indignant
at the artifice by which the shrewd Capellmeister had robbed
them of their last delicious night together, with its bitter-
sweet of farewells? However it was, she was as brisk and
bright at the last moment as if the departing guests had
been only setting out for a day's ride into the country.

"Practise your singing well," cried Amadeus to her, as
they separated; "when we come back, we will go on with
the lessons,"—and he added lightly in her ear—"with some
other things also!"

"Yes," replied Giuditta; and whispered, as she held him
back by his small white hand, "and when you get to Marino,
be sure to go to the grotto of St. Cecilia, alone—do you

bear? *alone*—and say a *Paternoster* for me! Be sure now!"

"You may depend on me, little wild-cat," returned Wolfgang, with forced cheerfulness, and trying to keep down a choking sensation in his throat, as he followed the long strides of his father.

The next day, after a rather dreary ride across the barren and desolate *Campagna*, they reached the Austin convent at Marino, where they were to rest several hours and take dinner. Wolfgang was very still, and apparently lost in lonely meditations the whole way: there was little in the wide plain, deserted and treeless, with its ruins, and here and there a wild-looking animal, to cheer and please a heart like his, which was born for songs, sunshine, and flowers. When dinner-time came, he begged to be excused from that meal, saying that he would dine on some oranges by himself.

For some hours, therefore, Amadeus was free to enjoy his solitude, and could now, without danger of interruption, fulfil his promise to say a *Paternoster* for Giuditta, in the grotto of St. Cecilia. This holy lady, as the guardian of all musical people, was his patron saint, and the legends of her wonderful music, and her organ-playing, had always had a special charm for him. One of the monks having showed him the path he must follow to find the grotto, he joyfully set out alone. The way led through a pleasant valley, which seemed all the more delightful from its vivid contrast with the dry and desolate *Campagna*, in the midst of which it lay like a bright oasis in the desert.

Through the valley a small, clear brook ran down from the rocks, among which the convent was perched, and slipped quietly along, now showing its crystal mountain-current, and now hidden by the large stalks and leaves of luxuriant water-plants. Waving cornfields and fresh meadow-green, starred with thousands of anemones and daisies, gave to the place a look of pleasant comfort, which Amadeus had missed throughout his morning ride from Rome. No human being was to be seen in the valley. Everything slept in the sultry noon.

At last our hero espied the entrance to the grotto, which was formed of volcanic rocks, hurled up and piled about in this confusion ages ago, by some fierce eruption of the nether world. The mouth of the cave was almost concealed by tree roots and ivy-stems, whose tangled web proved how rarely the shrine of the Saint was visited.

Amadeus with some difficulty made his way through, and stood still with wonder at the sight which presented itself. The cavern branched out in several directions into shadowy openings, and had from this cause alone an appearance of mystery. But this appearance was heightened by the dusky twilight which reigned on all sides, and by the bushes which grew down from the cloven walls, and veiled the entrance with their green curtain. Among the rocks, on a sort of rough altar, stood a stone statue of St. Cecilia,—evidently not the handiwork of a great sculptor, and much dilapidated under the touch of time.

Amadeus, true to his promise, performed his devotions, and then penetrated farther on into the depths of the grotto, where he found a sloping bank, carpeted thick and soft with moss. This was just the spot for his solitary picnic, and drawing the oranges from his pockets, he did justice to his frugal meal. Then he stretched himself at full length on the deep moss, and closing his eyes, allowed his imagination to retrace the last pleasant weeks, as in a waking dream.

Suddenly, from the depths of the grotto, he hears the first bars of a well-known song,—well-known, for it was of his own composition. Still more familiar was the contralto voice of the singer. He sprang up—the ear of a Mozart could not be deceived; but—how could she be here?—it was impossible! Taking a few hasty steps forward, there stood before him a girlish form, hidden in the garb of a pilgrim, which is the universal disguise of solitary wanderers in Italy, since this dress is sacred, even to the bandits. Quickly the wide-brimmed palmer's hat flew off, and the long necklace of cockle-shells was thrown down, and—Giuditta lay upon his breast!

"Giuditta!" cried Wolfgang, beside himself with amazement; "is it possible that you are here?"

"I appear to be!" she answered, with a saucy smile; "the dear Capellmeister thought he had cheated us of our good-bye, so cunningly! Did you think I would let you go without a good farewell? and did he think an Italian girl was to be trapped so easily? You were both out, there!"

"But I don't see—" cried Amadeus, stammering in his bewilderment.

"How the 'little wild-cat' got here?" asked the fair Roman

" Yes !"

" Didn't your father say that you would stop for dinner at the convent here ?"

" Well—"

" And you travelled with monks, and when monks stop at a convent for dinner, it is the same as to say they will stop at least six hours—two at table, two in the wine-vaults, and two asleep."

"But how did you know that ?"

" Amadeo !" cried Giuditta, with a laugh, " that is one of your real German questions. In Italy every child knows it !"

" And how did you get here ?"

" Why, I knew that you would be here to-day, and as I always make four pilgrimages here, every year, I went to mother, and told her it would be a clear shame for an Italian to be so cheated, and that I was determined to have a good-bye from you by strategy. She laughed, for the idea just suited her—especially as your father's spending the night at the convent had piqued her a little."

"But how came you *here* so soon ?" insisted Amadeus, patting her round cheek impatiently.

" Well, I just took my pilgrim hat and shells, and trudged right after you."

" Not on foot ?"

" Yes, I walked all the evening and half the night. Then I slept a few hours at Novelli with my aunt, and I have been here now for these three hours, and have been praying to the holy Cecilia."

" But you must be terribly tired !"

" That is nothing : I was bent on stealing a last kiss from you,—and I have shown your father that 'tisn't so easy to cheat an Italian girl. Then, too, Father Frattina, my confessor, will count the pilgrimage as a penance, I know."

Amadeus shook his head, in smiling reproof. Much as it pleased him to see Giuditta once more, yet his conscience troubled him a little on account of the trick which—though without his design—was being played on his father; for Father Mozart's will had not only been a law to the boy, but he had never concealed any plan or action from him,—in such mutual respect and confidence they had lived together. Never until now had he suspected anything in the remotest degree wrong in his brotherly affection for Giuditta, but this secret meeting put a doubt into his head, and that made him observant, and so, all at once, he saw, as the ripe young Italian pressed her kisses on his lips, that it was no sister he was holding to his breast!

Yet were these kisses so sweet that they rippled through him in tremulous thrills—never had her caresses so intoxicated him—and for the first time he felt that with the charming maiden he held a heaven in his arms.

Many a time he had petted, and kissed, and embraced Giuditta in their madcap play. But his part of the experience had only been the joy of a wild boy at play with another boy, or with his sister. But now it was different. The man within the boy began to know what it is to clasp a beloved and beautiful girl. The witchery of this new impression was strong enough to drive out everything else. And had not Giuditta for his sake plodded the whole long way from Rome? Had she not spent a day and night merely to have a farewell from her friend? And could his generous heart remain untouched by such a proof of her warm sisterly love? In his operas he had often written love-songs, but without any real knowledge of his subject, that is certain. Now it came to him, like a revelation, what love really is.

Giuditta, meantime, had seated herself on the soft moss, and drawn Amadeus down by her side, where he lay with his fair head in her lap. Long would they remain in this way, smiling into each other's faces in silence; then, like two rosebuds which the wind moves, their heads would bend together, and join in happy kisses.

Hours went by in this manner, in banter and confidential talk, and the boy and girl were all the more beautiful and blessed, because no further longing came to their consciousness, and the Angel of childlike innocence sanctified their joys. The morning-glow of love was over them—rosy, golden, ineffably tender and fair. And into its delicious haze they looked, and in dim presentiments caught the rapture of the heaven which lay beyond.

At last it was time to separate. Giuditta was the first to remember it, for she must be back before midnight to her aunt's abode in Novelli. And she said:

"Now, Amadeo, we have had our farewell; but there is one word more. You will come again, and I know you will never forget me." Then she drew forth from her bosom a little cross of gold and gave it to Wolfgang, saying—

"Take this amulet; it has been blessed by the Holy Father

4

himself. It has lain on my heart since I was six years old;
let it lie now on yours, and when you look upon it, think of
me !"

Then with one wild sob she flung her arms about him,
kissed him passionately, and was gone.

CHAPTER VII.

THE MAGIC RING.

" SEE Naples, and die !" an English writer has said; as if
it were the crown and summit of all earthly beauty.
To the Mozarts it indeed seemed as such.   The splendid situation of Naples, the beauty of the city and its surroundings,
the wonderful atmosphere, and the warm welcome they received at all hands, made it appear, as Madame Uslinghi had
said, almost a Paradise.

A few days after their arrival they were sitting at home,
awaiting the coming of two of their new friends, who had
promised to take them to the famous Conservatory *Della
Pieta*, where they would meet a circle of distinguished Nea-
politans, and hear the musical performances of the artists
and pupils of the Conservatory there assembled.   The expected friends were Doll and Jomelli;—the former a German
composer of distinction; the latter, one of the famous musicians of his time, whose opera *Cajo Mario* was just at that
time being given before crowded houses in Naples.

It was now seven o'clock in the evening.   The extreme
heat of the day was over, and through the open windows a
fresh, reviving breath from the cool sea stole in.   Father
Mozart had seated himself on the balcony, in quiet enjoyment
of his fragrant German pipe, and the ravishing view which
lay spread before his eyes, taking in its sweep the whole magnificent Bay of Naples.   Amadeus was sitting at the piano,
playing a new minuet of Haydn, which he had just received
from Nannerl.   Haydn was his very ideal—his joy—and, as
a German, his pride; and the piece before him filled him with
delight.   At that moment the two musicians entered the

room. Amadeus did not cease playing, but cried, in his peculiarly bright and enthusiastic tones—

"Just hear this! It is a new thing of my glorious Haydn's! —what a voice of joy there is in that! Do you hear? It is as if we were in a crowd of happy people; and now—it is a flock of children, laughing, romping, and pelting us with flowers!"

Then he rose, and with a look of almost inspiration on his bright face, browned a little by the southern sun, said he—

"What a noble sphere is that of the tone-artist! I see it anew in this creation of the divine Haydn. It is not alone that he ravishes the souls of thousands and thousands with the sweet mysteries of his harmony: he exalts—purifies—comforts them; and when he dies, he is not dead—his works live on to bless thousands and thousands more."

"Yes," replied Jomelli, gravely; "it is the only common language of all peoples and lands. If there were a second Babel, and all earthly tongues were confused again, music would still remain as a speech which every ear would understand."

"Only," said Amadeus, "it must not speak of *things*—but only of *feelings*. It is because it rules the realm of the emotions with such absolute sovereignty, that music goes so deeply to the heart; while for the head it has, directly, no message. Therefore all descriptive music is an abomination. Oh! I am sure—I am sure, that music is the voice of the heart, and for the hearing of the heart alone!"

It was delightful to the old Italian composer[1] to hear the young *maestro*, standing there with his blue eyes so earnest, and his face lit up with enthusiasm, speaking like a new evangelist in art. As much to test his wisdom, as for any other reason, he asked:

"What, then, would you give as the meaning of music?"

Amadeus thought an instant; then, as if it were a part of his new evangel, he replied:

"Music is the melody, to which the world is but words."

"Will you explain that?" asked Jomelli, with a puzzled expression.

"Explain?" returned Amadeus, with a little shrug of his shoulders: "if there were only no such thing as explanation!

---

[1] Jomelli was a martyr to his efforts at reform in the Italian school of music. He died four years after this—in 1774—broken-hearted at the persecutions of his enemies.

I *feel* it all, but 'tis a harder matter to explain it. Here is my idea: The relation of the tone-art to its particular expressions, —marches, dances, chants, operas, and so on—is like the relation of pure æsthetic architecture to its practical applications: we know it only as applied to human uses. A temple is to be built, or an opera-house, or workshop, or palace, and in their plan must be considered at once the object of the structure and the principles of beauty. So stands music in relation to life and the world. I can conceive of the ideal music, but it is unearthly, unattainable. For us earthly beings it only appears as a melody set to such words as life and the world furnish. The mother sings her baby to sleep: the battalion shouts a war-song: a group of girls must dance: pious souls will pray: there have we the words for cradle-song, march, mazurka, and psalm.

"Therefore, the freer it can be from such a definite employment—the farther removed it can be from its words, the diviner it is. And so the sonata, and higher still, the symphony, stand at the head of our music!"

In the mean time the hour for the gathering at the Conservatory had arrived, and they set out at once. It was a gloomy old edifice, and had rather the appearance of a cloister than an Institute for the culture of art. The huge dark door yawned like a lion's jaws, and the reception-saloon, in spite of the pictures of the saints along the walls, looked like a riding-school. The impression it made on Wolfgang, therefore, was by no means a pleasant one, and the mood into which it threw him was not at all brightened by the great throng of lords and dames who appeared here, besides the pupils of the Conservatory.

"Here is the bane of my life again," he said in a half whisper to his companions, and with a look of despair on his face, after the first formal greetings were over; "it will be all jugglery and musical tight-rope performance with these people! Little they care for the flight of imagination, or the summoning of musical ideas, if only the fingers hop and fly."

Amadeus was not himself: his temper was irritated, his look unsteady, his thoughts occupied with the conversation which their coming hither had broken off—till he was invited to sit down at the piano. As soon as he had taken his seat, he was another being. The people in the room had no longer any existence for him. Earnest and restful was his look, fixed straight before him; every muscle was concen-trated to the expression of what was within his soul.

He commenced, as he usually did, with an adagio move-ment. It was a simple melody, set in a still simpler harmony, which only after a time would become more interesting. He began in this way, partly to wait till his own spirit became aroused, and partly that his hearers might be drawn gradually to accompany him in his succeeding eagle-flights.

Wolfgang did not notice how the people near him glanced at each other with looks which said, half jeeringly, half in contempt—"Very ordinary!"

Then Mozart's playing grew more fiery, till the harmonies massed themselves, and tossed like a stormy sea under his hands. But their turbulence was for common ears too intri-cate. It wearied many of his audience, and several of the dames began to whisper to each other: soon others followed, till at last half the company was talking.

Finally, it attracted the attention of Amadeus, who had before been too deeply withdrawn into himself to notice any-thing but the tones which filled his spirit and busied his hands. His blood, which was at any time sufficiently excita-ble, rushed to his face.

"Dummköpfe!"[1] he muttered, half aloud, but in German; "they gab and chatter, because I do not make the tones turn summersaults on their ear-drums. Wait a bit: I will bring them to terms!"

Then at once giving the *motif* a new and unexpected turn, he suddenly struck into a most brilliant variation, and his hands smote out the swift tones like sparks, and mingled them with glittering ice-drops, till the whole company stood spell-bound in silent amazement. But the more they won-dered and admired, the wilder grew Amadeus with anger and contempt. His fine little hands now flew over the keys, in pranks and entanglements which seemed to have been let loose in a very madness of mockery and derision, till the fin-gers were no longer visible, and only the diamond in his ring showed their arrowy flight by its incessant flash.

The company was dumb with astonishment. Many of the pupils of the Conservatory had anything but a comfortable feeling in their hearts, and especially some of the older ones, who had travailed for long years with their piano practice

---

[1] Blockheads.

and brought nothing out of it after all,—they saw their noth-
ingness so vividly in contrast with this young stranger from
the barbarous land of Germany. When Amadeus had ended,
and a loud applause greeted him, several of these musical
mechanics, half-dead with envy, shrugged their shoulders,
and whispered something in their nearest neighbor's ear.
Then you could hear—" Ah ha !"—" Now I understand !"—
" Of course !"—" Pretty skill, that is !"—till the murmur
seemed to go all through the room.

Wolfgang was talking with the Director of the Conservatory, and knew nothing of what was going on ; but Jomelli
noticed it, and said at last to Father Mozart : " I must see
what that is all about." Then approaching one of the pupils,
he asked him what it meant.

" Oh, nothing !" the gaunt fellow answered ; " only, any
one could do that if he chose to use the same means !"

" ' Means ?' " said Jomelli, " I see no ' means,' except a
frightful amount of finger-power, with genius behind it !"

" Ah ?" returned the long pupil, smiling scornfully.

" What do you mean by your ' ah ?' " thundered the old
Italian, with such fierceness that the Director and Amadeus
both turned to see what was the matter.

" You are a friend of the gentleman !" responded the other,
shrugging his shoulders.

" I am a man of fifty years, with an established reputation," answered Jomelli, haughtily ; " and I ask you what
you mean by your grimaces at the performance of an artist
like the young *maestro* yonder !"

" They say he wears a magic ring on his finger, and plays
by witchcraft !"

Jomelli and the rest of Mozart's friends laughed aloud at
the absurdity of this. A little smile of pity and contempt
passed over the beautiful face of Amadeus ; then slipping the
ring from his finger, he laid it in the Director's hand, and
went again to the piano, where he played for a few moments
more wildly and wonderfully, if possible, than before. Then,
a little languidly and wearily, as if too tired with the stupid-
ity and baseness of these fools, he motioned to his friends to
come away.

CHAPTER VIII.

SIGNORA BERNASCONI.

SIGNORA BERNASCONI, at that time the greatest singer of Italy, had just dined. The costly Neapolitan soup of snails and muscles, the *frutti di mare* (oysters and little shellfish), the lobsters, lettuce, fish, and roast game, had all been removed, and there stood on the table only the oranges, figs, peaches, and grapes, with some flasks of *Capri* and *Falernian* wine. The table was set for ten; but apparently only one had dined. It was the Signora's command that it should be always thus, whether ten, two, or no guest at all, were present at dinner.

The latter had been the case to-day. The heat had been so oppressive to the Prima-donna, that she would not subject herself to restraint from the presence of guests. Therefore, although plenty of cavaliers had been announced, and among them such names as Prince Francavilla, and renowned artists, to whom her lavish table was usually open, they had all been sent away with the cool answer: "Signora Bernasconi dines alone to-day."

A famous prima-donna, in Italy, rules like a tyrant; for not only the composer who writes operas for her, has everything to hope if he obeys her commands, and every thing to fear if he shows himself a rebellious slave; but over the manager, also, as well as each of her admirers, whether he be artist or nobleman, marquis or prince, her sway is absolute.

Signora Bernasconi was now reclining on a sofa, her finely moulded form only clothed in a white *négligé* of some light and costly material. She was beautiful and proud as a Juno, and on her face lay not a May-day expression, but rather a midsummer look, suggestive of sun-glow and storm.

Boundless hauteur was throned on her lofty forehead; the arched nose, the boldly-marked eyebrows, the flashing eyes, and the faint hint of a spiritualized moustache on the curved upper lip, all betokened fire, force, and determination. Whoever looked upon this woman, could not but feel that it required a little courage to have anything to do with her,

The lofty forehead was, just at present, gathering in somewhat portentous folds, for *ennui* and a petulant humor were threatening the Prima-donna. No one was there to notice it, to be sure, except her maid, who stood in the farthest window niche, with one hand pressed anxiously over her beating heart, for she expected every moment that the tempest would break above her head. The poor maiden shrank in fear, when now she heard, in a sharp tone—

"Arabella!"

"Signora," she answered, tremblingly, as she took a step forward.

"Come nearer!" bade the singer; "am I to crack my voice in speaking to you?"

The abigail meekly obeyed.

"Give me some ice-water!"

Arabella reverently handed her a goblet, and the Signora drank: then she stretched her round arms apart, as if terribly *ennuied*, and asked—

"Is there no one in the ante-room?"

"No one, Signora."

"And why, in heaven's name, have they refused all visitors to-day?"

"*Grazia*, Signora," stammered Arabella, "your ladyship commanded it!"

"Stupid!" she returned; "I said I would dine alone, but I said nothing about visitors after dinner."

"Madonna—"

"Silence!" commanded Bernasconi: "your stupidities will be the death of me!"

There was a little pause, in which the Signora moved her beautiful shoulders impatiently, and let the laces fall a little lower from her neck.

Then the Juno called again:

"Is that old fool of a philosopher my uncle at home?"

"I think so," replied Arabella: "he scarcely ever leaves his study."

"Go and tell him I want to speak to him."

The maid departed, and Bernasconi said to herself, while a derisive smile played around her mouth—

"That's a good idea; he shall come and amuse me. Kings and kaisers used to have their court-fools—why shouldn't the Bernasconi have a philosopher for hers?"

The uncle appeared. He was a small, unsightly man, with

a morose and misanthropic expression on his dry face. Scrubby white hair covered his head, and his careless clothing sat crooked upon his body. His beautiful niece lay hidden on the sofa, as he entered, and the old fellow began to mutter to himself—

"Not here! Pretty way to do, that is!—disturb my studying for nothing!—that's woman's fashion!—oh, women —women!"

He had approached a little round-topped table, which the Signora had received a few days before as a gift from Prince Francavilla. It was of great value—an imitation of those found in Pompeii, and inlaid with antique mosaic.

"Ah ha!" he muttered; "that's a beauty! No place for it here, though—what do women know about art! There —there—there!" he cried, as he whisked off some ribbons and laces which lay on the table; "the finest mosaic in the world, and they cover it with such stuff as that!"

Suddenly he perceived the Signora, who had raised herself on the sofa, and was laughing at him. The old man started in terror, not so much at having been overheard, as at the unexpected loveliness which confronted him; for the singer's black hair had fallen down over her full bosom, and she was a picture for a painter—and naturally somewhat astonishing to a dry old gentleman like her uncle. He commenced an apology, but she cried—

"Not a word, I heard it all; but what makes you think so ill of us women?"

"It would be a waste of time to discuss that with you," he growled. "What did you want of me?"

"Never mind now, I want you to answer my question first."

"Well, women are frivolous, and unreasonable, and—"

"What would you do without us, I'd like to know?"

"Do? We would be happy," the old philosopher replied with lively gestures and enthusiastic tone—"happy as kings!"

"And what do you think about marriage?"

"H'm! I call it halving one's rights, and doubling one's duties!"

"Excellent! excellent!" cried the Bernasconi, heartily laughing; "and now for the proof that woman is inferior to man."

"Well, look you! The higher a thing is in the scale of being, the longer it is in coming to ripe maturity. This is a

4*

universa. principle in nature. Now, what more proof do you want? Man scarcely reaches the maturity of his reason at the age of twenty-eight years; woman attains hers at sixteen or eighteen."

"Nonsense, uncle!" replied the Signora, threatening him with her uplifted finger; "you mean that it takes you slow creatures thirty years to get your reason, while we get it at fourteen!"

"Yes, and what a thing it is, when you've got it!" growled the philosopher. "When did a woman ever have any genius in art, for instance? All their cultivation of music, even, is only an imitation and affectation, for the sake of making them more pleasing to men."

"You're pretty nearly right, as a rule, I must admit," laughed the Signora.

"Every one knows that, who has looked below the surface at all. You can see it in their behavior at concerts or the opera. Who can help wishing them to the devil when they break in upon the most splendid music, with their idiotic chatter, chatter, chatter! The Greeks kept their women out of the theatre, and showed their sense—for then they could hear something. Never was a woman yet who knew enough to keep quiet before a beautiful thing, be it in music or art."

"And you say that to *me*, uncle?" asked the Prima-donna, contracting her brows.

"H'm," replied the philosopher, shrugging his shoulders; "all I can say is, that you are a wonderful exception!"

At that moment Arabella entered, and announced "Maestro Caraffa."

"Let him wait!" answered the Bernasconi in a hard voice.

"And now," asked the old uncle impatiently, "may I know what you wanted with me?"

"I am getting what I wanted without your knowing it!" she replied, laughing.

"What?" he cried, pushing his hands angrily over his stubby hair—"you have only used me as a puppet, to kill time for you?"

"Oh! uncle," she replied with a mocking smile; "who could rate a man's shrewdness so low as to attempt such a trick as that? Your male wits would of course see through .t at once, if it were tried!"

The old philosopher made a face as if he had been drinking vinegar.

"Ass that I am!" he muttered to himself; "I have been made a pretty fool of—by a woman, too!"

"No, no, uncle!" cried the Bernasconi; "you have given me one piece of wisdom—that marriage is 'halving one's rights and doubling one's duties!' and in return for it, I beg of you to accept the little mosaic table yonder, which you admired so much."

"Signora!" cried the uncle, "you can't mean it! The table is of enormous value!"

"I am glad if it has value for you and your art-collection," replied the Prima-donna, with some hauteur; "a Bernasconi recognizes no other value in it. Stephano shall take it to you;" and she nodded adieu to him. But the old man preferred to take his prize at once, and departed, carrying it hugged in his arms like a mother with her child.

Maestro Caraffa, who was waiting in the antechamber, biting his lips with vexation, was no more thought of. He was a young composer, sprung from one of the best Neapolitan families, and numbered among his ancestors the great Cardinal Anton Caraffa, who, under Pope Gregory XIII., was librarian of the Vatican library. Handsome, gifted, and of a sensitive and refined organization, he had given himself up wholly to music, and had lately written an opera called *Thisiphone,* for the Neapolitan stage. The Bernasconi was to be its prima-donna, and the principal parts had been written especially for her peculiarities of voice, form, and manner. With her, therefore, hung the success or failure of the work. But, unfortunately, Caraffa had failed to find favor with the imperious singer, and she would not consent to give the opera a rehearsal. With one excuse and another she put it off, till the young composer was nearly driven mad with anxiety for his darling composition. It wanted now but three days to the king's birthday celebration, on which occasion the opera was announced to be given before the court and people. It was at present the hoarseness of the Prima-donna which was alleged as her reason for delay; and Caraffa had called to make one final appeal to the great singer.

After an hour's waiting in the antechamber, the Signora at last deigned to admit him to an audience.

The young Italian entered the room, pale, worn almost to a shadow, and with a look of haggard desperation on his face, which had so altered him in the last few weeks, that his friends scarcely recognized him when they met on the street.

Signora Bernasconi still lay on the sofa, in a careless and languid posture. She had not thought it worth her while even to rearrange the laces which showed her round shoulders and the swell of her bosom, nor to gather up the disordered wealth of her black hair; still less to apologize for keeping her visitor waiting so long.

" Maestro Caraffa," she began, roughening her voice a little, " you hear how hoarse I am; but it is somewhat better."

Caraffa bit his lip in ill-concealed anger, and replied—

"I am glad it is better; but that is small comfort to me, when the king has commanded that the *Thisiphone* be given three days hence, and you will not rehearse it even once."

"I *will* not?" cried the Prima-donna, with a black look.

" You *can* not, I should say," the young composer corrected himself, though with an angry sarcasm in his tone, despite his efforts to hide it.

" That is better," said the singer. " You have written me such awkward airs, too!"

" But, good God!" cried Caraffa, "you declared them beautiful at first."

" So I did, till I found out their vices. They strain my voice!"

"I will alter them."

" Then they will lose their interest."

" Are they too high for you?"

"For *me?* Do you know whose voice it is that goes a whole octave above other sopranos?" she asked, smiling scornfully.

" I know they call you 'Italy's Nightingale;' but—"

" Well then, this nightingale will not let herself be heard in any rehearsal of your opera!"

" What do you say?" stammered Caraffa, white with de-spair, as he foresaw the shattering of all his musical ambition, in that hard, merciless tone.

"I say that I will not rehearse it! and that is my last word upon the matter;" and the Bernasconi rose, turned her back carelessly on the composer, and disappeared into an inner **room.**

CHAPTER IX.

LIFE AND DEATH.

THE next day was the one on which Signora Bernasconi had promised to go with her young friend Amadeus, to whom the great singer had taken a wonderful fancy, to the beautiful and famous island of *Ischia*. The party was to consist only of the Signora, the two Mozarts, Jomelli, and the constant attendant of the Prima-donna, Prince Francavilla, who had a magnificent residence on the island.

There are two pearls in the Gulf of Naples. One is the blue *Capri ;* the other, beautiful *Ischia.* Out of the deep, unbroken azure of the sea these two islands rise, covered with flowers, balmy with fragrance, and spicy with all delicious fruits. They lie near each other, the fair children of that moment when the sea flung its strong arms around the land, aflame with inner volcanic fire, and mingled its waves of power with earth's creative glow. And this fiery life still remains in these islands; it gushes in their hot springs; it ripens the glowing grape-bunches; it darkles in the deep eyes of the islanders; and burns in the pomegranate and cactus blossoms.

The little company reached Ischia in a yacht belonging to Prince Francavilla. It was a sparkling introduction to a splendid evening—that tossing ride over the crisp blue waves, dancing and flashing under a light breeze and the clear afternoon sunshine. The Signora sat on a handsome raised seat at the stern of the yacht, and at either side reclined the Prince and Amadeus; while from lip to lip flew jest and retort, wit and compliment, with now and then the fragment of a song, broken in upon by banter or merriment.

At the island everything seemed to have been prepared to greet them with especial gayety, for it was one of the festival-days of the Church, and the islanders were all arrayed in their holiday garments, with their black-ribboned straw-hats stuck jauntily on one side, and their scarfs, bright with all the colors of the rainbow, flying from their hips. All the way-side images and crosses were adorned with wreaths of flowers and here and there, in open grassy places, nimble fisher maidens were dancing the wild *Tarantella* to the rattling thump of tambourines.   Everything was in a glow with life and gayety—from the blossoming vines to the ripe cheeks of the Italian girls, with their slender though voluptuous forms.

At the villa of the Prince there was as merry, if a more refined and exalted festivity among the little company, who prolonged their meeting until late in the night.   The gayety had increased from hour to hour.   Glowing wine, glowing eyes, glowing words and hearts—all was fire, life, pleasure. Wonderful had been the Bernasconi's singing of her finest *arias;* deliciously had Amadeus improvised upon piano and violin; divinely beautiful the star-strewn Southern sky glanced down on the revelling company; when suddenly Jomelli, who had strayed away to the sea-beach, came back pale, and with a face like that of a man who has seen a spirit.

"Jomelli!" cried the Bernasconi, whose falcon eye nothing escaped, "what has happened?—you are white as Death!"

"Because I have just encountered Death!" replied the old Italian, gravely.

"How so?" asked all.

Jomelli was silent a moment, while he regained his self-possession, and then said in a voice low with emotion:

"Signora! Heaven has granted us to-day a merry meeting: your kindness and that of the Prince have heaped joys and pleasures upon us, and all about us over the fair earth God has poured out balm and peace and blessing. I know that your heart feels this, for only with depth and greatness can a Bernasconi feel, think, and act. Signora! prove this now—call back an unhappy one, battling with himself and with the world—call back a dead man to life!"

The Bernasconi laughed, half scornfully. "Jomelli," said she, "I knew you were a cunning musician and composer; but I never knew before that you were such a famous tragedian!"

"He means to give us a little serio-comic charade!" jested the Prince. "That is well—for over Death and his terrors, life and joy rise all the more glorious!"

"Make them, then, bloom forth again out of the gloom of darkness!" said Jomelli, gravely yet softly, with his eyes still fixed on the Signora. "I do not jest: on your magna nimity hangs, this moment, the life or death of a human creature!"

"I do not understand you!" said she, her face growing pale, and an unspeakable solemnity gathering about her heart.

"I will tell you what I have just seen," he returned. "I went down, as you know, to get a breath of the cool sea-air. Hardly had I gained the beach, when I saw a crowd of people collected at the water's edge. Moved by curiosity, I drew nearer, just as a boat, with several men carrying lights, touched the shore. Out of it, the fishermen lifted and bore to land the body of a young man."

Jomelli paused: a deathlike pallor overspread the Signora's face.

"Well," said the Prince, in an indifferent tone; "it was some fisherman or sailor, I suppose, who had been unlucky enough to be drowned."

"No!" cried the Bernasconi aloud, with an expression of certainty in her voice; "it was Caraffa!"

All started.

"Yes!" repeated Jomelli slowly, and deeply moved—"it was Caraffa!"

A moment's deep silence ensued; then the Bernasconi asked:

"And he is dead?"

"No!" replied Jomelli: "the fishermen had seen him plunge into the sea, and made haste to rescue him. He lives, but—I know the young man, and only you can save him. His life and his future lie in your hand!"

Again deep silence.

"Be generous, Signora!" commenced Jomelli's voice anew. "Let me go and tell him, that to-morrow you have promised to rehearse his opera."

"I have given my word that I will never sing in a rehearsal of the *Thisiphone!*" replied the Prima-donna, with a frown darkening upon her pale face.

"And you will keep it, when it means death to a young, hopeful life?"

The lightnings began to flash in the Signora's dusky eyes and the storm to gather on her brow, when wondrous tones fell upon the ear,—tones so pure, so sweet, so imploring, that it seemed a wounded spirit praying, in the death-struggle, to God for pity.

It was Amadeus, who, moved to the depths of his heart,

had slipped away, and, with the tears standing in his eyes, was breathing forth a wondrous " *Kyrie eleison* " from his violin. And the tones swelled upward, pleading and beseeching, "Lord, have mercy upon us! Christ, have mercy upon us!"

Then deep, deep in the soul of the Bernasconi it grew dim, as with a twilight of youthful recollections—a glimmering dusk as of those times when the words had held significance for her,—when she, a little innocent maiden, had pressed her hand upon her breast in humility, as she sung it in the church choir, "*Kyrie eleison!*" And still the imploring tones arose— " Lord, have mercy upon us!"—soft, and sweet, and pure as an angel's voice from heaven.

"Jomelli!" said now the Bernasconi, "go you, and tell Caraffa, that I will gratify his wish, and to-morrow there shall be the rehearsal, and his opera shall be brought out with all the power at my command."

Jomelli thanked her joyfully, and quickly turned to go.

"And," called after him the Signora, vehemently, "tell him 'tis not because of this silly prank of his I do it, but of my own free accord."

When Amadeus joined them again, she pressed his hand in silence. Soon the prince and she had disappeared, and did not return.

It was after midnight when Jomelli came back from the beach. Caraffa was not out of danger, but the message had given him new life, and the friends only left him when, in accordance with the Signora's commands, the young composer had been brought to the prince's villa, and cared for with all needed attention.

The gray of dawn was in the sky when Jomelli and the two Mozarts returned to the main-land. The light, fresh breath of the morning fanned their heated foreheads with a delicious coolness; and as the lights of the vessel, at the first ruddy streak in the east, were all suddenly extinguished, it seemed to them that they had just awakened out of a strange and troubled dream.

CHAPTER X.

A BATTLE AT MILAN.

THE day had come on which Wolfgang Amadeus Mozart's first great dramatic work, " Mithridates, King of Pontus," was to be given at the *Theatro ducale,* in Milan. All Milan was in commotion, and divided into two parties;—the one composed of friends of Amadeus, eager for his success; the other of his enemies, who had, ever since his arrival there, been secretly intriguing for his defeat and ruin. If it is easy for a genius to make friends in Italy, it is as easy to make enemies. The fire which warms is very much the same thing as the fire which burns; and the southern temperament that is quick to kiss, under one set of circumstances, is quick to stab, under another. Amadeus had already gained a multitude of enthusiastic supporters at Milan, and the Bernasconi was so warmly attached to his cause, that no efforts of his enemies (and they had tried every means) could prevent her from being the prima-donna of his new opera. Not only with her, but with Santorini, the great *tenore,* and others who were to take a part in the opera, every expedient had been tried—anonymous letters, bribes, threats, cajolery—to induce them to desert the young maestro, whose success drove his enemies mad with envy. With little hearts, to be a rival is to be a foe, and too many of the second-rate Italian musicians were of that character.

Fioroni and Grimani, both eminent musical characters, and the former the Milanese Capellmeister, were the most dangerous enemies of the Mozarts, because neither father nor son suspected their being other than good friends to them Not alone their jealousy of the sudden popularity of Amadeus, at Milan, but the contemptuous repulse they had received from the Bernasconi, in their efforts to seduce her from his cause, had aroused their bitter hatred to the young artist, and their determination, by fair means or foul, to make the forthcoming opera a failure. The most dangerous hate is that which is still, like the deepest water—still, like the deepest joy, the greatest virtues, and—the ugliest dogs.

Father Mozart was in a fever of anxiety for the success of the "Mithridates,"—so much depends with the Italians, and indeed with any public, on the first impression which a thing makes upon them. It might determine the entire future career of his son as a composer, whether the new opera at its first presentation should go *alle stella* or *a terra*—to the stars, or to the ground.

Amadeus himself, on the other hand, was full of the music alone. No shade of anxiety crossed his face. While the work was incomplete he was all diligence and earnestness, scarcely taking time for sleep or food; and when it was finished, an Olympian serenity was throned on the high white brow, and his presence was a living sunbeam wherever he went. It was not pride, or self-seeking, or vanity,—Mozart never knew these from the beginning of his life to the end,—but a perfect certainty of the worth of his work. This opera, "Mithridates," once finished, he recognized as far above the common tragic operas, such as were produced at that time on the Italian stage. He knew it as well—and as unconsciously—as he knew light from shadow, or heat from cold.

So it was, that Amadeus was in no such fever as composers usually are on the eve of a new work's presentation. His eye was clear, his look restful and serene as ever, and only appeared on his face the cheerfulness of pleasant expectancy.

The hour for the opening of the doors of the *Theatro ducale* was now near at hand. A throng of people was already collected in front of the building, and constantly increasing. One side of the crowd, nearest the door of entrance, seemed to have some purpose or plan in common, which united them in a more compact mass, and kept them talking to each other in low tones, mingled now and then with half-repressed laughter. Most of them—men, women, and girls—seemed to be from the lower classes, though not all; and among them was slipping about a small man, in handsome clothing, but with a dark, sinister face,—gliding like a snake hither and thither, with a word to say in every one's ear, or a meaning wink or gesture to each one of the throng. At last he approached two good-looking girls, who stood together a little on one side of the crowd, close to the building.

One of them belonged to the chorus of the *Theatro della Scala*, the other appeared to be a stranger in this company. The former was pretty, but with an evident consciousness of the fact; the other was beautiful, but seemed not to know it

In the look of the little chorus-singer appeared the seductive charms of a fallen angel: the face of her companion showed a childlike innocence, united with great energy. She was a sweet maiden—a Roman, one could see at a glance—blooming with youth and radiant with life. Her lips evidently were made for good-natured smiles; but no such smiles wreathed them now: on the contrary, she wore an expression of unrest, and earnest anxiety.

"What are they all saying?" asked the fair Roman of her neighbor; "what is it that is to happen at the opening of the opera?"

"Hasn't Maestro Grimani, your singing-master, told you about it?" replied the other.

"No! All I know is, that he says 'tis bad music, and he would like to have it fail—and I hate him for it! For I know he lies, and that Signor Amadeus writes beautiful music."

"You know him, then?"

"Yes, at Rome!" said she, turning away to conceal the glow which passion brought to her cheeks. To her happiness they were that minute interrupted by the small, sinister-looking man, who now glided to their side. It was none other than Grimani himself.

His first motion was to slip his hand into his pocket; and, as he turned to the little chorus-singer, the Roman girl thought she saw something like gold glitter between them.

"Remember!" he whispered; then turning about, he greeted his fair pupil, and said in a low and wheedling tone—

"And you, my beautiful young scholar, you will now have an opportunity to do your teacher a great favor. Go up on to the stage with your pretty neighbor here, and there you will find a crowd of other girls who have been instructed by me just what to do. The Capellmeister Fioroni will be there, behind the side-scenes, and you are all to watch his movements. As soon as the Bernasconi advances to the footlights, in the beginning of the first act, you will hear a great coughing, shuffling of feet, and hissing. Then Signor Fioroni, hidden behind the scenes, will give a loud laugh. That is your signal. You and the rest of the girls must then laugh as loud as you can, and hiss, and cough. If the Prima-donna retires in rage, our game is won; but if she should happen to persist in singing (for her pluck is tremendous), then you are all to break in again in the middle of the song, at Fioroni's signal: you will hear it echoed from the parquet and the gal-

leries, and the opera is gone to the dogs! And Signor Fioroni and I will make sure that you are well rewarded for
your share in it!"

"Hold!" cried the little Roman, and her eyes shone like
those of an enraged lioness—but it was too late; Grimani
had vanished in the crowd, which now streamed past them,
for it was time for the opera to commence.

The theatre was nearly filled: the momen. for the beginning of the overture was at hand, and Father Mozart, with
Amadeus, were hastening along the narrow passage beneath
the stage which leads into the orchestra—the former to seek
his box, and the latter to take his place on the conductor's
stand.

Suddenly a veiled figure stopped them. "For God's sake,
one moment!" a voice cried.

Both stopped in astonishment: the voice was that of a girl,
and sounded familiar to them.

"What is it?" asked the Capellmeister, the thought flashing across his mind that they were in Italy, the land of sudden revenge.

"Maestro Mozart is ruined!" cried the veiled figure, in a
hoarse whisper.

"How ruined?"

"A crowd of men have sworn to kill your opera, and to
beat back the Prima-donna by a tumult. Fioroni is to give
the signal—"

"Fioroni?—Impossible! He is our best friend!"

"Friend or enemy, he is to stand behind the scenes, and
give the signal for the uproar to begin. There is but one
salvation—"

"And that is— ?"

"The father must stand close to Fioroni, and never let him
out of his sight for an instant! And the Bernasconi must
know what awaits her!"

"True—and God bless you!" cried Father Mozart, hastening away to find Fioroni.

But Amadeus stood rooted to the spot. That voice—did
he not know it? And it said "the father"—

"Who are you?" he cried, trembling with emotion.

"First, a reward for my warning!"

Amadeus instinctively reached after his purse.

"Not so!" cried she, almost indignantly. "I ask only an
answer to one question. Do you wear an amulet?"

" Yes," answered Amadeus, and with trembling hand he tore open the ruffles on his breast, and showed the little cross of gold which hung next his heart.

" Thank God !" cried the form ; " then I need not despair !"

" Giuditta !" broke from the lips of Amadeus—but she had disappeared, and from the orchestra there were anxious calls for their leader : the overture must begin.

How he got to his place, Amadeus knew not. Giuditta *n* Milan—she, his guardian angel, who hovered near him, though he had almost forgotten her—she, who loved him so well !—And then, too, Fioroni his enemy, who had pretended such warm friendship ! Enemies on the stage, and enemies in the audience ! And the Bernasconi ? will she have the courage to stem the storm of hisses and laughter ? All this whirled through the brain of the young maestro in a chaos, till his head burned.

Quickly Amadeus grasped his baton—a sharp blow on his desk, and the house was still as death. The baton was lifted, and the overture began.

The orchestra of sixty performers played finely, for they played with delight. The overture was a success, and the curtain rose. Now began the composer's heart to beat fast and thick, for the moment had arrived for the Bernasconi to enter as *Aspasia*. She came on—but what a magnificent appearance was this !

A universal exclamation of astonishment arose from the whole audience. A more beautiful woman never had been seen upon the Milanese stage; a more commanding glance an empress could not have thrown over her slaves; more annihilating and resistless looks could scarcely be expressed in human eyes. It was apparent that those looks sought out expected enemies, and as they flew over parquet and boxes, hundreds of eyes dropped in shame, and not a sound was heard in the great audience. And now, after a fine Recitative, the witching voice began the *aria*. Ah ! that was no such old-fashioned affair as they were accustomed to hear, with its inevitable snarl of trills and roulades : it was passion—passion in the music and in the voice ; it was a song out of nature's very heart, ringing out with a sweetness and fire that carried every hearer irresistibly on its wings.

The crowd listened in utter silence, holding its breath, lest it lose a syllable. When the Bernasconi had ended, a tempest of applause burst forth, and would not lull or diminish till she had come back, sure now of the double triumph—of the music and her own rendering of it—and repeated the *aria*.

Fioroni, meanwhile, stood with an ashy face by the side of Father Mozart, who had laid his arm through that of the Italian, and held him fast. His rage burned within him like a fire, for not a hiss, cough, or murmur was to be heard in the whole house, and the accursed Salzburger held him so tight and watched him so intently, that not a sign could be made to his hired troup on the stage. He was beaten—completely defeated—in spite of all the gold he had spent, and his enemy's triumph was complete.

He endured it nearly through the first Act; but when the bursts of applause became more and more frequent and tremendous, he tore himself away from Father Mozart, and rushed from the theatre. Unfortunately for him, he came upon Grimani, who had also been driven out by his rage. And now began an angry quarrel: Fioroni insisted that Grimani must have embezzled the money which he had so lavishly furnished him for bribes. Words of fiercer and fiercer hate and fury passed from one distorted face to the other, till at last it was well that neither had a stiletto, for Milan had surely lost one, or two, of its notabilities.

When the opera was over, a tempest of applause filled the theatre,—no longer for the Prima-donna, who had already received her laurels, but for Wolfgang Amadeus Mozart; and shout upon shout rent the air, of " *Evviva il maestro!*" " *Evviva il maestrino!*"

The slender, boyish form came before the curtain, and bowed again and again its thanks. And now out at the doors and down the street it still echoed, " *Evviva il maestro!*" " Long live the master!"—" Long live the little master!"

As Amadeus took his seat in the carriage, trembling with joyful excitement, a veiled figure suddenly was at his side— a swift arm was about him—a passionate kiss burned on his lips. He cried out—" Giuditta!"—but the vision was gone, and only a bunch of flowers lay in his bosom; and on its ribbon was written, "True love till we meet again."

PART III.

ILLUSIONS.

CHAPTER I.

AT COURT.

IT was a festival day at the court of the Elector Maximilian
Joseph of Bavaria; for His Royal Highness Prince Clement of Saxony, Elector of Treves, was on a visit in Munich.
Nymphenburg, the elegant chateau where the court resided,
was then at the perfection of its richness. Splendid fountains
threw their streams eighty feet high into the air in front of
the palace, which crowned the summit of a sloping park, and
was built in five detached castles, united by galleries. About
it were broad gardens and running streams, with cascades
and rocky grottoes; and at one side orangeries and conservatories transported the visitor into Italy and the tropics. In
the wide park were herds of deer and flocks of pheasants, and
in the banks of the water-courses a whole colony of beavers
had been domesticated.

Nymphenburg had been fitted up by Max Emanuel, former
Elector of Bavaria, in the most wildly extravagant manner.
No expense was spared, in gorgeous upholstery, in gilding
and carving, in statuary and paintings, or in the laying out
of the grounds, with pleasure-houses, costly fountains, and
the like. A ruinously expensive horde of courtiers had been
maintained at this magnificent chateau, and in all respects it
had been the aim and determination of the Elector to rival
the splendor of Louis XIV., king of France.

Thirty millions of debt and a ruined country were the result of this royal imitation.

Max Joseph, the present Elector, had set out with wholly
different intentions. He was possessed with that noblest
ambition which a prince can cherish—the wish to see a happy

people round his throne.   First of all, his effort was to repair
the not only emptied, but shattered exchequer, and to reduce
the public debt.   He began, therefore, with cutting down the
riotous splendor and ostentation of his court.   To set a good
example, he even reduced his own personal expenditures to
the lowest possible figure.

But what are the noblest resolutions worth, when force
fails, to carry them into action?   His mother, and all his relatives, as well as his counsellors, did their best to outwit
these resolutions, and to restore the court of the Elector to
its ancient splendor.

Max Joseph's youth came at that time when the new philosophy of which Voltaire, Rousseau, Diderot, Holbach,
Grimm, etc., were the priests, was just being transplanted from
France into Germany, and when Frederick the Great had
taken up its patronage.   The Jesuits—and particularly the
tutor of the young Elector, Father Stadler, one of the most
learned Jesuits of his time—could not entirely keep their
young sovereign from breathing the atmosphere of the new
spirit of the times.   What they could do, they did; and
succeeded so far as to prevent Max from fulfilling his ardent
desire to travel abroad; and to so order his education, that
he knew far more of Judea and Rome than of his own fatherland.   His father confessor kept daily before his mind this
satanic aphorism: that it is dangerous to know too much of
temporal affairs, for the greater the knowledge, the greater
the responsibility before God!

But a noble nature is not so easily to be buried.   Amid
the seductions of a luxurious court, he had kept his heart
pure; and at the age of eighteen years, inexperienced, but
uncorrupted, he had taken the throne.   Between that time
and the one of which we speak, two-and-thirty years had
intervened, and the fresh and courageous boy had given
place to a man of fifty years, whose will was subservient to
the beck of those who surrounded him.   A troop of worthless favorites kept him continually in terror of being poisoned;
and by means of this fear they drove him to everything which
they wished.   In this way alone was it possible that the once
noble will should be broken and brought to naught; that
Bavaria should be left in poverty and wretchedness, at the
mercy of pitiless bloodsuckers; and that the old ruinous
splendor of the Electoral Court should be restored.

So it was, that now the court at Munich glittered like a

golden star among the other German courts, and Nymphenburg had become again the magnificent chateau which it was in the time of Louis Quatorze; and here to-day, as we said, there were extraordinary festivities in honor of the visi of Prince Clement of Saxony, Elector of Treves.

It was early in the day, but already an unwonted bustle prevailed in the whole chateau. Every limb among all the army of servitors was in activity. In the great room of the garden-house stood the Chief Marshal and Steward, Count Von Tattenbach, with the Chief Silver Chamberlain, Count Von Törring, surrounded by a throng of persons belonging to the lesser nobility, who carried out their orders; while the five-and-sixty officers of the kitchens and wine-vaults, together with the twenty butlers and table-keepers, stood in solemn silence, and at a respectful distance, awaiting the arrival of their respective charges. In the park and garden were the head gardener, the grotto-master, the marble-keeper, and the landscape gardener, accompanied by a swarm of underlings busy in their several cares.

The drives and paths, on which the autumn had strewn its withered leaves, were all swept clean; the water-works all inspected once more; the arbors and trellises minutely cleared of the least suspicion of rubbish. Garlands of flowers festooned every available arch and pillar; and marble vases and statues were washed white as snow.

The long avenue between Munich and Nymphenburg was all astir with carriages and foot-passengers; for other distinguished guests besides Prince Clement had been invited for the day, to a hunt, a dinner, and a court concert in the evening. The carriages of the Munich nobility and the court officials rolled, closely following each other, along the broad and handsome drive, flanked at each side by the city people who had come out on foot to see what was to be seen.

Among these aristocratic equipages was that of Prince Zeil. It was a new and elegant Viennese carriage, in one of whose luxurious corners the prince leaned idly back, while at his side sat Amadeus Mozart.

"But, my dear Mozart," said the prince, "why wouldn't you stay in the service of the Prince-Archbishop of Salzburg? You have already the position of concertmeister?"

"Yes, your Excellency," replied Mozart, with an ironical smile, "if that can be called a position!"

"Why, what is your salary?"

"My salary? I'm afraid your Excellency would take me for a slanderer or a foolish jester if I told you."

"Not at all : tell me frankly."

"Well, then, my salary as concertmeister to his Grace of Salzburg is a hundred and fifty florins a year!"[1]

"Outrageous!" cried the Prince.

"But that isn't the worst of it!" continued the musician, a frown gathering on his fine face.

"How so?" asked Prince Zeil.

"His Grace the Archbishop is a pious man, and of course knows that the world is full of evil," returned Mozart, smiling ironically; "so, in order to cut down our pride and shield us from the seductions of a well-larded purse, he not only forbids us musicians to have concerts, but treats us like valets, giving us language which would better become a street-ruffian, than an archbishop! Of course I can't stay there."

"You are right!" replied the Prince, with some indignation. "But will you do me the favor not to speak of these facts commonly? The whole nobility will be compromised!"

"Prince Zeil is the first stranger to whom I have spoken of it," said Mozart, slightly bowing. "There is another thing," he continued : "I must have a broader field to work in than at Salzburg. I have set my eye on either Munich or Paris."

"Well, whatever I can do toward getting a position for you from the Elector," said the Prince cordially, "you can rely upon my doing. Have you seen Count Sceau and Baron von Berchem, both favorites with the Elector?"

"I saw the Baron last Friday," replied Mozart.

"And what did the old knave have to say to you?"

"He had but little time for me," said Mozart, with a derisive smile; "for just as I had entered the splendid room, fitted up in oriental voluptuousness, his servant announced that his warm bath was ready."

"Everybody knows what that meant," said the Prince, with a look of disgust. "There was little to be hoped from him after that. Didn't you try it again?"

"Yes, and the next time a widow of one of the Baron's officials was there with a pretty-faced daughter, to obtain an order for her perquisites. I waited with the good mother two hours in the ante-chamber, while she prattled to me of her

---

[1] Historical. Nissen, p. 360.

misfortunes, till the daughter came back. She had evidently been crying, and looked pale, but she held the order in her hand. The Baron was not to be seen afterward. The servant announced that he was weary, and must sleep!"

"Well, well," said the Prince, with a stern look in his eyes, which was evidently not for his companion: "It is a thousand pities that such men as you are, by the grace of the devil, made dependent for success on a 'nobility'—save the mark!—which contains such dogs as he!"

The carriage had now reached the chateau, and as good luck would have it, they obtained audience of the Elector at once. It was an anxious moment for the young composer. He had now passed his twenty-first year, had used with the utmost diligence every advantage for musical culture, and could see before him a career, not only of fame and what the world calls "success," but of a nobler success in carrying out his own noble aspirations,—if only the Elector would help him to the first step.

Oh happy countries, where genius is free to follow its own way, independent of the aid of some bestarred and betitled fool! In Mozart's country and time the aristocracy held down the people like the slaves in a slave-ship, smothered beneath the hatches, letting up only here and there one, as chance or favoritism directed, to the free air of his own possibilities!

If he could only get from the Elector the position of concertmeister or court-composer, it would be the standing-place from which his influence in the musical world could fall with effect; a working-place, where he could pursue his art unharassed by anxieties or the necessity of unworthy labor, and where his darling plan could be worked out—of establishing a new and nobler style of operas in Germany. How happily he would toil! How beautiful would be his life—devoted, untarnished by other cares, to his art! And what a new and purer atmosphere he would create for music in the world!

"Mozart?" repeated the Elector slowly, when his name was announced in introduction—"the Salzburg concertmeister?"

"At your Excellency's service!" replied the young composer, with a joyfully-beating heart. "I have approached your Excellency to offer my services as musician."

A little pause ensued. Max Joseph took a pinch from his golden snuff-box, and answered:

"Ah, yes! There is no vacancy just now—no vacancy!"

"And could not your Excellency *make* some modest place for so talented a young man?" asked Prince Zeil.

"'Tis too early!" replied the Elector. "He must go and travel in Italy, and make himself a name. I don't promise anything; but 'tis too early now."[1] And Max Joseph turned and walked away.

Mozart stood as if petrified. He knew not whether he dreamed or waked. Had he heard straight? "He must go to Italy!" where he had already been for seven years—whose darling and pride he had become. He, whom the Pope had made a Knight of the Golden Spur, who had been elected a member of the Academies at Bologna and Verona, whose operas had been received with such enthusiasm in Milan?

It seemed impossible; but the Elector's icy words were yet in his ear. It was the first real disenchantment of his life. The consciousness of his inner worth triumphed, to be sure, over the slight which had been put upon him. He knew it was because he was not seen as he was, but judged from the majority. And with this thought in his mind, he left the chateau. But the sun-gold had all faded out of the day for him. He had witnessed in his heart the first clash of battle between his life that might be and his life that must be. To lose temporary success is a small thing: to lose the opportunity for future success, or what seems such a loss, is hard enough.

Still, it was, as we said, the first real disenchantment of his life; and the losses of early years are only as those of a child, in a spring meadow full of flowers, who sees here and there a blossom trodden under foot. But later on, how is it then? When the autumn has but a few daisies left—it is another thing to see the scattered darlings trodden down. And later still, when the shadows have grown long, and the twilight comes early—then, far as our eyes can reach, stretch the ice-fields of winter, under whose snowy shroud lies the quiet burying-ground of all our hopes.

[1] The Elector's very words.

CHAPTER II.

TWO SISTERS.

AT the time of which we write, the fine city of Mannheim, round which the Rhine and Neckar are extended like protecting arms, had, on the side toward the former stream, an imposing entrance-way, surmounted by an elegant stone arch, and called the Rhine-gate. On the keystone of the arch is cut the coat of arms of the Elector who built it, Karl Philip, and beneath the shield these words:

BONUS PRINCEPS NUNQUAM
UT PACI CREDIT NON SE
PRÆPARET BELLO.

"A good prince never trusts peace so far as not to be prepared for war."

Close by this Rhine-gate of Mannheim stood, in the year 1777, a small, unpretending house. It made no display of size or expensiveness, but it was pretty and home-like, and showed at the first glance that its inhabitants believed in order and neatness. Two five-sided bay-windows, rising into turrets, projected on the sides of the house, as if there were eyes within which liked to see out; and from the gable windows above, those eyes could enjoy a splendid view across the Rhine.

The owner of this dwelling was an open-hearted, honorable man, named Weber. His position was not indeed among the high ones, but he had an office under the Elector, which he had filled with the greatest fidelity for many years: his salary had, until recently, been only two hundred florins a year, which was little enough, with wife and six children—five daughters and a son. But now the household circumstances were a little less straitened, since, as a reward for his long faithfulness in the service of the Elector, his salary had been raised to four hundred florins. Fortunately, too, he owned the pretty house of which we have spoken, and had a little side-income from two of its chambers, which were rented to an old friend of the family.

But small though his house and his salary were, the con
tentment and happiness of the Weber household were great.
There was not one of the family who made any further demand on life than for health, cheerfulness, daily food, and, as
the spice of all these, the heartiest affection for each other.
And, in truth, fate was so friendly as to richly satisfy these
modest demands. The father and mother both had the firm-
est health, the children bloomed like fresh roses, and since
bodies were sound and souls were satisfied, of course cheerfulness and contentment were not wanting; while the pleasant
family-life made all desire for outside pleasures superfluous.

Herr Weber was no dry and juiceless husk of a man, such
as so many lawyers of that day were; on the contrary, he
loved art and science, and though his limited means made
the purchase of books or the enjoyment of concerts a rare
indulgence, yet the good man had many a friend who was
glad to lend him choice volumes, and give him invitations to
feasts of music. Music was one of the great pleasures of the
Weber household, and the father spent many an hour in
playing the old clavier, which it was the hope of his life to
exchange for one of the new piano-fortes, at that time just
coming into vogue in Germany. His scholarly and musical
culture was kept constantly burnished by his duties as teacher
of his children. For in those times a man's education was
prevented from becoming rusty by the necessity of being his
own family's schoolmaster. Some idea of the facilities for
school-education may be got from this fact: that even at the
court of the Elector, the teacher of the young nobility ranked
below the head hostler. The court coachman got a salary
of three hundred florins; the vice-coachman and the twelve
trumpeters each two hundred and fifty florins; the teacher—
Professor Philosophiæ—two hundred florins, annually!

Herr Weber had, in his wife, a priceless assistant in the
education of his children. She was good troops in every
respect;—notable as a housewife, simple, economical, unweariedly diligent, bent upon good order, and sincerely pious;
without in the remotest degree belonging to that class of
women whose piety runs to a sentimental playing with religious feelings.

The oldest two of the children were girls. Aloysia was
fifteen years old, Constanze fourteen. Both were beautiful,
and blooming as fresh rosebuds on which the morning-dew
still trembles.

They loved each other devotedly; yet their characters were strongly contrasted. Aloysia, who had a fine voice and was educating herself for a singer, was full of life and fire. Nothing appeared to her too difficult or unattainable; her zealous diligence bore down all obstacles to reach a chosen end. And this end the maiden had already determined upon—to charm the world with her voice. She was therefore passionately enthusiastic in music, and revelled in dreams of being herself a priestess of it.

It was quite otherwise with Constanze, who seemed much more restful, quiet, and spiritual than her sister. She was still a child, in the strongest sense of the word. She lived like a modest and lovely flower, born to bloom only for its own little forest-nook. That which especially characterized her was a tender sorrowfulness, to which she seemed inclined by nature. To a keener insight it was apparent that this disposition to melancholy was nothing but the reflection of a deeply-sensitive soul, exalted and moved by its inner unfolding, as it passed from childhood into womanhood.

Constanze had continually a vague, undefined consciousness of *something*, she knew not what, unfolding and developing in body and soul. She sought to understand it, but in vain; yet often its tenderness and yearning melted her even to tears. When, at such times, her sisters would banter and rally her, she could be as gay and merry as any of them; but the gayety on her part always seemed a little overstrained. Constanze had, perhaps, more docility and patience than Aloysia, and loved music as well; but her voice, though soft and sweet, was not powerful.

All the Weber children had pure hearts behind their pure faces. They had but little to do with people outside of their own household; and of the world's wickedness they knew nothing. Never had they heard a word or a tale at which their cheeks must redden or their eyes be cast down.

Of finery in dress they had no notion in that household. What they understood by "dress" was only extreme neatness and tidiness applied to the simplest materials. Therefore whenever Aloysia or Constanze completed their dressing, by putting a flower in their fine hair, they had no thought of how they were made more beautiful by it, but only how beautiful the blossom looked upon them. So lived they, in pleasant, quiet contentment, with hearts warm to each other and friendly toward all the world.

Aloysia had already made her *début* on the Mannheim stage in the opera of *Lamori*, and had been well received. There seemed to be nothing to prevent her taking the position of prima-donna at once, except her lack of dramatic power. But this entrance upon the somewhat perilous life of the stage, had made no difference in Aloysia's character. Her girlish bashfulness, of course, was removed; but the childlike modesty of her heart remained untouched. She possessed a great safeguard in her teacher, Wendling, who was conductor of the orchestra and a warm friend of her father's. Neither had her entrance into a public musical life made any great changes in the household. She could not, it is true, so regularly help in the housekeeping as before, on account of her practising and rehearsals; and at such times Constanze took her place at her mother's side. But in keeping the house tidy, in making the younger children's garments, in the evening employments of spinning and knitting—all was as before. She was the same diligent, simple-hearted, cheerful daughter of the house; only, there was a little tinge upon her face of increased dignity, and a certain respect paid to her by the others, as to one who had been out in the world.

The mother's true heart was a little disturbed at the future prospect which seemed to open up before Aloysia. It was such a seductive career, that of a public singer, and the child knew so little of the temptations which were in store for her! Sometimes her motherly anxieties would express themselves in silent shakings of the head, or words of regret that the loud world would claim her oldest darling.

At such times father Weber would bring to her comfort the calm, restful force of his reason, and show her how it was a true gift from God, that Aloysia possessed such a voice and such aspirations; and how it was unchristian to be otherwise than thankful for it. The maid had good principles, and so long as she held fast to them, he had no fear for her.

" You are right, dear husband!" frau Weber would reply— " you are right! I am a foolish woman; but you know how Aloysia has grown a part of my very heart!" and she would brush a tear from her eyes with her apron corner.

Not less so, indeed, were the other children to the good mother; but naturally the anxiety which the eldest caused, made her doubly dear. Is it not always so?

Nothing could be pleasanter than the group in the comfortable sitting-room, especially of an evening, when the raw autumnal wind beat and shook the round window-panes in a ghostly way. Then the smaller children would be clustered near the fireplace, where a bright fire crackled and glowed; while Johanna and Maria sat knitting warm garments for themselves or the others, and the mother, with Aloysia and Constanze — sometimes, too, Wendling's daughter, Gustl — kept their spinning-wheels whirling and humming. Herr Weber, meantime, would be playing the old clavier, or walking up and down the room, in his long dressing-gown, his pipe in his mouth, listening to the talk or singing of the others.

Not for tons of gold would Weber have given up these hours at home; and if now and then a friend, as Wendling, joined the group, and the conversation became more interesting, he was happy as a king.

On such an evening the family were so gathered together about the cheerful fireside. November had set in, raw and fierce, and an icy wind came whistling from the Rhine, beating and rattling about the bow-windows, so that now and then a single slate tile from the gable roof would fall cracking into the street, and the staid old weathercock was whisked around till it squeaked with anger.

A fine rain blew against the windows, as if mocking spirits of the night were beckoning and making signals to the maidens, who from time to time would glance up, as an unusually spiteful gust whished against the panes.

"Nice weather, this!" said father Weber, cheerily, stopping before the fire as he paced up and down in his gown of flowered chintz, and puffing a fragrant cloud from his long pipe. "You'll have no calls to-night, girls!"

"None made of sugar or salt, Papa, that's certain!" said Constanze, looking up roguishly.

"None at all, I hope!" said the mother: "we are pretty well off, as we are."

"Yes indeed—yes indeed!" replied Weber, with heartiness: "but how I pity, such nights, those human creatures who stand alone in life, and never know what a home is!"

"Poor souls!" returned frau Weber: "no one knows better how to pity them than we women; for no one can appreciate so well as we what they miss."

"Yes, the family life!" said the father, standing in front of Aloysia, and laying a hand lovingly on her shoulder. "Mark this well, you girls! that woman has the family life to thank, for what she is to-day. What was she in the early times of all nations? Nothing but a slave! Even with the Greeks exalted as they were, woman was shut up to the narrow circle of the one house and its petty concerns—shut up, for that matter, in a few rooms, called the 'female apartments!'"

"And mustn't they see even their papa?" asked little Sophie, in surprise.

"Yes, the father and the husband — nobody else!" answered Weber, with a smile.

"With the Romans, though, it was better," said Aloysia.

"Perhaps—a little," replied her father; "but with them, as with our own chivalrous ancestors, there was, in the very reverence paid to woman, an implied contempt. The Egyptians worshipped their cats, you know!"

"How horrible the Oriental life must be to women!" said Constanze.

"Body and soul in chains," replied her father,—"iron chains or golden ones, it matters little which. Where there is a family life, there only is woman's position secured."

"Ah!" exclaimed Aloysia, "if we only had the strength and independence of men! I feel, every day, that there is no lack of good purpose in me, to do something great and distinguished; but the strength, the strength is wanting!"

Herr Weber smiled at his daughter's eagerness. Taking her by the chin, he lifted up her glowing face and looked down into her eyes for a moment; then releasing her, he said—

"I thought my Aloysia never lacked for courage, strength, or confidence."

"That is not always true," replied the maiden; and in her earnestness she made her spinning-wheel hum so swiftly, that the thread broke in her fingers.

"Nor need it be," said the mother, at that: "otherwise many a thread in life would be snapped. Strength, for men: patience, for women!"

At that moment came a loud knock on the street door. All listened while the old servant, Kathrina, went to the door, with her keys rattling in her hand. They heard the lock turn, and then a hearty voice inquire, "Are they at home?"

"That's Wendling!" said father Weber; "but what does he stop on the steps to ask that question for?"

But Kathrina's answer had already been returned, and they heard two people come into the hall.

"He is not alone!" muttered Weber, a little put out at the idea of having his pleasant evening disturbed by a stranger. But at the familiar tap on the sitting-room door, he called out, "Come in!" and the door opened.

It was indeed their old friend Wendling; but to their surprise, there stood at his side an unknown young man, of slight and not particularly imposing form, with a face not beautiful certainly, but peculiarly interesting, the brow high and swelling out at the temples, the mouth finely cut, and the eyes deep and full of soul.

Wendling, who was evidently in the best of humor, cried out gayly—

"Haven't I surprised you? In such abominable weather— you ought to see the soaked hats and cloaks we gave to old Kathrina!—at night, too, and especially in company with a strange visitor!"

"Who must beg your forgiveness for the intrusion," said, with a courtly bow, the young man; "but the Herr Orchestra-conductor—"

"Led you astray," interrupted Wendling, laughing; "because he knew that he would be giving a great pleasure to the Webers, and at the same time showing his young friend something pleasant."

"At all events, you are both heartily welcome," said father Weber, shaking hands with them cordially: "Wendling knows it for himself; and as for you, Sir, you could not have had a better introduction into our quiet household."

"My dear fellow!" cried Wendling, with such a beaming face as they were not accustomed to see on him, as he brought one hand down on Weber's·shoulder, and pointed to the stranger with the other, "our friend here needs no intro duction—his name and his works are recommendation enough."

"Herr Conductor—"

"Hush!" said Wendling, smiling delightedly, while the whole family gazed in curiosity at their guest, who began to feel quite embarrassed.

"And whom, then, have we the pleasure of greeting?" asked the mother.

The young man would have replied, but Wendling clapped a hand over his mouth.

"Not a word!" he cried, threatening him, with mock ferocity. "You must guess!"

Then all of a sudden, Aloysia sprang up, pushing aside her spinning-wheel, and cried—

"Mozart! I bet it is Herr Mozart!"

"So it is," said Wendling. Then there was an enthusiastic greeting from every one; for that name, already so renowned in the musical world, was well known in the Weber household.

"But, girlkin!" at last said Wendling to Aloysia, "how came you to guess it?"

Aloysia blushed, as the attention of all was suddenly turned to her by the question; but immediately recovering herself, she replied, that it had flashed upon her like a revelation. Besides, she had heard them say yesterday, at the opera, that Herr Concertmeister Mozart was present in the audience.

"And so I was," said Mozart; "and was right glad to hear you sing, for your voice is exceedingly sweet and pure."

"You heard and saw only a beginner," replied Aloysia, with sincere modesty.

"'Saw'—yes!" returned Mozart, with his own peculiar frankness; "but I *heard* a cultivated singer. Your style is excellent, and when your acting is a little better, you can go where you please as prima-donna."

Possibly this judgment, expressed by any other young stranger, might have seemed arrogant to the family, and been somewhat resented; but the tone in which the words were said, full as it was of the same hearty frankness and straightforwardness which shone in the young man's face, allowed of no mistake as to his good meaning. Besides, there is in all men of genius a certain something which acts as an overmastering power over common persons. Their souls feel instinctively the presence of a mightier spirit near them, and they yield willingly to it, even before they are conscious of this natural submission.

So was it here, while the lovable and genial nature of their guest put forth its unconscious winning influence on the Webers. It was evident that the characters which met here were naturally adapted for each other;—frankness met frankness; truthfulness met truthfulness; sincere friendliness met sincere friendliness in return.

It was no wonder, therefore, that Mozart had already, before half an hour had expired, clean forgotten where he was;

at least he felt as much at home as if he had grown up with the family. At Wendling's request he had brought with him several songs of his composition, which Aloysia now sang, while he accompanied her on the clavier.

Most enviable gift of genius, that it can so delight good hearts! While the music was going on, there stood father Weber, blowing clouds of smoke from his pipe, as though he had undertaken to hide all Olympus with them; the orchestra-conductor expressed nothing but beaming delight from head to foot; while the mother's eyes were full of tears, and the children sat as if at church.

When at last Aloysia came to a terribly hard passage, which Mozart had written in Italy for the famous *De Amicis,* and went through it with extraordinary skill, then Amadeus also was carried away with delight and surprise. Forgetting where he was, he sprang up from the clavier, took the maiden by the shoulders, and exclaiming, "Wonderful! I must give the girlkin a kiss for that!" he carried out his words without an instant's hesitation.

Every one laughed aloud; and little Hermann, clapping his hands and spinning round like a top, cried—

"Now Aloys will have a beard! She has let herself be kissed!"

Aloysia herself was red as a rosebud, and so half-terrified that she fled to her mother's side like a scared fawn; but the father, who usually failed to see the fun of such proceedings, recognized its harmlessness on this occasion, and cried, laughing—

> "A kiss in fun
> Harms never a one!"

Then to give things another turn, and relieve her daughter's embarrassment, the wise mother gave orders for tea, and quick as a flash both the girls had disappeared—one to set the table, the other to give directions in the kitchen. Meantime the gentlemen talked about music, and at last came to speak of a man who was just at that time very noted in Mannheim, and afterward famous throughout the musical world—Abt Vogler.

Weber praised him, but Wendling held fast to his assertion that Abt Vogler was a musical mountebank. In support of this he pulled a paper from his pocket, and unfolded a huge poster; then turning to Amadeus, he said, in a tone of indignation·

" Herr Mozart, what sort of a man and composer can he be who announces the programme of his new work in enormous letters after this fashion: 'A Sea-Fight!—The Fall of the Walls of Jericho!—Stamping-out Rice in Africa!'"

Here a merry peal of laughter from Mozart interrupted the reading: "'What sort of a man?' I should say he was a fool *or* a mountebank, certainly!"

"Didn't I say so!" cried Wendling in triumph. "When a man tells me, as Abt Vogler did, that he can make a composer in three weeks and a singer in six months, I call him the biggest swindler and wind-bag in the world!"

"Well," said Amadeus quietly, "I am curious to see the man and hear his music. I hate to judge a thing without a fair trial. There *are* people who push their originality to the point of *bizarrerie.*"

"Yes, and hide their quackery under it!" said Wendling.

After the simple meal—the "Evening-bread"—was over and the tea-things removed, the remainder of the evening was passed most pleasantly. Mozart was never in better spirits, and entertained the whole company with wit and odd tales and an inexhaustible stream of droll verses. The last thing before they said good-night, he sat down to the clavier, and improvised for a long time, till the whole witchery of his presence seemed to be transmuted into music and sink into their hearts.

But wherefore sat Aloysia so long without disrobing, at the window of their sleeping-chamber, gazing out through the round panes into that rainy midnight? She hardly knew wherefore, herself. Her mood was one she had never experienced before: joyful—almost happy; and yet so oppressive, that her heart trembled and palpitated.

"Why don't you come to bed?" asked Constanze, now for the third time, and half-asleep.

"Because I am so excited!" answered Aloysia: and her sister turned over, and softly slept.

CHAPTER III

CHRISTMAS GIFTS.

WINTER had come down upon the earth with might and
main. The Rhine hurled along upon its current great
blocks of ice; the bridge of boats which united Mannheim
with the other bank, had been taken away; the streets were
full of snow, and whosoever could, kept close by stove or
fireplace; while about the door-yards could be seen single
ravens, sparrows, and yellow-hammers, driven into town by
the cold, hopping hither and thither in search of their scanty
food.

But frosty as it was without, in many a heart there was
warm June weather; as, for example, in those of all the
Weber household, and in that of Mozart. He had brought
his true-hearted mother to Mannheim, and they lived at the
house of Capellmeister Cannabich, who had long been a devoted friend of Father Mozart, and had received his wife and
son with open arms. A good share of their time, however, was
spent by the warm fireside of the little house near the Rhine-
gate. Everything there was so simple, homely, and good—
so frank, yet unassuming! Two months had not passed since
the evening of his introduction to the Webers, yet Amadeus
seemed an integral part of the family. Through him, too,
their household life had been broadened into something more
earnest than it was before his arrival, while Wendling's and
Cannabich's more frequent presence added to its attractions.

It may be imagined how the confidence and friendship
between these warm-hearted people day by day grew greater.
Amadeus brought a new influence into the musical education
of Aloysia, who began to think that she never before had
really known what singing was. To Constanze, Johanna,
and Marie, also, he gave lessons on the clavier, and many a
pleasant evening passed in having little household concerts,
of which he was, if not a very stern, at least a very popular
conductor. His imperturbable cheerfulness, his whole-souled
way of entering into life and art, his wit and his unselfish-
ness, attached every one to him. Such a friendly expression

of countenance, such a serene brow, clear eye, and smiling mouth, always brighten up our surroundings, as a sunshiny day does the earth. The hearts of the children were completely stolen away to him, and little Hermann often talked in his sleep about "Unkie Wolfgang."

It is a well-known fact, that we never completely know and trust a person, till we have had a hearty laugh together. Perhaps it is in the perpetual gayety of youth, that we are to look for the cause of the long endurance of youthful friendship, often lasting into old age. Cheerful people are not only happy, but, as a rule, good, well-disposed people—free from envy and peevishness, not apt to sneer or slander, and disposed to keep out of the way of evil persons as much as possible. This was the case with the Weber household, who found the key to their little Paradise in this: that they were sound in mind and body, always fresh and vigorous, ready to take a warm part in everything good and beautiful, and possessed of this magic amulet—"He is not happy who has what he wants; but he who does not want what he cannot have!"

But it was the presence of the two girls, Aloysia and Constanze, which especially bound Mozart, from the very first, to the Weber household. Both were so charming, and indeed so united in their sisterly affection, that at first they were hardly distinguished apart in his mind. They filled his heart, without his taking the pains to separate them. But soon there arose within him a consciousness, which attracted him with irresistible force toward the maidens: he loved!— But which one? Each was as dear as the other—yet a different charm crowned each.

When he heard Aloysia on the stage, and watched her in one of her favorite *rôles*, or when he was sitting at the clavier, at home, and she stood by his side, singing with her glorious voice, it seemed to him often as if he must catch her to his breast, and, with one burning kiss, cry out: "O thou sweet angel! it is thyself only that I love! Without thee I can no longer live!"

But when at other times he observed Constanze, the warm-hearted childlike nature in its still cheerfulness, over whose heart there seemed often to hover, as it were, a dim veil of vague longing,—when he saw how she accomplished all her household duties, young as she was, with such a quiet grace, which suited so well her childlike absence of restraint,—

when his eyes met hers, which were so pure and clear, and yet again so delightfully deep and darkling, as if they would betray to him the existence of a hidden wonder-land,—then it seemed to him as if he must draw Constanze to his side, and murmur in her ear: "Oh, let me find it—this enchanted wonder-land; let me find it—on thy heart!"

If Aloysia's sparkling exuberance of young life often carried him away on its current, in a sort of heavenly intoxication, yet, as often, the thoughtful sympathy which he always found in Constanze for whatever interested him, drew him wholly to her side; and it seemed as if the sparkle and dash of her older sister was like that of champagne, bubbling up into misty foam, and leaving nothing in the glass when it has flown. Yet, on the other hand, what an enthusiastic worshipper of art was Aloysia—how her aspirations mounted upward, hand in hand with his own! Seemed they not to have been created for each other? He—perhaps soon to be court-composer to the Elector, or Capellmeister at one of the great capitals; she—the famous prima-donna, for whom her beloved one writes such splendid airs! What a thought was that! and what a future—of common aspiration, common enthusiasm, common renown! And all this beatified through the bliss of love.

When such thoughts crowded forward, the image of Constanze must necessarily retire in his mind. She was younger, too, and less developed physically than her sister, whose graceful figure and fresh beauty already had won the heart of all Mannheim.

This hesitation endured not long with Mozart. So strong a spirit as his ill brooks a prolonged indecision. Art again won the victory; and, as after a long battle between clouds and sun, the latter often suddenly breaks through, so it came to him at once as a revelation—"Thou lovest Aloysia!"

And how was it with her? Ah, she had long known very well how it stood with her little heart! One image had been enthroned there ever since that fateful kiss on the first evening—Herr Wolfgang Amadeus Mozart—as sole and absolute monarch.

With her, too, art had filled the place and done the duties of the little roguish blindfold god; for she had also cherished the thoughts of a common future in music, to be attained by them together. Besides, Amadeus—so charming on a nearer acquaintance—was the first young man who had ever ap proached her closely. Was it any wonder that her heart opened to receive him at once?

"To receive him," but only in secret. Neither of them had ever breathed even the lightest whisper of their love. In both hearts the fire burned, but it was fed only by the still happiness of a first and secretly blossoming love.

Christmas Eve was now drawing near; and all over Ger many great preparations were being made, in every household, for the great festivity of the year. In the little house by the Rhine-gate there was an especial activity,—each member of the family making ready their gifts in secret for every one of the rest. In the daytime there was not much opportunity for the children to prepare their presents for the father and mother, without being seen. But at bedtime, which was pretty sure to come very early during the last week before Christmas, they all scattered to their rooms, and the little fingers flew busily at their sewing, knitting, drawing, or embroidery.

Every night, as soon as Aloysia and Constanze had reached their chamber, out came work-boxes and divers unfinished articles, and they set to work.

And how cheery it was in the clean little room, with the lamp burning brightly on the low table, the stove getting red in the face with its excitement against the cold, and the warm curtains shutting out the starlight and the frost! Here their nimble fingers would ply, for an hour after their good German bedtime.

But why was Constanze always up so early in the morning? Why did she steal so softly out of bed, leaving Aloysia to enjoy her sound morning sleep, while she lit the lamp quietly, and, wrapping herself in a thick double-gown, sewed on a little pocket-book?

It was a little gem of an affair, and on it, in silk and chenille, was embroidered a landscape, in the middle of which stood an altar under a rose-tree. On the altar lay a laurel crown, and about the whole wound the words—"*For the worthiest, the crown;*" and underneath only this—*From a faithful heart.*" Was this gift for the father? No one knew, for before her sister was awake, each morning, there was no more trace of her work to be seen.

Christmas morning at last came, bringing joy and merriment—for that one day at least—to every household in Germany, little or great. For that one day, it was indeed a realiza ion of Christ's coming—the coming of love and joy on the earth. In the Weber house the celebration was simple enough, ye' full of happiness to all. It was to each one not so much the gifts they received, as the gifts they gave, which delighted them—not so much their own pleasure, as it was that pleasure reflected back to them from the faces of the others. No one was forgotten in the distribution of presents. Amadeus brought with him for Aloysia several songs, which he had been writing for her voice, beautifully transcribed and illuminated with pen sketches. For Constanze he brought a rondo for the clavier, also copied in the neatest manner; and his pockets were stuffed with nuts and sugar-plums for the children. For Herr Weber he brought an elegant meerschaum pipe, on which he had carved the five lines of a bar of music, with the three first notes of a smoking-song famous at that time.

But the most precious of all the gifts which he himself received was reserved for the last. Just at nightfall, he was sitting at home, trying some new music which was among his morning gifts from the Webers, when a little packet was brought to him by the servant. It had been left, she said, by a little girl, unknown to her. He opened it with some curiosity, and found a beautiful little pocket-book, of light blue silk, on which was embroidered an altar and a laurel wreath, with the words—"*For the worthiest, the crown ;*" and, "*From a faithful heart.*"

"From Aloysia—surely from Aloysia !" he cried, in perfect delight. "Who else could have sent it? And if it was Aloysia, then she loves me!—then she loves me!" And he danced about the room, rejoicing like a child, and kissing his gift.

At last, it occurred to him to look into his pocket-book. There he found only a card, on which was written in a disguised hand : "No one must know of this gift, and no one must be spoken to about it—not even the giver, if the giver is guessed."

"Guess?" thought Amadeus; "who else could I guess but Aloysia? Oh, then, I have not deceived myself in thinking so many times, when I have caught her look, that I read love in it, so quickly were her eyes cast down ! And has she not, of late, always colored when I entered the room, or addressed her? Did not her hand, at my departure yesterday for the first time tremble in mine ?"

Then a crowd of incidents rushed to his recollection, every one of them a fresh proof that he had guessed correctly. It seemed to him as if Heaven had suddenly opened to him. He could have embraced the whole world: he trembled with excitement and pleasure; and it was well he was alone, or surely he had betrayed himself that moment. But no! he was not alone! there stood his beloved instrument, his trusted friend in sorrow and joy, and he must talk with it of his new happiness. Opening the piano, he sat down and played. Crash and clang, ripple and trill, tangle and maze of intricate harmony—trumpet-blast and fountain-plash—ocean-beat and triumphant storm—all streamed forth into the gathering night. No one heard but his own heart; and that heard not, for it was speaking itself.

At last he sprang up, with an impulse to go to the Weber house; but as he rose, something tinkled on the floor. He stooped to find it, and lo! it was Giuditta's little golden cross—his amulet. In his excitement, he had fumbled with his hand inside his waistcoat and had snapt the already worn cord.

The occurrence struck upon him a little unpleasantly. He became quieter, and laying the cross on the piano, he paced slowly up and down the room.

Giuditta's image was floating before his mind; he was thinking of those delicious days in Rome, of the farewell in the grotto of St. Cecilia, of the strange meeting in Milan, and the words, "Till we meet again!"

But had not seven years gone by since then? Poor Giuditta! where was she now?

"We never shall meet again!" he said to himself. "But to thy remembrance, true heart! I will be faithful. Thou wast my guardian angel in Milan. Thou art and shalt remain to me a dear far-off sister!"

And he took up the little golden cross, fastened it anew to the cord, and hid it on his breast. But this accident remained as a discord in the pure harmony which had so intoxicated him. He could not drive away the thought, "What if this were a warning from thy guardian angel, who sees thee walking in the wrong path!" Amadeus sat down again at his instrument. At first his fingers followed out an earnest, almost sorrowful melody, now rising to an eager protest against some unknown fate, then sinking into sadder resigna tion—till suddenly his eyes fell on his Christmas gift. Then leaped the tones out like sparks, till the sparks were lightning-flashes, and everything exulted again within him. "She loves me—Aloysia loves me!" and springing up, he hastened away toward the Rhine-gate.

He entered the house just as Aloysia was about to try the new songs which he had given her in the morning. She was overjoyed to have him at the clavier to accompany her. The first piece they took up was an air to those words of Metastasio, "*Non sò d'onde vienne,*" etc., to which Bach had already composed an air. But this one was Mozart's own, peculiarly adapted to Aloysia,[1] and it expressed the feeling of a young maiden who stands in innocent wonderment before the new emotions of her heart, which she cannot understand—which she scarcely dares attempt to understand.

Aloysia sang it gloriously: it was as if the dumb and yearning soul had found a voice—not consciously to itself—but so unconsciously natural in its laying hold of this new-found voice, that Amadeus felt his heart beat hotly in his breast, and his hands tremble as he followed the accompaniment.

The two immortal sisters—Art and Love—were there; both half-dumb, and each the interpreter of the other!

Then came the duett which Amadeus had written for this evening and for their two voices. Aloysia had at first a solo passage, which she sang charmingly; her voice only in one place trembled, and a deep glow covered her fair face. It was where the beloved whispers to her friend in sweetest tones: "Yea, thou knowest, O Beloved, that my heart is ever thine!" She could scarcely stand—her knees trembled, and her voice threatened to fail. But, fortunately, the clear voice of Amadeus broke in. But when he, too, with an unspeakable depth of meaning, repeated the same words, "Yea, thou knowest, O Beloved, that my heart is ever thine!" and both voices in lingering tones sank together in one long cadence—then, for both, their holiest secret was expressed; they knew that even as each loved, each was beloved. It was very well that, at the end of this song—which was loudly applauded by the little audience—the "Evening-bread" was announced. As they took their seats at the table, each was in a peculiar mood. Frau Weber seemed wholly lost in thought—Wolfgang was all wit and gayety—Aloysia appeared strangely confused, and gave her father the pepper

---

[1] Historical.—Jahn. Part II.. p. 168.

when he asked for the salt, and abstractedly passed him his box of tobacco instead of the wine-flask. Only Constanze, who had been busy in the kitchen during the singing, and her father, were quietly serene as ever. The latter smiled contentedly at the merry chatter of the children, and the former hung with an expression of still happiness on the looks of their young guest.

At last came the hour for departure. Aloysia went into the anteroom to bring frau Mozart's cloak and hat; and, to spare her the trouble of looking for them, Amadeus hastened after her. But, strange to say! before they had found the cloak, in the dark room, they found each other. There was a low whisper—"Aloysia!" an answering one still lower—"Amadeus!" and two happy hearts were beating on one another, and a close, burning kiss said, "Yea, thou knowest, O Beloved, that my heart is ever thine!"

But embrace and kiss were the work of an instant. At the next moment Aloysia brought in the cloak and carefully put it about good mother Mozart; but a peal of good-natured laughter followed this friendly act—Aloysia had put the cloak on inside out, and frau Mozart stood, like a Chinese picture on a tea-chest, gorgeously arrayed in flowered calico.

Frau Weber shook her head thoughtfully, as the guests bade good-night amid jests and laughter. Then all the Weber household went to rest.

Only one had no thought of sleep, and that was Aloysia. Constanze could not but see her sister's strange mood, and when both were in their chamber, she asked, in an affectionate tone—

"Why are you so disturbed and restless to-night, Aloys?"

Aloysia looked at her sister with all the golden sunshine of happy love in her eyes, and putting her arms around the slender young form, caressed her: then, as if her heart was too full of its bliss, and must brim over, she sank her head upon her shoulder—

"Constanze! I love him; and he loves me, also!"

Constanze believed herself to be dreaming.

"You love him?" she answered, in a constrained voice: "Who?—who is it that you love?"

"How can you ask!" said Aloysia; "who is there but Amadeus?"

The words smote like a stinging sword through Constanze's

soul. A deathlike pallor overspread her face, and with white and trembling lips, she repeated, slowly—

"And he loves you, also?"

"Yes!"

"And he has told you so, himself?"

"This evening—a little while ago! Oh, I am so glad!" And Aloysia pressed her little sister to her heart, and kissed her again and again. But suddenly she drew back, and cried—

"Constanze! what is it? Your forehead is cold!—you are pale as death!"

"It is nothing," she answered. "I am tired to-night. I am so tired!"

"Can't I do something for you?" asked Aloysia, anxiously. "Mayn't I brush out your hair?"

"No, darling," answered Constanze. "You must go to bed. Only let me sit here awhile quietly."

"But you will be cold: there is no fire in the stove!"

Constanze shook her head. "'Tis no matter, darling. I will come to bed pretty soon."

Aloysia disrobed herself, talking all the while of what had happened, and of the bright future which her love-dreams painted for her and Amadeus. She was too much preoccupied to notice, meanwhile, that her sister made no reply. Soon she bade good-night, and sleep closed her eyes and cradled her in sweet dreams.

But Constanze sat still at the window. Tears glittered in her deep calm eyes, that gazed out through the round panes into the starlight above, and the thick night that overshadowed the earth below. From the Rhine the mist crept slowly across the sleeping city, and all life was sunken in stillness and darkness.

Dark and still was it also in her young heart, which had enjoyed such a happy day—which had this very evening beat so joyfully with its tender secret.

Constanze sat long in silence there. At last she rose, and kneeling down, said her evening prayer humbly and fervently. What this childish heart prayed, who knows, except God? It may be that she asked forgiveness from her heavenly Father, that—for the first time in her life—she had done something in secret from her good parents and her dear sister. It may be that she kissed the chastening hand, which had so wonderfully reached down out of the clouds, and turned her own secret against her.

When she arose, it was all still and peaceful in her heart, but sleep would not come for a long, long time. And when, toward morning, her eyelids fell, the dear child's weary head rested on a pillow wet with tears.

———◆———

CHAPTER IV.

A NEW ENEMY AND A NEW FRIEND.

FROM that day, Mozart was a new man. A more manly life, in the worldly sense of the word, must naturally be begun from this time; for it was of more importance to establish himself in some permanent position, that he might as soon as possible claim Aloysia for his bride. Father Weber saw this practical direction of Mozart's thoughts with pleasure; for, though both the young people supposed their secret to be strictly their own, Herr Weber and his good wife both knew it very well. They had needs been blind and deaf not to have guessed it from that duett on Christmas night, and the behavior of them both.

The mother was for some time quite anxious and disturbed about the state of affairs; but her husband's calm good sense soon quieted her motherly apprehensions. For, certainly, young Mozart was so stanch and true a character, and so highly gifted, that nothing was to be feared with regard to him. And what a fine outlook it was for Aloysia, if her eminent talents in music were united with his!

Meantime the new shoots of this growing plant of love were as yet so tender, that they were not trusted to the cold winds of the world, but kept sheltered, almost from the eyes of its possessors even. No words of fondness passed their lips; and only passing looks, or at most a light pressure of hands, told what was in the heart. Besides, the careful mother always made it a point to be present whenever the young people met. Even to rehearsals and concerts she accompanied her daughter, for propriety's sake; which she could the more easily do now that Constanze began of her

•wn accord to assume almost the whole burden of the house-keeping. This the mother intrusted to her with perfect confidence, for Constanze, in spite of her youth, had already almost a mature measure of discretion and housewifely wisdom. Indeed, she might have passed for a maiden of eighteen years. And with what gentleness and tender affection she met them all—her parents, her younger sisters, and Aloysia! Her days were one unceasing watchfulness for their comfort and happiness, even in the smallest things. Mozart, too, found as ever a friendly welcome at her hands; only, it seemed to him that now-a-days she was somewhat more retiring than usual in her manners toward him, and sometimes, when he looked at her with more than ordinary kindness, he almost thought her downcast eyes grew suddenly moist. But just at present he had little leisure for such observations—he was busily occupied with plans and endeavors for a permanent situation as musician.

"So it seems you are going to stay in Mannheim?" had said to him lately the governess of the Elector's children, Madame von Zoller: she was a good friend of his, and the tone in which she said it seemed to hint a pleasant piece of news under the form of a question. Mozart knew of nothing which would keep him there permanently, though this would have chimed with his wishes exactly. Upon his saying so, the governess exclaimed in surprise—

"Why, I thought you knew. The Elector said to me, the other day, 'By the bye, Mozart is to spend the winter here!'"

This was good news to Mozart. He hurried at once, full of joyful anticipations, to Count Saviola, whose official position at court made him the readiest way of access to the Elector. He supposed, naturally enough, that if Karl Theodore wished to keep him in Mannheim, it was with some other view than that of having him spend the remnant of his small means in forced idleness there—perhaps with a view of engaging him as musical instructor for his children, since that had already been spoken of.

As he went up the steps of the Intendant's mansion, he met Abt Vogler, just coming away from an audience with the Count. He was accompanied by a handsomely dressed stranger, whose intellectual face, and powerful eyes, notwithstanding their somewhat sad expression, denoted a man of distinction. Vogler was engaged in close conversation with him, and, as Mozart came up to them, introduced him with

6

a patronizing air to the stranger, as the future director of the Mannheim theatre, Dr. Gotthold Lessing.[1]

Mozart was delighted at the opportunity of knowing the renowned author of " Emilie Galotti," and " Minna von Barnhelm," which had long ago awakened his youthful enthusiasm. In the fulness of his heart, he at once spoke to Lessing of his own hopes of securing a position, either at court or in the theatre;[2] but as he spoke, there passed over the face of Vogler such a freezing, derisive—almost diabolical—smile, that all Mozart's hopes, if he had seen it, would have taken flight. But, happily, his own look was fixed on the noble countenance of Germany's great poet, while his fearless fancy already was picturing a delightful winter to be passed in the companionship of so noble a soul.

Abt Vogler allowed no time for longer conversation. He had just been honoring Lessing with the announcement that he was engaged in writing a treatise on the philosophico-musical question, " Whether tones sound best in a white room or a black one ?" and now, taking leave of Mozart with a careless nod, he proceeded with his companion on their way.

Amadeus laughed to himself at Vogler, and hastened up the steps, now doubly hopeful. But alas ! the Intendant was too busy to see him, and he had to return without any satisfaction. Again and again he had the same luck. Count Saviola was either occupied with State affairs, or away from town, or giving an audience to some great personage or other. At last, when Mozart's patience was pretty nearly exhausted, he gained admission one day. It was evident, as soon as he set eyes on the Count, that he was no longer as friendly to him as formerly. At once it flashed across Mozart's mind that this change had some connection with Abt Vogler, whom to-day again he had met as he came through the antechamber, and from whose supercilious face he had scarcely received a look of recognition. Little did he suspect, however, the wiles and intrigues by means of which Vogler had prevented his success at court—intrigues which the ingenuous nature of Mozart would have blushed to employ, even for the holiest purpose, much more for the envious undermining of a rival's success.

[1] This attempt to secure Lessing as Director at Mannheim fell through, because he was dissatisfied with the prevailing sentiments at court there.
[2] It must be remembered that the "theatre," in all the German cities, belonged to the opera, and music generally, as well as to the drama.

When now Amadeus pressed the Intendant for a straight answer, whether or no there was any position for him from the Elector, that nobleman only shrugged his shoulders. This French gesture always had a specially irritating effect on the frank young German, and it was just now the last straw on the camel's back of his patience.

"What!" cried he, "still no answer?"

Saviola gave his shoulders an enormous shrug, as if he would draw his head in like a turtle, and replied—

"Excuse me, but there is no place for you!"

Mozart's blood flew to his head with indignant anger—

"*Eh bien!*" he cried; "the Elector had done well to say that before. I beg you to thank his Excellency, in my name, for the somewhat late, but gracious intelligence!"[1] and with an ironical obeisance he left the room.

It was a bitter disappointment. Here was a whole month gone for nothing; and his hopes of a speedy marriage and of a musical career all dashed to the ground, because a few titled jackanapes chose to be ignorant of him and careless of his art. There, across the street, stood the elegant mansion of Abt Vogler, the Elector's Vice-Capellmeister, who dwelt there like a prince. He, whose flimsy veil of affectations Amadeus had pierced through at their first meeting, who was a mere awkward boy at composition or in playing the organ and piano, whom every true musician despised as a mountebank,[2]—there he dwelt in luxurious leisure, petted by the court and praised by the people. And here in the street stood Mozart, without position or employment,—he who had left Italy as its darling *maestro*, and returned to his fatherland only to be coolly repulsed by the three German princes from whom art had most to hope!

There needed a little time to cool his temper and restore his blood to its usually serene current. He felt this himself, and set out at a rapid pace, in spite of ice and snow, for the neighboring village of Neckarau.

It was a splendid day. The sky was clear as a bell, and from its bright blue depths poured down a flood of sunshine over the boundless sheet of sparkling snow that stretched away to the horizon. From the mountains, whose long out-

---

[1] Mozart's own words.
[2] *Vide* Mozart's Letters (N. Y.: Leypoldt & Holt, 1867), Vol. I., pp. 116, 125 157, etc. But Abt Vogler afterward reformed and became, late in life, a fine musician.

line was cut clean against the clear blue, a fresh air was
blowing, whose bracing vigor cooled the blood and made
every muscle of the body elastic as a steel spring.

Had it not been for his relations with Aloysia, which made
the idea of a departure from Mannheim so painful, Amadeus
would have recovered his good-humor in the first ten minutes; for was it not true that

"The world was all before him where to choose?"

and had he not the serene consciousness of his own worth
within him? Yet now, with the little house by the Rhine-
gate holding out its hands to him, how could he leave Mann
heim forever?

It was no wonder, then, that neither the splendid blue sky
nor the gay sunshine and glittering snow-scape could smooth
the frown off his forehead so easily. With unusual seriousness, therefore, he strode rapidly forward, and it was but little
past noonday when he reached Neckarau. Anger always
makes vigorous people hungry, and as it would be too late
for dinner in Mannheim, he turned into the "Swan," and
called for a glass of wine and something to eat.

The "Swan" at Neckarau was a queer little tumble-down
inn, whose dilapidated appearance might well have prevented
any but the boldest wayfarer from entering, unless he knew
how many years it had stood stanchly against all weathers
in that same condition. The tap-room was so low that a tall
man must perforce be polite enough to remove his hat before
venturing under its ceiling. The walls were black with
smoke and the savory steam of many dinners, while the
small and dingy window-panes let in a very meagre portion
of the bright daylight outside. The room was innocent of
any adornments except two or three remarkable prints, pinned
on the wall, of an ancient and murky appearance, which would
have done credit to an "old master." The furniture consisted
of a venerable sideboard, a few tables and chairs, and a huge
stove, surrounded on three sides by a bench, and sending out
a comfortable glow from its open mouth.

The room was empty as Amadeus took his seat at one of
the tables, except for the comely and buxom hostess, and one
guest, who sat on the bench by the stove. This person excited Mozart's interest, as soon as his eyes fell upon him.
He was a young man, with a finely cut face, handsome blue

eyes, and an abundance of brown hair, which was neither powdered nor *queued*, but left to go its own graceful way upon his well-shaped head. But what struck one at first sight was, that his dress, notwithstanding the frosty weather, was adapted rather for summer. The thin gray coat showed melancholy marks at the elbows, and the rusty waistcoat of blue silk, buttoned suspiciously high in the throat, was a shivery sort of garment to look upon, considering the ice and snow outside—through which he must have come on foot for some distance, judging by the looks of his shoes, whose chinks seemed to bespeak an inquiring mind inside the leather. A battered hat and an old blue cloak lay near him, but there was no appearance of his having ordered anything to eat or drink. The warmth of the stove seemed to be his only refreshment, and that indeed must have been considerable; for he looked frosty enough, though upon his face, despite its paleness, lay a humorous expression mingled with its disconsolateness—as if he were aware of a certain comic side to himself and his circumstances.

Amadeus was hungry enough to be very well pleased when the amiable hostess spread his table with a snowy cloth, and laid thereon a hot steak, with bread and a glass of wine. The savory smell of the meat struck his nostrils with an appetizing fragrancy, which—O happy time of youth!—entirely drove from his mind Abt Vogler, Count Saviola, and the frustration of his plans. Just at present he had no plan, except to enjoy a good meal; and that, fortunately, no courtier's machinations seemed likely to disturb. But he had no sooner taken the first bite, than his eye fell on something which drove still further away, if possible, any recollection of his own disappointments. The young man still sat there by the stove—but what a face!

If Wolfgang had not been such a thoughtfully kind-hearted soul, he must inevitably have burst into a laugh, so tragico-comical was its expression. The savory odor of the steak had appealed to another empty stomach besides his own, and its owner seemed to be trying to subdue its clamors by holding both hands across it. But this did not prevent his nostrils from expanding, and his eyes devouring the platter, while the eyebrows were raised dolorously, and a deep sigh was just escaping him. As his look caught that of Amadeus, he had to smile at the ludicrous figure which he was suddenly conscious of making, and he exclaimed:

"It *is* rather pitiful—the absurd plight a man is in with his nonsensical body! Here is his spirit, merry as a May morning—and it only takes a twenty-four hours' fast to turn May into December with him!"

Mozart looked at him in astonishment. This was not the language of a vagabond; and then, "I hope you don't mean," he exclaimed, "that you haven't eaten anything for twenty-four hours?"

"*I* hoped I shouldn't mean it, too, yesterday!" he replied; "but as the play hath it, you know,

> "'Who trusts in hope, or a woman's oath,
> Is tipsy, or in love—or both.'"

This, with the indescribable play of the features which accompanied the words, showed Mozart two things plainly enough,—first, that it was an actor whom he had to do for; and second, just what he ought to do for him. He at once ordered a second repast like his own, and invited the stranger to take a seat at the table with him.

This he did with a delighted alacrity, and before the meal was finished he had told his whole history, at Mozart's request. His name was Lange, and, as his companion had guessed, he was by profession an actor. The world had never turned its soft side to him, but had shown itself, so far as he was concerned, a sharp-cornered and hard-grained affair. His purse never had been long enough to reach more than a few weeks ahead; and if fortune had at times put some bright streaks in his sky, it had generally clouded up again very shortly. Yet his troubles had never altered his cheerful and rather self-confident disposition; but had, on the contrary, added to his cheeriness by giving it a philosophical turn. If he could not always order a dinner, he could quote abundance of dramatic authority for his hunger; and if garments sometimes failed him, passages of Shakspeare never did. A spicy proverb was sweeter than a cigar in his mouth (when he could not buy the latter); and the trolling of some rollicking old song was as good as champagne to him, at any time. There was at the same time a shrewd sense, and a goodness of heart about the man, which pleased Amadeus exceedingly, and made him promise Lange that the very next day he would introduce him to the Intendant, and try to secure him a place at the Mannheim theatre immediately. The actor was delighted with this offer of assistance; and when he confided to Amadeus, with a comical expression of mimic despair, that his only difficulty lay in making himse.f presentable for an introduction to Count Saviola, his new friend allayed his anxiety by an agreement to send him a small bundle in the morning.

After several hours' talk, which had the effect to make his own troubles seem of very small account to him, Mozart shook hands with the actor, and set out for a brisk walk back to Mannheim, in the fading afternooon sunshine.

"A handsome fellow he is!" said Lange, as he watched the disappearing figure, close-buttoned from the cold; "and a noble soul.—But pshaw! I forgot, like an ass as I always am, to ask him who he is! Never mind—'the rose by any other name, etc.' He's a trump, and that's enough for me!"

CHAPTER V.

DISCORDS.

THE next morning Mozart carried to the Swan at Necka rau, with his own hands, a bundle containing divers essential garments and a new hat. When Lange was duly arrayed in these he made an exceedingly fine-looking figure, and if he wore his hat a little too jauntily and had a little bit of the stage stride in his walk, yet these were not unbecoming to his slender form and long flowing hair.

Amadeus took him straightway to the Intendant, who was so much taken by his good appearance, and some slight proof of his abilities as an actor, which he very willingly gave, that a position was given to him at once. The nobleman who had only yesterday repulsed the greatest musician of his time with a shrug of the shoulders, now engaged this stranger with almost no knowledge of him and very slight trial of his qualifications.

Another man than Mozart would have been deeply incensed and mortified by the behavior of the Count, and by this irony of fate; but not Amadeus! He was as genuinely pleased as a child at the success of Lange; and when the latter requested a small loan from him till he should receive something from his engagement, Amadeus gladly gave it to him.

And now came up again his own perplexities. Repulsed by Karl Theodore, what better could he do than to try Paris! Undoubtedly he would find at the French capital a warm welcome; and notwithstanding the discomforts of a journey thither in mid-winter, he would have determined to start at once—but, his heart was chained at Mannheim! The thought of a long, perhaps final separation from Aloysia and the Weber family, to every member of which he had become so deeply attached, was insupportable. Wolfgang did just what we all do when there is a path which our judgment persistently points out to us, but which we dread to walk in—he looked under every possible stone for an excuse to stay where he was. A considerable number of such excuses he found; for the hostility of the court had the effect of making all his friends so much the more obstinately bent on serving him. Cannabich promised to find pupils for him; Serarius, the privy-councillor, another devoted friend of his, offered him and his mother a home at his own house;[1] and Wendling urged upon them to take seats at his table. Finally, a wealthy Hollander, who was a great patron of music, gave him an order for three short clavier concertos and two flute-pieces, at 200 florins. They persuaded him, also, to write some duetts for flute and piano, to be published by subscription. That would give him employment for at least two months; and so he decided, by no means reluctantly, to remain in Mannheim.

Aloysia was now no longer a " beginner" on the operatic stage, but a successful singer. The Mannheim public received her ever with increased favor, and her reputation was excellent with the Elector and his court. Rehearsals and appearances now absorbed most of her time, and her old duties as vice-housekeeper received very little attention at her hands. But while Aloysia, on account of rehearsals or invitations to the court or aristocratic houses, was, many an evening, not to be found in the quiet little home-circle, yet Mozart never failed to find Constanze there, the same as ever—always the soul of the household, and still the dear, childlike, simple maiden, with her deeply sensitive heart, and ready interest in every good and beautiful thing. With her, Wolfgang always felt

---

[1] Mozart's Letters, Vol. I., p. 150.

calm, contented, and *at home.* There was a peculiar rest and peace which came over him when near her. And a close observer might have noticed the same thing in Constanze. When Aloysia was at home, her sister always quietly drew back, and busying herself about household affairs, was in the room but little. When Aloysia was away, however, she was tenderly devoted to the happiness of their guest, yet never for a moment overstepping that maidenly reserve, which, in its union with womanly loveliness, was to Amadeus so wonderful and charming.

There was but one feature of his life in Mannheim which was utterly disagreeable to him. This was the giving of lessons at set hours to all sorts of pupils. "This accursed schoolmastering!" he would say at night, as he flung himself into a chair at the Webers', and recounted the stupidities of some bungling creature who was *trying to try* to learn to play. At such times it required all the gentle influence of Constanze to set his jangled nerves in tune again. This she would do, perhaps by the mere silent magnetism of her presence; perhaps by reminding him that the teachers are the true monarchs of this world—the earthly creators, whose plastic chaos is the unformed soul. At another time she would soothe him, merely (for in this, some human souls are like a musical instrument) by being played *upon*—by listening and drinking in his music or his impassioned talk on art.

It was at such a time of disgust with his *brod-wissenschaft* ("bread-and-butter-work") that he wrote to his father at Salzburg: "I could not get on passably without pupils, which is a kind of work that does not suit me. Of this I have a strong example here. I might have had two pupils: I went three times to each, but finding one of them not at home, I never went back. I am willing to give lessons out of complaisance, especially when I see genius, and inclination and anxiety to learn; but to be obliged to go to a house at a certain hour, or else to wait at home, is what I cannot submit to, if I were to gain twice what I do. I find it impossible, so must leave it to those who can do nothing but play the piano. I am a composer, and born to become a Capellmeister, and I neither can nor ought thus to bury the talent for composition with which God has so richly endowed me (I may say this without arrogance, for I feel it now more than ever); and this I should do if I were to take many pupils, for it is a most unsettled *métier:* and I would rather

6*

neglect the piano than composition, for I look on the piano to be only a secondary consideration—though, thank God, a very strong one too. My head is full of opera-writing—French rather than German, and Italian rather than either."[1]

His father, meantime, was constantly urging Amadeus to go to Paris, where he foresaw more fame and profit for his son than in a precarious and haphazard life in Mannheim. But this advice, wise as he could not help suspecting it to be, Amadeus would hardly have taken, if it had not been for two circumstances, which brought a harsh discord into his life there.

In Kircheim-Boland, at the palace of the Princess Von Oranien, an acquaintance had sprung up between Aloysia and young Lange, the actor, as could not fail to happen during a week's residence under the same roof. She met him on the Mannheim stage also, and at concerts, etc., but without being familiar with him at all. Though Lange came to Mannheim as a friend of Mozart, and all the women united in enthusiastic admiration of him—calling him the "new Adonis"—yet the first impression he made on Aloysia was unfavorable. The serious, quiet, almost severe tone of her own education, and of the household life, had moulded her tastes; and Lange, notwithstanding the amiability of his character, was the opposite of all this. She could not but recognize his personal beauty, but his manner frightened her at first, and repelled her. Her father and mother did not hesitate to express their dislike of this "rattle-brain," as they called him; for before he had been a month in Mannheim, the town was full of stories of his pranks and exploits. Mozart himself received more than one lecture from the Weber parents, for his kindness to the man; especially as Lange appeared to have forgotten the little debt he owed him. Into the house by the Rhine-gate, therefore, the actor never had been admitted; yet it seemed to Amadeus that his light-headed friend had cast an eye upon Aloysia. He sought every opportunity to meet her on the street or in the theatre, and whenever he succeeded in gaining access to her, he seemed to put forth all the fascination of which he was capable to win her favor.

Aloysia gave him not the slightest encouragement; on the contrary she avoided him, and treated him with more persistent coolness than any man of her acquaintance. It seemed clear enough to Amadeus, that a man with all the attractions of this "new Adonis," must eventually succeed with so inexperienced a maiden as Aloysia, if he persisted in his advances. He felt that in all outward appearances Lange had greatly the advantage of himself. So it came about that a little demon of jealousy slipped into Amadeus's heart, without any fault on the side of Aloysia. As some one has said, "Jealousy is the hypochondria of Love." It has a thousand eyes, each of them quick to see a great deal more than there is to be seen. This, therefore, made one of the discords in Mozart's life at Mannheim. To this was added a doubt, and the two together quite broke up the harmony. The doubt was in this wise:

Amadeus constantly carried with him that pledge of love —the little silken pocket-book which he had received on Christmas night. Yet he never had disobeyed the injunction of the "true heart," not to mention the gift, even to the giver. He was sure it came from Aloysia, but great as had been his temptations, he never had hinted a word of it to her. But to-day came a temptation which he could not resist.

He had taken dinner with the Webers. Notwithstanding the hearty appetite which he usually brought to this substantial meal, to-day he had only played with his knife and fork, and had remained in a monosyllabic condition of glumness all through the repast. It was plain enough that he was in ill-humor; and plain, too, that he thought he had a good right to be, about something that had happened. It was simply that Lange had presented Aloysia, during rehearsal in the forenoon, with a lovely bouquet. The gift of such a bouquet in mid-winter was peculiarly significant. But he did not know how Aloysia had done her best to refuse it, nor that Lange had by no means premeditated giving it to her; since it had only just been given to him by some lady of the court, as a reminder concerning a tender rendezvous they had appointed. But jealousy never stops to find out any of these little particulars, which in reality make all the difference " 'twixt tweedle-dee and tweedle-dum."

As soon, therefore, as he was alone with the two girls for a few minutes after dinner, it occurred to Amadeus to remind Aloysia of their happy Christmas evening. He drew her into one of the window-niches, so as to be out of hearing of Constanze, who was busy in clearing the table, and began:

"You wanted to know why I was so still, all dinner-time?"

"Yes!" replied Aloysia, in her usual friendly tone: "'tis something extraordinary to see *you* in that mood."

"But don't you know," whispered Amadeus, "that you hurt me terribly by taking those flowers from Lange?"

"I am very sorry, if I did!" answered Aloysia with perfect sincerity. "I saw no way to refuse them without offending the man. I held out against it a long time."

"If you only felt now, as you did that Christmas night—"

"Amadeus!"

"And if you but knew how holy I have kept your dear gift—"

"My gift!"

"I have kept silence, as the 'true heart' bade me; but now let me once speak of it. It has made me so happy—"

"What has?"

"The pocket-book, which your darling hand embroidered, and sent me so secretly."

"There is some mistake, Amadeus!" replied Aloysia, shaking her head in perplexity.

"What!" he exclaimed, forgetting himself, and drawing out the pocket-book—"you won't acknowledge your own precious gift?"

But at that moment they both started in momentary terror. Constanze had let fall a pile of dishes, which flew into a hundred pieces with a great crash. She stood leaning on the back of a chair, pale and trembling. As Mozart hastened towards her, with the pocket-book still in his hand, the pallor of her cheeks gave way to a burning flush. She no longer had the strength to stand, and sank weeping upon the chair.

"You are frightened, dear Constanze!" said Mozart, his sympathy being at once excited.

"Yes!" she answered in confusion: "the mistake—with the dishes, I mean!"

"Oh, well!" cried Aloysia; "that isn't the dreadfullest thing in the world: never mind it, child!"

But Constanze went out, sobbing as if her heart was broken.

It seemed to Wolfgang a little occurrence to disturb so weighty a conversation; and he returned to the charge at once—

"Aloysia! answer me on your word of honor—was this gift from your hand or not?"

"It was not!" she answered, positively.

At that instant the mother entered, and the conversation was broken off. Mozart remained a few minutes, stiller than before, and then left the house. There was but one thought in his mind as he hastened homeward, and having arrived there, as he paced up and down his room with long strides: "Not from Aloysia! From whom then?" Suddenly the strange behavior of Constanze occurred to him. Was it not strange that her usually steady and careful hand had let fall its burden? And then her paleness, and blushes, and weeping—and at that moment, too, when he had held the silken present in his hand. Could it be from her? "Impossible!" he thought; and yet—

But just then came the postboy's knock. It was a letter from Salzburg. His father urged him most earnestly to set out at once for Paris. The case seemed a plain one to the eyes of Amadeus. He almost believed that he heard the voice of destiny upbraiding him—as if his guardian-angel called to him, "Yes, forth into France! There, in the central city of the world, which once already has received thee with acclaim, *there* is thy place! Keep thy troth with Aloysia, if thou wilt, but forget not, in love, the mission with which God sent thee upon the earth!"

His conclusion was formed at once. His friends could no longer blame him; for, sorry as they were to part with their comrade, they could not but see that Mozart was born for something better than to dry up in giving lessons at Mannheim. Weber, especially, strengthened him in his resolution, and more than hinted that, though he seemed like a son to him already, when he should have acquired a position and income which would justify the founding of a new family, he would be doubly dear to him as a son-in-law.

The separation from his beloved was painful indeed; but sacred promises on both sides assured each of a proud and happy future. Constanze had been unwell ever since the mishap which has been related; and Amadeus had to take leave of her, in the presence of her mother, as she lay in her own chamber. She bade him farewell affectionately; but that veil of soft melancholy, which always seemed to lie upon her heart, now had fallen thicker about her. Amadeus trembled though he scarcely knew why, as he reached his hand to her. She held it fast a moment, pressed it gently—then hid her face in the pillows.

"I don't know what it is!" said the good mother, as they went out: "The child never was nervous, yet everything now seems to move her so!"

Two hours later Mozart and his mother were on their way to Paris. Lange, mounted on a fiery black horse, kept them company as far as Heidelberg. Here he had bespoken a famous breakfast for them. Glasses clinked and wit sparkled: there was many a merry reminiscence of their first meal together, in the dingy tap-room of the "Swan;" then hearty adieus and "good luck!" and they separated.

———————◆———————

CHAPTER VI.

DISENCHANTMENT.

OH morning of youth—golden, glorious youth! Beautiful time, when the glowing imagination pours out the sun-gold of happiness over the whole earth; levelling every mountain that would block the future way; strewing the path, instead, with laurel-wreath and treasure, honor and renown, friendship and love! The world lies just wakening in the rose-odors of fresh dawn, and the whole future is one flower-chain of joys, courageous actions, and proud hopes. Certainly youth is the brightest period of our existence; for then we live in a world of our own creation, which knows not that there is such a thing as illusion—and therefore is Paradise! And is it not beautiful to be "poor in the knowledge of men, rich in ideals?" How merrily the boat rocks over the waves that dance in the morning wind! Rock on merrily—for, alas! the waves dance slowly and more slowly, and only too soon the thunderous "fortissimo" of youth sinks into the "pianissimo" of age. Xerxes rushed upon Greece with a million conquering warriors; and how disheartened he stole back home, secretly and alone, in a fisherman's skiff! How many a man, like him, dreams in that golden time of overmastering greatness—and enters Charon's skiff at last, naked and poor, with a whole graveyard of broken hopes in his chambered heart!

Mozart was twenty-one years old, when he now left Germany the second time for Paris—that city in which his famous childhood had won so many laurels. Tl en, he was only a wonder-child, while now his many musical works and his successes in Italy had secured his reputation as a master. Had he not a right to have high expectations from Paris? Was it not natural that the fairest anticipations filled his mind, and the most daring hopes built fairy palaces in his heart, and enthroned Aloysia amid their splendor?

In France, at this time, the strife was between the national style of music and the Italian style. Lully had long ago originated a French music, introducing bolder harmonies and new flights of melody into such antique music as he found before his time. He wrote nineteen operas, some of whose choruses are grand. But after him there followed no other such genius to continue the work he had begun. In 1733 came Rameau, who was in many respects a national and original composer, but notwithstanding his fiery independence, and his thorough knowledge of effects, he did little for French music. He composed more than twenty operas, but his originality degenerated into affectation and mere effort to be *unusual.* Then came the introduction of Italian opera, by that splendor-worshipper, Louis XIV.; and, literally, "after him the deluge;" for at the time of which we write, 1778, Paris was full of Italian music—the works of Pergolesi, Jomelli, and Leo—while the national school was only represented by the *Opera Comique* under Philidor and Monsigny.

But, four years before this date, there had come to the French capital the great German reformer in dramatic music, the Chevalier Von Gluck. He had great genius, and therefore he excited at once great hostility. He made enthusiastic friends and bitter enemies. His especial rival was Piccini, whose talent lay in originating pretty melodies; and all Paris was at once divided into two parties—the Gluckists, and the Piccinists.

The Italians could not prevent Gluck from gaining a partial triumph; and now might not Mozart be still more successful, and accomplish his great ambition, to ennoble and elevate French music?

Unfortunately there was one element, and it played a large part in his own life, which Mozart never took into his calculations. That was the existence of enemies. He never could believe, till the proof was forced upon him, that any one hated him But envy follows worth, as the smoke does dame; jealousy clings to success, like the shadow to the body: and out of them comes hatred, like a poisonous snake, and not only stings its living victim, but coils, hissing, in the dust of his grave. If, in Milan, Fioroni and Grimani had undertaken the *rôle* of the snake, and in Mannheim Abt Vogler, just so Piccini and Gretry were ready for it in Paris. By plots and wiles of every conceivable kind they prevented Mozart from obtaining either position or employment, or even getting a fair hearing. He could not so much as get a libretto written for his projected opera. Friends he did have, and some influential ones, but indifference and *laissez faire* were stronger than love in Paris.

The following letter to his father at Salzburg, gives his own account of one of his Paris experiences.

"PARIS, May 1, 1778.

"The little violoncellist, Zygmatofsky, and his unprincipled father are here. Perhaps I may already have written you this; I only mention it cursorily, because I just remember that I met him at a house which I must now tell you about—I mean that of the Duchess de Chabot. M. Grimm gave me a letter to her, so I drove there. . . . . . I waited half an hour in a large room without any fire, and as cold as ice. At last the Duchess came in, and was very polite, begging me to make allowances for her piano, as none of her instruments were in good order, but I might at least try it. I said that I would most gladly play something, but at this moment it was impossible, as my fingers were quite benumbed from the cold: so I asked her at all events to take me to a room where there was a fire. 'Oh oui! Monsieur, vous avez raison,' was her answer. She then seated herself, and drew for a whole hour in company with several gentlemen, all sitting in a circle round a large table, and during this time I had the honor to wait. The windows and doors were open, so that not only my hands, but my body and my feet were cold, and my head also began to ache. Moreover, there was *altum silentium;* and I really did not know what to do from cold, headache, and weariness. I again and again thought to myself, that if it were not on M. Grimm's account I would leave the house at once. At last, to cut matters short, I played on the wretched, miserable piano. What, however, vexed me most of all was, that the Duchess and all the gentlemen did not cease drawing for a single moment, but coolly continued their occupation; so I was left to play to the chairs and tables, and the walls. My patience gave way under such unpropitious circumstances. . . . . . Give me the best piano in Europe, and listeners who understand nothing, or don't wish to understand, and who do not sympathize with me in what I am playing—I no longer feel any pleasure.

"You write to me that I ought to pay a good many visits, in order to make new acquaintances and to renew former ones. This is, however, impossible, from the distances being so great; and it is too muddy to go on foot, for really the mud in Paris is beyond all description. To go in a carriage entails spending four or five livres a day, and *all for nothing.* It is true the people say all kinds of civil things; but there it ends, as they appoint me to come on such and such a day— when I play, and hear them exclaim: 'Oh! c'est un prodige, c'est inconcevable, c'est étonnant!' and then, *adieu!* At first I spent money enough in driving about, and to no purpose, from not finding the people at home. Unless you lived here, you could not believe what an annoyance this is. Besides, Paris is much changed; the French are far from being as polite as they were fifteen years ago: their manner now borders on rudeness, and they are odiously self-sufficient."[1]

In another letter, dated *Paris, July* 3, 1788, after giving an account of the *Concert Spirituel,* he writes: "I went home, where I am always happiest, and always shall be happiest— or in the company of some good, true, upright German, who, so long as he is unmarried, lives a good Christian life, and when he marries, loves his wife and brings up his children properly. I must give you a piece of intelligence that you perhaps already know, namely, that the ungodly arch-villain Voltaire has died miserably, like a dog—just like a brute. This is his reward! You must long since have remarked that I do not like being here, for many reasons; which, however, do not signify, as I am actually here. I never fail to do my best, and to do so with all my strength. Well, God will make all things right."[2]

After vainly seeking some vantage-ground from which he might exert an influence there—after repeated cool receptions from this and that one of the nobility, he looked back with utter homesickness to Germany. Paris would have none of him—why should he stay there?

[1] *Verbatim.*—Mozart's Letters, Vol. I., p. 196   [2] *Ibid.,* p. 214.

Then another blow smote his heart: his mother—his dear counsellor and companion for so many years—died in his arms. This filled the measure of his weariness of Paris, and he shook off the dust of his feet, and turned his face homeward.

Just as he was leaving he received a letter from his father, announcing that he had obtained for him, from the Archbishop of Salzburg, the position of cathedral and court organist, with a salary of four hundred florins a year! So this was the fruit of all these journeyings, thou great musician! Thou, for whose possession kings and peoples should have contended, and in whose renown they should have taken pride—thou art to go back to little Salzburg as organist!

The old cheeriness returned to Mozart's face only when an intervening ascent had hidden Paris forever from his eyes. And before him—what lay? Ever the world of the ideal—and foremost in its landscape a sweet welcome awaiting him in Mannheim!

CHAPTER VII.

DISAPPOINTMENT.

IN the mean time great changes had taken place in the Palatinate. Mannheim was threatened with the loss of the court, which was to be removed to Munich; and since in that case the opera and all its *attachés* must accompany the exodus, there was in the Weber household a painful anxiety as to the future. The occasion of this removal to Munich was this: Karl Theodore, Elector of the Palatinate, was the heir of Max Joseph, Elector of Bavaria.

An hour and a half after Max Joseph had breathed his last, on the 30th December, 1777, just before sunset, the Chancellor of State, Kreitmayr, opened a little private casket, known only to himself, and took out the last will and testament of the deceased Elector, together with a previously prepared announcement of the accession of Karl Theodore, which was to be proclaimed in the streets of Munich by the trumpet of a herald.

The courier who brought the news from Munich, found

Karl Theodore at church assisting at the mass for the close of the old year, 1777. The intelligence seemed to move him painfully. He was fifty-three years of age. " Now are thy best days over !" he said to himself, half aloud; and all Mannheim echoed the prophecy, which proved only too true.

Karl Theodore left unwillingly—as George I. left Hanover for England—his beloved Palatinate; but since go he must, he set out the same night. Baron Hammerstein came half-way from Munich to meet him and offer his congratulations, but got only the curt reply : " You're much too hasty—much too hasty !"

Arrived in Munich, the old Elector found that Austria also laid claim to Bavaria; and the report came that her troops were already in motion. Apparently careless of his new realm, he at once signed a treaty ceding a lion's share to Austria, only taking care to secure good places for his illegitimate children, who were dearer to him than his Electorate.

Then rose up to save the integrity of Bavaria one of the splendid women of history—the energetic sister-in-law of Karl Theodore, Maria Anna, widow of Duke Clement, a nephew of Kaiser Karl VII. In righteous indignation she wrote to her friend, Frederic the Great: " I, old woman as I am, must be a man now, since all our men have become old women !"

Frederic replied : " Ah, Madame, que n'étiez vous Electeur ? nous n'aurions pas vu arriver les honteux événemens, dont tont bon allemand doit rougir jusqu'au fond du cœur !" [1]

And the great man and the noble woman did their best together to save the disgrace of this cowardly treaty with Austria.

These events had not yet taken place when Mozart left Paris, though the Elector had already gone to Munich; but throughout the Palatinate, and especially in its capital, there was great anxiety. If the court left Mannheim, it was hard to see where Weber, Cannabich, or Wendling were to look for a livelihood.

Mozart knew but little of all this. Since he went to Paris, the political affairs at home had disturbed him but little, and Aloysia's short and unfrequent letters, which at last ceased altogether, had naturally devoted very small space to politics.

[1] " Ah, Madam, why are you not Elector ? then were we saved such shameful events, at which every true German must blush from the bottom of his heart !"

His heart beat fast as he approached Mannheim, on his way from Strasburg. He had purposely left Bruchsal, where he had passed the night, early in the morning, so as to reach the Rhine-gate by noon. The clock was just striking eleven as he raised the knocker on the familiar front-door.

Old Kathrina answered his summons, and gave a joyful cry, as she recognized young Herr Mozart.

"Come in—come right in!" said the good old soul, shaking hands with him heartily. Without waiting to ask after any one, he opened the door of the sitting-room; but there were only the two youngest children there—little Sophie and the six-years-old Hermann. When the first jubilation of the delighted children was over, Amadeus asked after their father and mother. Both were out, but the mother would soon be home.

"And Aloysia and Constanze?"

"Why!" exclaimed both the children in surprise, "don't you know, then?"

"Know what?" asked Amadeus, and the question already set his heart to beating hard.

"Aloys and Constanze are in Munich."

"Where?" cried Mozart, thunderstruck.

"In Munich," repeated Sophie. Then she continued, with an important face, and that sage and *naïve* expression peculiar to little maids—

"You know the Elector lives in Munich now. And all the court and the business and every thing has gone with him, so it is awfully dull here now. And two weeks ago the order came that all the players and opera-singers should go to Munich.

"And that is a great ways," interrupted the small voice of Hermann.

"Of course," said little Sophie, reprovingly, to her brother; "as if Herr Mozart didn't know that! Now—mother would have gone, too, and Constanze kept house for us; but because—"

"Mother had to make a dress first, " broke in Hermann.

"Now, Hermann!" cried Sophie, in a reproachful tone. "Because mother couldn't leave us children and father—"

"And Aloysia mustn't go alone on account of Herr Lange," added the youngster.

"On account of Herr Lange?" asked Mozart, growing pale a little. "Why so?"

"Oh, he is just talking his nonsense!" said the little maid.

This imputation touched Hermann, and he cried hotly—

"'Tisn't nonsense either! Hasn't father scolded lots of times because Herr Lange—"

"He hasn't scolded; no such a thing. He only told Aloysia—"

"He has, too!" persisted Hermann: "he has scolded because Herr Lange keeps coming past the house, and I've seen him when I was up in a chair at the window; and he comes home with Aloys, too—"

"Who says he does?" cried Sophie, zealously.

"Father says so!" answered little Hermann, bending forward in the heat of conflict: "don't you s'pose I've heard him when I was abed?"

"That was naughty!" said his sister: "you ought to have been asleep, or at least not heard him."

"I couldn't make myself deaf, could I? and father talked so loud."

". Well, well, children!" said Mozart now: "never mind about it. 'Twasn't Aloysia's fault, however it was. Is she well?"

"Oh, yes!" replied Sophie, joyfully. "You don't know how much the people like her! She often brings whole baskets of flowers and beautiful wreaths with her from the theatre."

"Has she thought of me and talked about me much?" asked Amadeus, with a very sober look on his face.

"She hasn't had time," cried Hermann. "She was always at rehearsals, or somewhere!"

"But," said Sophie, warmly, "Constanze has talked about you all the more. When we sat together here, the winter evenings, and father was out, and mother was with Aloys at the theatre, and each of us had some work before us, then Constanze would always speak of you;—what you were doing to-night in the great beautiful city; and how you were enchanting the people with splendid concerts; and how the king and queen had perhaps that very day had you play before them, and given you ever so many pretty things: and all this she would tell as beautiful as the stories in our red book."

"And was it all true?" asked Hermann, eagerly.

"No!" said Amadeus, with a mournful smile; "not quite

true. Constanze's thoughts were illusions—as mine have been !"

When frau Weber came in, and soon afterward her husband, Mozart felt a little brightened up by their hearty welcome; and as they sat at dinner, he received a full and particular account of the recent changes. It seemed sad to have to break up their pleasant little home, where they had anchored their hearts in so peaceful a haven, but they consoled themselves with the hope of soon being all reunited at Munich. Amadeus, however, could not but notice a tinge of anxiety or sadness in both the Webers, more than could be attributed to the mere change of residence. This, with Hermann's innocent prattle about his eldest sister, put a very uncomfortable doubt into Mozart's head.

This doubt was strengthened by another consideration. When he went home to Cannabich's, he found the Capellmeister himself gone to Munich; but his wife received him cordially. She could not say enough of the wonderful progress which Aloysia had made, and her popularity both as singer and actress. " Already," said frau Cannabich, " I have no doubt the Munich nobility have become as enthusiastic about her as every one was here."

This, too, was a wound for Amadeus. Was it likely that a prima-donna, now the first ornament of the German stage, surrounded with adulation and homage, would give a thought to him—the poor organist—who had brought nothing back from Paris, except shattered hopes and disappointments?

But Mozart's was not a nature for sentimental sorrow; and he had a perfect hatred of all doubt or vacillation. His resolution was formed at once—he must start for Munich instantly. He must see with his own eyes; and then—if Aloysia loved him, his happiness and his future were secure. If she loved him no longer, then away with the withered rose-garlands !

CHAPTER VIII.

AND AGAIN DISENCHANTMENT.

ALOYSIA WEBER would sing to-night at the Munich theatre, in Salieri's opera, "Axur." Lange, the actor, had spent a good hour before the long mirror in his elegant chamber, making himself ready to go to the theatre—not to take a part upon the stage, but to see and hear his idol, at whose appearances he never failed to be present. It would have been difficult to find a handsomer man, so far as *physique* went, than Lange was when fully dressed. The slender, firmly knit figure, the regular and well-cut features, the blue eyes twinkling with good-humor, the waves of brown hair that fell upon his shoulders, the rich garments made in the latest fashion, and fitting to a nicety—all made up a fine-looking man. The Munich dames were by no means blind to his attractiveness, and he had won many a gay victory over their hearts. His was a nature which was as little capable of forethought for the happiness of others as for his own. Consequently, he had plucked all the roses that came in his way, whether with thorns or not. The present was all of life to him; the past was too disagreeable to remember; the future too uncertain to anticipate. Yet all this did not prevent his adoring Aloysia, and paying court to her, to such an extent as her coyness would permit. Light-minded, reckless as he was, this love for a pure-hearted girl was to him a religion: it seemed to lift him above the trivial plane of his life, when, at times, he thought he saw an instant's gleam of answering love in Aloysia's eyes. Such momentary glances were, hitherto, the extent of his triumph with her.

But to-night, to-night!—he hoped to gain something more. Where and how, were as yet his secret.

The theatre was full to overflowing: nobility and courtiers, officers civil and military, all the wealthy and cultured classes of the Capital had their representatives in full force in the crowded audience; and with all of them Aloysia Weber won new laurels that night. Her voice was glorious, and her appearance enchanting: such a union of talent, beauty, youth,

innocence, and modesty was a rare spectacle at that time in
Munich. Every one knew that the richest and most capti
vating cavaliers had made advances to the Prima-donna, and
had got only mortification for their pains.

Indeed, Aloysia lived almost as retired a life in Munich as
she had in Mannheim; she was with Capellmeister Cannabich, under whose care her parents had placed her, and the
public admiration had no access to her in its homage, except
before the footlights.

It was at that day, in the Munich theatre, peculiarly difficult to maintain a good reputation, since it seemed to be the
particular business of the *bon-ton*, both at court and in the
town, to trample all morality and good repute under its feet.
The original impulse in this direction no doubt went out from
the French court; but at the German capitals it found a delighted echo; and Munich was, least of all, an exception.
Karl Theodore, so far from showing any shame for his noto-
riously dissolute life, had his audience-chamber decorated
with the portraits of his mistresses. And if the chiefs of
society were thus, the less said of its lower ranks the better.

Under these circumstances, the stage furnished, of course,
an unusually slippery footing for a girl's feet. So that
Aloysia's spotless and modest behavior was doubly noticeable
and well-known—as Amadeus was rejoiced to hear, upon his
apparently casual inquiries among those who sat near him in
the parquet. But glad as he was to know that Aloysia was
the same pure maiden as ever, how was it with her relations
to him? He knew only too well how attractive Lange was
in manners and appearance; and that between the handsome
actor and himself there could be no comparison in this respect. At the same time he knew as well how much the
worth of his inner nature outweighed that of the fickle and
frivolous man who was his rival. Yet Lange had talent, too,
and was as popular in his department as Aloysia in hers.

Amadeus had arrived in Munich only just in time to reach
the theatre before the first act of the opera was over, and he
was determined, if possible, to see his beloved at the close of
the performance, if only for one minute, alone. So, being
familiar with the building from his former experiences in
Munich, he went to the door which led from the ladies' robing-
room into the street. Opposite this door, he remembered,
stood an old half-ruined house, with broad projecting eaves,

under which were kept buckets, ladders, hose, etc., to be ready in case of a fire in the theatre.

Here it was so dark that if one stood under these eaves it would be impossible to see him; for Munich at that time was innocent of any such thing as street-lights, and it would have been hard enough to recognize a person even in the middle of the street. Over the entrance to the green-room, to be sure, a lantern swung, bnt this burned very dimly, and scarcely lit the steps below it.

Wolfgang stationed himself deep in the shadow of the overhanging eaves, and awaited with beating heart the appearance of Aloysia. Several female forms, cloaked and hooded, came out from the green-room and passed him on their way home. Some of them were accompanied by servants; some were joined by expectant cavaliers, and taken charge of with jest, and kiss, and titter; and all disappeared in the darkness like vanishing shadows.

What he saw put Mozart in an uncomfortable mood. For the first time he now had plainly before his eyes the dangers to which Aloysia was constantly exposed; and he determined not to step forward and announce himself when she appeared, but to remain hidden and watch her conduct. She was long in coming. "Well," he thought impatiently, "she must be changing her dress entirely; or perhaps she is worn out with her fatiguing *rôle* in the opera, and is resting awhile."

Just then a girl appeared from the door; she certainly had Aloysia's figure—But no! *she* would not be going home entirely unaccompanied, through the darkness. And is not that snatch of a song, which she hums half aloud, meant for a signal? Even so—for a man's form emerges from the shadow of the building across the street. It is an officer's uniform which now and then gleams in the dim light of the lantern. He approaches the girl, and the soft report of a kiss betrays the character of the meeting.

Wolfgang smiled, but the smile turned into a humorous look of anxiety as the pair betook themselves to the same sheltering shadow which concealed himself. Noiselessly he drew back a little farther, and, unmarked by them, had the benefit of a little love-scene.

The ancients enumerated three sorts of kisses: the "Basium," which passed between relatives and friends; the "Osculum," which was a mark rather of respect, and used by priestly persons; and the "Suavium," or love-kiss, which

7

was the only true and *bona-fide* kiss. Our modern times, sc
much given up to the natural sciences, look upon the kiss as
a sort of physico-electrical experiment, whereby the kisser
and kissed become natural philosophers, investigating some
of those most hidden and interior laws which lie at the
foundation of all science. We would not claim that Wolf
gang considered this, in his present peculiar situation; but
he instinctively perceived that the kisses which he heard
were what Catullus would have classed among the "Suavia;'
and his modesty drove him, like an angel with a flaming
sword, out of this Paradise.

He slipped on tiptoe to the other side of the house, and
just then Aloysia came down the steps from the theatre.
He recognized her at once, and, forgetting all his resolutions,
he would have started toward her, when he perceived that she
was not alone. She had a maid with a bright lantern for
attendant. Quietly she proceeded on her way homeward.
Amadeus followed her, in silent joy, for he thought: "They
were mistaken after all—Lange has nothing to do with her!"
He had scarcely said this to himself, when Lange himself
was at her side.

"You have been very long, Aloysia," he said aloud, and
without the least embarrassment. "Did you think you could
tire me out, and drive me away with weariness?"

"I hoped," replied Aloysia, in her resonant voice, which
went straight to Wolfgang's heart, "that you would be
reasonable, and obey my request."

"What request?"

"To let me go home quietly and alone."

"Am I so burdensome to you?"

"No; but this nightly attendance will hurt my reputation,
and that ought to be sacred to you."

"To me everything is sacred, my angel," cried Lange,
"which concerns you. But where else could I ever see you
or speak with you, except when you are returning from the
theatre? In the daytime your sister is with you—and, at the
house, Cannabich is on guard. And see you and speak with
you *once* every day I *must*, or I am miserable."

Mozart trembled; these were at least the words of love,
even if Aloysia held strictly drawn the line of propriety.

"And you still are silent?" asked Lange, while he walked
close at the side of Aloysia, and Mozart followed silently in
their shadow.

"What can I say?" answered the girl. "You know that I am interested in you, my dear Lange, but you know also my fixed determination."

"Not to grant me a word of love," said he with a sigh, "until I change and become a steadier man."

"Even so!"

"Ah, that is asking a great deal, Aloysia. You know the play says, 'A snake may change his skin, but he can't become a camel.'"

"Lange," said Aloysia, as if much pained, "do not make yourself out worse than you are. Revere the strong will of the man in your heart, and become noble. God has given you unusual talent; you are an artist—make yourself now a good man!"

"And if I change, then may I hope for your love in return?"

Aloysia walked on for a moment in silence. In that silence it seemed to Mozart that an executioner's sword was lifting—lifting over his neck. At last Aloysia answered—

"My friend, there is but one safe path in any difficulty; and that is truth and openness. You know that I loved Herr Mozart. I think you do not need to make me confess that your image has crowded his out of my heart; but I will never give my hand to you—never! so long as you stand one jot below his noble standard of earnestness and uprightness. Perhaps it is wrong for me—" she went on; but the words now were lost in the distance, for Mozart stood stricken to a statue, with a heart cold as ice. He had heard enough—the sword had fallen.

This dream of love, too, was an illusion!

CHAPTER IX.

THE FUTURE'S BEAUTIFUL STAR.

IT is strange how man finds himself in this world in relations with a thousand different things; and every one of these relations is a shackle. It is pitiful how a noble soul finds itself fettered and hemmed in by them; and how through their tyranny, it has to cramp down all its greatness and aspiration, till at last it can no longer maintain them at all. In the mean time, just as speech is an art, but silence is a greater one,—as command is hard, but obedience is harder —so, although a man often wins admiration who boldly walks on over all the bounds of human opinion and custom, like a giant striding over the Alps as if they were only furrows in a field; yet unspeakably greater is that man who feels himself raised, by his inner worth, above all the little outward relations in which he finds himself, but none the less respects them and considers them, without allowing them to rule over him. Such a spirit never forgets that man, in spite of all his circumstances and relations, through the might of his own free will, is still his own master, creator of his fortunes and his destiny.

Mozart belonged to the number of these noble and beautiful natures. In him there was no trace of egotism; but his character was rounded out into symmetry by magnanimity, the purest generosity, and a wonderful capacity for self-sacrifice. That Aloysia should give the preference to Lange over him, seemed to him, in his modesty, very natural; but at the same time he could not but say to himself that she had neither understood him nor appreciated his inner soul.

Nevertheless, this breaking loose from a dear friend could not have taken place so easily, if it had not been that the bonds which united him to Aloysia had already been weakened. The first strain upon them was the discovery that the little silken Christmas gift, the secret message of love, had not come from her. Then came Lange's approaches, the gradual cessation of her letters, and at last the talk with the children. And now his own experience in Munich had shattered the already undermined palace of his trust. In the wreck and ashes of its ruins his heart lay smouldering; but he remained man enough to lift himself above his heart, and following the guidance of his strong will, to bite back the pain.

The night after his watching of Aloysia and Lange was naturally a sleepless one: the battle had to be, as always, fought out in his soul. When the smoke of the conflict had cleared away and left him in serene air again, there only remained the question, whether he should depart without a visit and a formal sundering of their relations.

His first impulse was to see Aloysia no more forever; but this was only an impulse. He had promised her parents to visit the two girls and deliver some letters to them; besides,

..e had become so bound to the Weber family that it was impossible to break with them entirely and at once; then, too (and it was one of those considerations which seem secondary and unimportant only because they lie so deep in the heart), he wanted to take leave of Constanze, the good, true soul, and to solve his doubt as to the Christmas gift. These were reasons enough for calling on the two sisters in the morning. He had no desire to see Lange; and lest any invitation or momentary weakness should overset his resolution to depart at once, he ordered a conveyance to be at Cannabich's door by twelve o'clock.

Fate seemed, however, to prefer to interfere a little with his plans. Cannabich and Aloysia had gone to rehearsal. Only Constanze was at home to receive him; but what a frank and hearty reception it was!

She could scarcely recover self-command from the surprise at seeing him, and her delight showed so plainly in her childlike openness, that Mozart was strangely touched by it. It was the reception from Aloysia which he had been anticipating: now, it was her sister—his sister—with whom he felt so restfully happy. Gladly he gave himself up to the joy which he found, almost forgetting that which he had wished. At last, after a hundred questions concerning his life in Paris, his present plans, the household at home, and so on, the conversation fell upon Aloysia. At once he perceived that at the first mention of her sister's name Constanze was embarrassed. Mozart detested everything like circumlocution, or strategic approaches; and as usual he struck immediately to the point, and asked Constanze to tell him, on her honor, just what relations existed between Lange and Aloysia.

Constanze grew pale. It was plainly to be seen how much she dreaded to wound her friend in his dearest feelings; yet, there was but one way for her, no matter what the consequences might be, and that was—perfect truth. After a moment's hesitation therefore, she said:

"If you wish to know it, then I must tell you, much as I hate to."

"Well—"

"They love each other."

Mozart heard it calmly. "I knew it!" Then he added, mournfully, "If this love might only make Aloysia happy! But I fear the contrary."

"And I also," said Constanze; "and what will father and

mother say? The truth is, that Aloysia thinks she sees the guiding hand of Heaven in this affair. She hopes to convert Lange to a nobler life, and then bestow her hand upon him, when he merits it."

"A dangerous experiment!" returned Mozart, shaking his head; "an attempt which may have succeeded once in a million times, but hardly so often."

"So I think," said Constanze, firmly.

"Lange is not a vicious man," continued Mozart; "but he is so light-minded, that even were he to change for awhile, it would not last. He belongs to those people who invent a curious sort of logic from their levity and selfishness. Whatever his nature cannot or will not abstain from, is in his view innocent: whatever will succeed, is good: whatever places '*me*' in the best light, and flatters '*me*,' is right: whatever goes against his inclinations, is evil: whatever can be hidden under any cloak, is perfectly excusable. All such things as sins are ignored, and Heaven—which might be angry—is denied. That is no husband for Aloysia!"

"No indeed!" said Constanze; and her eyes swam with tears as she bent them on Amadeus. But when he lifted up his head and looked into her gentle face, a glowing blush suffused it. Mozart saw it, and at once there came back to his recollection all which had passed between him and the dear beautiful girl who sat by his side. All the tender feelings, the wondering doubts, which her conduct had raised in him, now arose with double force. Pressing closer to her on the sofa where they were sitting, he laid his hand softly on hers and said:

"Dear Constanze, I must depart within an hour, for I cannot meet Lange here; but there is something in my heart which has disturbed me for months."

The sensitive girl answered nothing, but her eyes drooped, and her bosom stormily rose and fell.

"It is a mystery, on whose solution at least my future—perhaps that of another—depends."

He paused, and Constanze moved her lips as if she would ask what it was.

"Can you tell me from whose hand that pocket-book was, which I received so secretly last Christmas night?"

"A pocket-book?" stammered Constanze, while the rose in her cheek blanched into snow.

"Yes!" cried Amadeus, as the breaking up of a long nigh'

dawned before his soul. " *This,* which I have borne here on my breast since I received it. Oh, deny it not! I see and feel that it was from you. An unhappy mistake made me think it was Aloysia's gift; but for many months I have doubted. Tell me, Constanze, was this a love-gift from your hand? I beg of you, tell me truly; my life—the happiness of all the future—hangs upon it!"

"O Amadeus—"

"It *is* from you?"

"Yes!" whispered the maiden, and she sank sobbing on the breast of Amadeus, who clasped her close in his arms.

—So sat they long together. Mozart's kisses burned on Constanze's brow, while she wept and smiled by turns, like an overjoyed child.

"Strange world!" exclaimed Amadeus finally; "always kind and wise to its children at the last. You were both in my heart from the first day I saw you; and so near, that my heart erred in judging between you. But"—and his voice was mellow and rich with feeling, and his beautiful deep eyes were full of light and love—"that which led us apart has led us together again; and the same day on which I lose Aloysia, I find my Constanze!"

" *Your* Constanze?" she repeated, looking into his eyes with a smile that was sweet as the finest April day.

"Are you not?" said he, taking his answer as he spoke—"Mine now and evermore! Let our love be a secret as yet; but remember, that so soon as it is possible, I hasten to you and lead you home as my darling, dearly-loved bride!"

"So let it be!" said Constanze, enraptured, and they sealed the promise with a long and burning kiss.

At that moment they heard the street-door open and steps approaching.

"Aloysia!" cried Constanze, and Mozart sprang up as she entered. At the same instant he heard his carriage drive up before the house.

The scene which ensued was peculiar. Aloysia was naturally very much surprised at the appearance of her friend, and at first quite perplexed. But her experience on the stage prevented this from lasting more than an instant. She at once assumed the proper tone for the circumstances, which united with its politeness enough coolness to let Amadeus know that the tender relations between them were broken off

Mozart could not but smile at this little diplomacy; but

his nature, open and honorable as it was, could not be con
tent with no more explicit statement than a tone of voice.
He went, therefore, to the piano which stood in the room
opened it, preluded a moment, and then sang, while he looked
at Aloysia with a merry smile—"I leave the maiden gladly
who will have none of me!"[1]

Aloysia blushed: but just then the postillion blew his horn
before the door, and Amadeus seized his hat and took a hasty
leave of them.

"Fare you well!" he said, as they stood together at the
door. "May Heaven keep you kindly, and bring the wishes
of our hearts to a happy end!"

And kissing the hand of each, he hastened down the steps
and sprang into his seat. The postillion cracked his whip
the horses started, and in the midst of a jubilant flourish on
the horn, the carriage rolled away.

[1] **Historical.**

PART IV.

KING AND SLAVE

CHAPTER I.

IDOMENEUS.

ABT VOGLER was enabled, by his intrigues and jugglery, to drive Mozart away from the Electoral Court at Mannheim; but he could not prevent Karl Theodore, now Elector of Bavaria, from remembering the young composer with good-will.

Karl Theodore, notwithstanding the looseness of his morals, was in some respects one of the best princes of his time. He was a patron of artists and learned men, and often a generous one; he encouraged agriculture and industrial enterprise, and sought to maintain right and justice among his people. Music was especially supported by him. So that during his reign the orchestra of Munich was the best in Europe; and the opera had there the advantage of the best singers, both male and female. Among the former were Del Prato and Raff; among the latter, Aloysia Weber and the two sisters, Dorothea and Lisette Wendling.

The Elector often thought of Mozart as a most promising composer; and Cannabich—now Capellmeister in Munich—never neglected to keep alive the often expressed wish of the prince, to have Mozart write an opera for the Munich boards. At last Karl Theodore put the wish into action, and sent Mozart a commission to write an *opera seria* for the Munich carnival of the year 1781.

Amadeus was delighted; nothing could have pleased him more than this engagement. For three years he had been revolving the idea of composing such a work, and here was an opportunity to do it for the best stage in Europe, in Munich, where the Weber family—for so long a time his home

—where Cannabich, Wendling, and his beloved Constanze dwelt. But this pleasure, too, was at first put in question, and embittered at the outset. Mozart was still in the service of the Prince-Bishop of Salzburg, and His Grace was hardly to be prevailed upon to give his "court and cathedral organist" permission to accept the Elector's commission and go to Munich to compose his opera. With great difficulty Mozart at last obtained a leave of absence for *six weeks.*

But what happiness it was for him to be in Munich again! What a warm reception from his friends; and what joy to see Constanze, and be near her once more! It is delightful even to think of such a musician as Mozart, glowing with creative power, bent on his work, full of magnificent ideas, wrapped up in his art, and exalted by his love. The materials upon which he was working were in themselves inspiring. The libretto for the new opera had been furnished by the Abbé Varesco; it was taken from the Grecian story, and bore the title, *Idomeneo Re di Creto, osia Ilia e Idamente.*

The plot was as follows. Idomeneus, King of Crete, who has been for a long time absent at sea, is reported to be dead. Much afflicted at this mournful intelligence, his son Idamante ascends the throne. This prince is betrothed to Electra, Agamemnon's daughter, who has been selected as his bride, but whose deadly hatred is excited by jealousy toward Ilia, the daughter of King Priam, who was brought to Crete as a prisoner. Idamante, now absolute ruler, follows the dictates of his heart, and declares himself for his beloved Ilia. While Electra, mad with passion and rage, raves in her despair, a great storm breaks from the heavens, and in the midst of it Idomeneus reaches the shore of his kingdom again. But he has made a vow to Neptune, that if he is preserved from the perils of the sea, he will offer up to him whomsoever he first meets on the shore; and—fearful fate!—the first to meet him is his son.

What magnificent music this first Act already demands! But the knots are still further entangled.

Like Agamemnon, Idomeneus keeps his unhappy secret hidden in his own breast; and, like that king, he would fain spare his son. So Idamante and Electra are allowed to escape to the main-land of Greece. To avenge the broken vow, Neptune sends a monster, which, beating the waves of the sea into foam and tempest, brings a curse and pestilence upon

Crete. It draws near on mountainous billows, while the lightning's blaze, and the thunder, as avenger of the perjury, rolls, threatening and shaking the earth, over the heads of Idomeneus and his house. The people, deafened and terror-stricken, flee for safety.

Then the third act opens with the approach of the high-priest of Neptune to the king. He depicts for Idomeneus the grief and despair which overshadow the people, while the monster sent by Neptune fills the island with a breath of pestilential death. Then the king's conscience awakens, and avowing his oath, he dooms his son to death.

But hark! shouts of joy fill the air. Idamente, deeply moved by the people's despair, has sought out the monster, and delivered Crete from its ravages by his heroic arm. Nevertheless he waits in the temple of Neptune, prepared for the sacrifice, while Ilia, clasping his knees, is ready to die with him.

Then the invisible oracle of the god unlooses the knots.

Idomeneus is deposed from the throne. Idamante ascends it with Ilia at his side; and while Electra in her jealous fury utters her curses upon Crete, the much-tried father is blessed with wealth and honor, and the people unite in jubilant greetings to the young and royal pair.

Mozart's very heart was shaken by his study of this libretto. The inspiration of the story came over him as with the sweep of mighty wings. No longer far away in olden Greece, but here above his own soul rolled the thunder, and darted the lightning; out of the toppling mountain-crests of the waves sounded the voice of the sea-god, till earth trembled and the hearts of men shuddered in terror. And vieing with the roar of the storm and the rushing of the sea, rages the jealous wrath of a repulsed and despairing soul, till love and reconciliation shine out like a streaming sunshine, and the clashing chords of a great historic tragedy are melted into pure, sweet harmony.

From that moment Mozart saw nothing and heard nothing but his unwritten opera. He had heard in Paris the operas of Gluck, and especially his *Iphigenia in Aulis*, with delight. To follow in the same renowned path was his determination; and would not his *Idomeneus* form a fitting *pendant* for Gluck's *Iphigenia?* Here, too, were mighty reminiscences of Troy: here, too, a father, who is forced to lift the sacrificial sword over the head of his son: here, too, the tears of a maiden, loving and offering herself up, like Iphigenia Electra's madness, also, is the very image of that of Clytemnestra, her mother; and about these tragic forms group themselves the god-stricken people, the ghastly monster Jove with his thunder, and Neptune with the awful anger of the sea. What a theme for the young athlete, who, after yearning for such an opportunity for years, was now preparing to measure his strength with the great master, Gluck, the founder of modern tragic opera!

Amadeus worked day and night. His best friends scarcely caught sight of him. His only visiting was at the Weber house, where he would go when body and soul were fatigued, and find rest and fresh inspiration for his work in the quiet company of Constanze. Aloysia was at this time in ill health, and seldom made her appearance. Her sickness preventing her from attendance on the stage, Dorothea and Lisette Wendling took the parts of "Ilia" and "Electra." The principal *arias* were written with particular reference to them, and their rendering of them in the preliminary rehearsals was so excellent that Mozart felt sure of success so far as they were concerned.

So the composition of the first two acts of the opera went on with great rapidity, and was soon completed. Then Wolfgang's face grew brighter than ever and his hopes bolder; but his highest expectations were overtopped by the enthusiasm with which the musicians and *connoisseurs* of Munich received these two acts at their rehearsal.

Mozart swam in a sea of happiness, which expressed itself in every letter to his father, during these weeks. The praises of the nobility; the congratulations of his fellow-artists; the intoxicating excitement of genius, which sees itself in its first great work; the unerring presentiment of a deathless renown; and to crown all, love, happy love—what more could mortal soul have had? In the success which he saw before him in this new work, there was included much more than the mere temporary triumph; there was also in it the prospect of a permanent position in Munich, and a speedy marriage with his Constanze.

Little was he disturbed by the anxiety which his friends expressed, whether he would be able, in the third Act of his opera, to make the interest and power of the music rise higher still, in order to give the work a fitting crown. He felt and knew that he had in reserve more power than he had yet employed; and in golden letters before his eyes he seemed to read constantly, *Finis coronat opus.* And at last he uttered those words exultantly aloud, as one morning, after a night of sleepless toil, he threw down his pen beside the notes still wet from its touch.

Fourteen days after, Capellmeister Cannabich entered Mozart's room, and in his friendly and hearty voice, called out as he opened the door: "Well! are you ready for the grand rehearsal at the castle?" But the words died on his lips when he perceived the composer sitting bent over his table, in a loose gown, busily engaged in reading over his sheets of manuscript, and here and there crossing out and making corrections among the notes.

"What!" cried Amadeus, surprised and terrified at once; "is it so late as that?"

"It is ten o'clock!" answered the Capellmeister; "and at half-past eleven the Elector and court will be there, and the rehearsal must begin. What under the heavens has made you forget yourself and everything else?"

"Why," said Amadeus, beginning hastily to dress himself, "when I came back from the Webers last night, where you helped celebrate the finishing of 'Idomeneus,' I was so aroused and inspired—"

"Ah, yes!" put in Cannabich, with a sly smile, "by Mademoiselle Constanze's eyes!"

"Why not?" said Mozart, laughing. "Are they not beautiful enough to enchant a man?"

"Indeed they are!" replied Cannabich. "They would make an Idamante blind for Ilia."

"Of course they would; and I am no king's son either."

"And I will bet you I know what the result was last night."

"Guess then!" said Mozart, hurrying with his dressing.

"The Herr Mozart was too excited to sleep, and went on working, contrary to all reason and prudence, all through the night!"

"It was exactly so!" said Amadeus, as he confronted the mirror and hastily arranged a neckerchief. Then Cannabich said, in a tone of expostulation—

"You will not hearken to my advice till you are ruined. This everlasting sleeplessness and working in the night, is enough to pull down the strongest constitution; it shatters the nervous system from top to bottom!"

'But, my dear Capellmeister," answered Mozart in an apologetic voice, "I can't help it!"

"Why not?"

"Because I had to go over the score of the opera once more. It is my first work which has seemed to me of real importance; can you wonder that I am particular about it?"

"Of course not; but you have already *done* all—"

"Yes, but I kept finding things to improve, and at last"— and Mozart's blue eyes beamed here, as he clapped his friend on the shoulder—"at last, my dear Capellmeister, a divine idea struck me. You remember the *adagio* in the third Act, where, after the oracle of Neptune, the harmony goes through an intricate modulation in triplets with a subdued bass, and at last ceases upon C minor?"

"Do I remember it?" repeated Cannabich, with enthusiasm—"it is perfectly beautiful; and not an eye in the audience will be dry!"

"Well," continued Mozart, now wholly forgetting his dressing, "just there I have introduced a chorus—'*O voto tremendo! Spettacolo orrendo!*' I tell you it will make their hearts tremble when it rises in sombre majesty, with its shrouded harmonies, its muffled drums, and hushed trumpets —like an inexorable Fate." And the composer sprang to the piano and struck several chords.

"Splendid!" exclaimed Cannabich. "But you are forgetting the Elector and the rehearsal again!"

"So I am!" said Amadeus, as he jumped up and slipped into his coat; "and in writing this chorus I so forgot myself that I never thought of bed, and was only just through with it when you came in."

"And how will it go at this last rehearsal of the opera? You don't suppose the chorus singers can—"

"Never mind. We'll leave it out altogether to-day, and then the effect will be so much the greater on the night of the performance."

"All right!" said the Capellmeister, as he lent a hand to complete Mozart's toilet. "But promise me one thing, my young friend."

"What is it?"

"That you never again will work all night."

"I am young and strong!"

"*Now* you are, true enough; but, as an older and experienced man, and as your true friend, I tell you if you go on at this pace you dig your own grave. If you do not hearken to me, you never will see forty years!"

At this moment Mozart gave a little exclamation of pain, and turned pale.

"What is it?" asked Cannabich anxiously.

But Mozart had at once recovered himself, and said, smiling—

"Nothing, my dear Capellmeister! I have worn, since childhood, a little gold cross on my breast as an amulet. In my hurry in dressing, I suppose it got turned, and cut the skin a little. See—it bleeds!—But come on, it is late, now."

"And your promise?"

"If I should make it," cried Mozart, laughing, "I could not keep it. When genius commands, the dust must obey, though it be shattered."

The old Capellmeister felt the truth of these words; but his eye rested with solicitude on the wan, over-wearied face of the young friend who strode on at his side so lightly. Mozart's mind was already in the midst of his opera again.

CHAPTER II.

THE KING OF TONES.

THE rehearsal in the grand *salon* of the castle went finely. The Elector and the most cultivated and critical members of the court were present. Karl Theodore broke out with a hearty *Bravo!* at the end of the first Act; and when Mozart approached him, he said to the young *maestro* with a gracious smile: "The opera will be a great success, and do you much honor, young man. One never would think that so great a thing was hidden in so small a head!"[1] From the nobility, also, he received a shower of compliments.

The Webers, of course, as well as Wendling and Canna bich, were delighted and jubilant; especially as the musicians of Munich, most of them people of taste and talent, expressed on all sides their wonder at this work, which so far surpassed

[1] The Elector's own words.—Nissen, p. 430.

all which they had previously heard. The next evening, a
the levee, Karl Theodore declared to every one: "I was per
fectly astonished. Never has music had such an effect on
me. It was magnificent!"[1]

What a prospect this opened for Mozart! If such was the
Elector's enthusiasm, he could not fail to give him a distinguished place, with a good salary. Already he saw himself
in a position by the side of his friend Cannabich, as Capellmeister; already his energetic spirit composed in imagination
opera after opera; already he led home his darling Constanze
as a bride!

Ah, what boundless hopes youth has a place for! We sail
away on our argonautic expeditions for the lost Paradise,
fearless of storm or frost, but—a few years later—how many
hearts are stiff and frozen in the ice-fields of a selfish, commonplace existence—

> "The set gray life and apathetic end!"

But in Mozart there was no commonplace, no selfishness.
Standing now in the bloom of his years, with broadened culture and burning passion for his art, with swift blood, keen
nerves, and an all-conquering imagination, the falcon-wings
of his genius bore him far away above the dust of triviali-
ties.

Mozart was deep in dreams of a golden future, while Lange,
now the declared *fiancé* of Aloysia, drank champagne to his
success, and at his expense.

So came on the time for the first performance of "Idomc-
neus," which at last, after several postponements, was set for
the 26th of January. It was a pleasant coincidence that this
was the day before Mozart's birthday; and only an hour before the opera was to begin, his father and sister arrived from
Salzburg.

"Good heavens! why, this is unheard of!" said Count
Seinsheim, turning to Baron Lehrbach, who had entered the
box at the theatre with him. "Did you ever see the house
so full?"

"Never!" answered the other; "not even when Gluck
gave his 'Alceste' and his 'Iphigenia' here."

"'Tis nearly an hour before the curtain rises," said the
Count, "and there's hardly a place empty in the house."

---

[1] His very words.

"Empty?" replied Lehrbach; "there has been a crowd turned *away*, already."

"Well, no wonder," said the Count; "the opera is glorious. I never saw the Elector so enchanted with anything. Young Mozart stands very high in his good graces."

"Then he'll get a position here, won't he?"

The Count shrugged his shoulders, and answered: "There's only one difficulty about it, and that is—the money!"

"And what a shame it is," said the Baron indignantly, "that the court should have money enough to support a thousand-and-one infernal supernumeraries, and lack the means to hold on to such a man as Mozart! What the devil do we want of fifty court physicians and as many court cooks, and the Lord knows what all!"

"You'd better suggest retrenchment to the Elector," said the Count dryly.

"Not I!" said the Baron; "nobody has less fancy than I for pulling other people's chestnuts out of the coals; but the court's poverty is a devilish humbug, nevertheless!"

"It *is* outrageous," returned the Count, "that the Elector can find gold enough for fools and women, and can't afford any for the support of brains. There is one consolation, such genius as Mozart has always makes its own ways and means, helped or unhelped."

At that moment an old gentleman, accompanied by a pretty, but no longer young lady, entered the orchestra. Amadeus followed them, and placed two chairs in one corner of the space reserved for the musicians. Then, after pressing the hand of each affectionately, he disappeared as unmarked by the audience as he had come.

"Who may that be?" whispered Baron Lehrbach to the Count.

"How can you ask?" said the other; "don't you recognize that face?"

"By Jove, it is Mozart's father!"

"And his sister," said the Count. "He told me he expected them both."

Now the boxes began to fill up. Lords and ladies in rich dress made their appearance; as if the sea of commoner people had tossed them into the front boxes like sparkling foam. Fair, voluptuous women thronged in, whose costly dresses, very much cut down, left shoulders and bosoms free, or showed them half-concealed by handsome little cloaks thrown over them with careful carelessness. Rare laces and flashing jewels, like snow and glittering sleet, made elegant settings for the round arms and proud necks. The most prominent of all these court dames was the Countess Seefeld, a fair girl of sixteen years, who was at that time the especial beloved of Karl Theodore. She was fresh and beautiful as Aphrodite. Her toilette was fairylike in its delicate loveliness, and was crowned by a set of jewels which cost 300,000 florins, a gift from the Elector. Although they well knew her relations with the Elector, the whole nobility did homage to her, for they were well accustomed to such disgraces, which rather excited their envy than their detestation. At her side sat the old Prime Minister, father of Count Seinsheim, and it was ludicrous to see how his stiff old Excellency exerted himself to pay court to the all-powerful favorite.

But though the boxes were resplendent with twinkling gems, and gold-laced uniforms, and robes of state, and though the gay coquettes gesticulated with their flashing fans, and sought to attract notice by loud chattering, no one in the rest of the house paid the smallest attention to them. But one thought held possession of the whole audience : that was, the almost solemn expectancy of something wonderfully great—music which already, before its performance in public, had made itself a fame. All awaited in intense impatience the beginning of the overture. Their eyes seemed determined to bore through the drop-curtain, and when the instruments began to tune, a perfect hush fell upon the house.

In the corner of the orchestra sat silent and motionless the old plainly clothed gentleman who had been seated by Mozart. His long gray hair gave him a calm and venerable look, but on his fine, spiritual face lay an expression of almost feverish tension. His wide open eyes were fixed immovably on the curtain which concealed the stage, while his hands lay in his lap, folded as if for prayer. And indeed the old man, whose heart beat fast with expectancy, was praying. It was a father's fervent petition for his son, beseeching the Almighty to grant him success.

Suddenly there was a stir in the audience : nobility and people all rose up, while the Elector entered. For one or two minutes there was a rustling of garments as they took their seats again, and then—a stillness as of death.

Now the baton of the Capellmeister rose calmly—a little

flash of its silver tip in the air—and the opera, "Idomeneo Re di Crete," had begun.

And how the overture took all hearts by storm! What an unprecedented wealth of instrumentation! What molten fiery tone-masses, in which with ceaseless succession the rushing of many waters and the battling of the elements followed each other, while in the midst of it murmured still the loveliest and softest melodies. This was no artistic and cunning *manufacture*, but the incarnation of musical ideas—. mighty ideas, presageful of the story to come; as if gigantic cloud-forms were rising out of the grave of the past, and moving with grand and earnest faces into the distance. There were recollections of Ilium's greatness and fall; of Idomeneus's woe and despair; intimations of the frightful clash of the elements, of weapons, and of human passions, all given to the soul in tone-pictures which were painted—not on the events of this one story, the finite—but on the dim sky, the infinite, as a background.

As the overture ended, a thunder of applause burst forth all over the house, led on by the Elector, who gave the signal by a hearty cry of *Bravo!* and the energetic clapping of his hands. But the up-rolling curtain hushed every sound.

According to common usage in the old *opera seria*, which had neither *introduction* nor *finale*, the piece began with an instrumental recitative, followed by an *aria* of Ilia, in G minor, *Andante con moto*. The daughter of Priam is re-proaching herself for loving a Greek. Passionate action, pleasing melody, mournful accompaniment, responsive bass-es—the whole bears a character of mild and submissive sad-ness, which is the dramatic character of her who sings. Nothing is old-fashioned, but all is fresh, original, and charming.

Then enters Electra. What a vivid contrast between her, the proud, jealous, angry daughter of the "King of Men," and the mild Trojan captive! What a rush and rage of wildest passions in this fiery heart! It is as if one heard the hissing snakes of the Eumenides, as they coil and knot them-selves incessantly. Almost a shudder creeps over the audi-ence, while they lean back involuntarily in their seats, as if to escape from this witchingly fair but terrible woman, whose furious jealousy knows no bounds. Listen! her voice halts at every clause, as if caught by the convulsive tension of her throat; she trembles with rage, and her furious jealousy finds rent in the high *B*, which changes to *A*, with a strange effect, on the repetition of the theme at the words "*vendetta e crudeltà*." The audience trembled as she began her *aria*, and the old man in the corner of the orchestra, whose bony hand was closed round his daughter's arm, while he leaned forward with eyes wide open, appeared to catch eagerly every tone of voice and instrument. Now comes the *B*—then the repetition of the theme: now the *A*—then his eyes sparkle, his face grows pale, but not with anxiety, it is with ecstasy, and in a trembling voice he cries, "Victory! Electra surpasses Clytemnestra!"

And in very truth Electra had surpassed Clytemnestra; Mozart had triumphed over Gluck. Hail to him, king of tones!

Then comes the meeting of Idomeneus with his son on the beach. The old king, who had been wandering ten years and now returns, seeking anxiously his son whom he left a child, finds him only to be his fated murderer. The scene is one which has few equals on the stage. When the curtain descended at the end of the first Act, after the splendid concluding chorus, a tempest of applause burst from the whole house.

The old man in the orchestra rubbed his hands with delight. He could not speak, but his eyes expressed his joy. Only once he leaned over to his daughter's ear and whispered, as he brushed a tear from his cheek—"If the good mother could have been spared to see this!" Then he appeared sunken in deep thought, but a contented smile brightened his face. He stood in the evening of his life like Moses on Nebo's top, looking over into the promised land of a new musical world—into a promised land whither his son would lead the people.

Then, for the second time, the great curtain rustled upward—

> "Se il padre perdei
> La patria, il riposo
> Tu padre me sei,
> Soggiorno amoroso
> E Creta per me."

Ilia, whose fetters Idamante has broken, expresses her gratitude to the king, and lets him guess the secret of her heart The melody is bewitchingly sweet, and the instru-

mentation of the *cavatina* speaks forth the Trojan maiden's
love, because it is the very voice of the composer's own soul
in communion with his beloved Constanze.

In the background of one of the boxes sat Constanze herself, sobbing with ravishment at this voice so familiar to her.
At her side, and sitting at her clavier, her dear friend had
found this melody, that (as he had whispered in her ear) all
the world might know that he loved and worshipped her!

But now these tones are ended: a stately march, heard
behind the scenes, leads us to the harbor of Cydonia, where
everything is ready for the departure of Electra and Idamante. The sailors sing the fine chorus, "Placido è il mar,"
which, with its peaceful music, makes a happy transition be
tween the foregoing and following scenes. A pure blue
deeply colors the clear harmonies; flutes and clarionets
waft over them the fresh sea-air, while the quartette points
out the rippling and rocking of the waves; and borne up on
these waves of sweet sounds every heart hears the assurance,
"Peaceful calm on wind and sea!"

All at once the chorus is silent. A siren-song reaches the
ears of the sailors. It is the voice of Electra, in a rare
melody, tender and caressing as the breath of a zephyr, beseeching for favorable winds. The strong will of the Greek
princess seems to compel the elements to her bidding. Swelling breezes sigh and wave from the violins. Then they
murmur softly in the sextette, repeating, "Placido è il mar!"
After this chorus the applause was tremendous; and the old
man in the orchestra moves about nervously on his chair, till
Nannerl asks him what is the matter. "Ah, the devil!" he
replies; "I must get my arms round that young sunbeam,
and hug him to my old heart!"

But what now? Why storm the violins so suddenly and
the brass instruments moan in long-drawn sighs? Why this
fearful confusion in the music, as the wood instruments rend
through the tone-masses with their cry of terror? Why this
mighty storm so grandly given by the orchestra, till the
foundations of the immense building seem shaken, while the
chorus shouts in fear, "Quel nuovo terrore!"

Neptune has struck the sea with his trident, till it bellows
and tosses to the clouds, while on its crests swims the deadly
monster toward the shore of Crete.

Then Idomeneus declares, amid the crash of thunder-peals,
that he himself is the guilty one. He bares his own head to

the unearthly power of the god, and beseeches Neptune to spare the innocent. But in the muttering of the muffled drums and the wandering, searching chords of the brass, there seems an intimation that Idomeneus is not the offering which the god desires. Something darker and more solemn appears to possess the orchestral harmonies, as if an ominous shadow were approaching, growing ever greater, borne on the wings of the storm.

The people seek safety in flight. "Corriamo! Fuggiamo!" echoes the cry. But while they flee, a hail of triplets lashes them, darkness surrounds them, the tempest drives them asunder; and as they escape in different directions, blinded by lightning-flashes, the chorus of "Fuggiamo" grows fainter till it is hushed to a pianissimo, and ends with the solemnity of organ music as the curtain falls.

In the third and last Act the interest and beauty of the music increase from scene to scene. Ah! with Mozart, for the first time since the beginning of the world, there came music which will never cease to be rich and classic—a dramatic perfection, a complete knowledge of counterpoint, which Bach himself failed to attain; an instrumentation planned in complex combination, as we find it in "Don Giovanni;" musical unity, purity, and truth, such as had waited all the centuries to find expression through his God-given genius.

When now Idomeneus can no longer hold concealed his terrible vow, and he names Idamante as the victim, the recitative dies away in sorrowful murmurs, and as the *C minor*—that key which is sacred to tears—is reached, then breaks in the chorus with its wondering awe: "O voto tremendo! Spettacolo orrendo!" The splendid chords oppressed the hearts of the hearers as with the approach of an inexorable fate. Not a soul in the vast audience but thrilled with that harmony, sounding forth among the hushed trumpets and muffled drums like the passing bell of a whole people.

It needed the sweet and happy conclusion of the opera, with its beautiful final chorus, "Scenda Amor, scenda Imeneo," to brighten and refresh the over-strained hearts of the audience, like sunshine after a sublime storm. And when the curtain descended, such a tempest of applause arose as the Munich theatre had never known before; and, above the thunder of voices and feet, the name of "Mozart!" "Mozart!" was heard in deafening shouts.

In the corner of the orchestra sat an old man, pale and trembling with joy. He did not stir when the storm of applause burst forth: he remained motionless as the throng poured out of the building in enthusiastic conversation over the new opera: he sat silent when the theatre was wholly empty. And when the lights had been nearly all extinguished, the few remaining ones in the orchestra threw a dim and ghostly glimmer over a memorable group—on his knees before his venerable father lay the great composer of Idomeneus, and the old man kissed him on the forehead; and neither spoke, for very intensity of happiness. On either side stood, like two guardian angels from a better world, Nannerl, Amadeus's sister, and Constanze Weber. Their eyes were wet with proud and joyful tears. And Constanze placed softly a crown of flowers on Mozart's head, and whispered, blushing at her own boldness, "For the king of tones!"

CHAPTER III.

LIFE IN VIENNA.

KING—and slave! King in his own beautiful realm of music: slave of circumstances, and the conditions of this world! Once over the boundaries of his own kingdom, and he was supreme; but the powers of the earth acknowledged not his sovereignty.

The Archbishop of Salzburg was a prince with the soul of a boor. He was now in Vienna with all his rich establishment, and Mozart was still in his service. The salary attaching to the position of court and cathedral organist was a sufficiently meagre one, and the office would have been one of little advantage to a composer like Mozart, at the best; but now he had it at the worst. The contemptible meanness of His Grace the Archbishop made his service worse than the yoke of a slave. Mozart was treated like the lowest servitors of the palace; he ate at the same table with the headcook and the valets, who considered him only their equal, or, as having less pay, their inferior in rank. This could not last forever, and after some unusually bitter experiences of insult from the little great man who employed him, Mozart threw off the shackles forever.

It seems strange that he bore such a situation so long as he did; but, with all his pride and sensitiveness, Mozart had the patient humility of true genius. He loved his art, and so long as he prospered in its service, worldly considerations were of small moment to him. If his soul had this morning caught a melody sent down from heaven, it mattered little at what table his body dined this afternoon. Besides, he was determined to be exceedingly patient in the pursuit of his hopes. "Patience, and patience! We shall win at the last!" was all through life his motto. Perhaps if it had not been for his longing to be able to have a home, where he might at last call Constanze "wife," he would still longer have borne with the vexations and mortifications of his position. But his own letter to his father at Salzburg tells of his emancipation.

"VIENNA, May 9, 1781.

"My patience has been so long tried that it has at last given way. I have no longer the misfortune to be in the Salzburg service, and to-day is a happy day for me. Three times already has this—I know not what to call him—said the most insulting and impertinent things to my face, which I did not repeat to you, from the wish to spare your feelings. . . . . He called me a knave and a dissolute fellow, and told me to take myself off. And I endured it all, though I felt that not only my own honor but yours was aggrieved by this; but as you would have it so, I was silent. [His father had constantly urged him not to break with the Archbishop.] . . . . Then came all in a breath, that I was the most dissipated fellow he knew—no man served him so badly as I did. It was impossible to get in a syllable, for his words blazed away like a fire. I heard it all with calmness. He actually told me to my face the deliberate falsehood that I had a salary of 500 florins—called me a ragamuffin, a scamp, a rogue. Oh! I really cannot write all he said. At last my blood began to boil, and I said, 'Your Grace does not appear to be satisfied with me.' 'How! do you dare to threaten me, you rascal? There is the door, and I tell you I will have nothing more to do with such a low fellow!' At last I said, 'Nor I with you.' 'Begone!' said he; while I replied, as I left the room, 'The thing is settled, and you shall have it to-morrow in writing.'

I put it to you, my dear father, if I was not rather too late than too soon in saying this. .... So long as the Archbishop remains here I will not give a concert. Your fear that this will bring me into bad odor with the Emperor and the nobility is quite unfounded. The Archbishop is hated here, and most of all by the Emperor. In fact, not having been invited to Luxemburg is the cause of his rage. By next post I mean to send you a little money, to show you that I am in no difficulty here. .... Publicly abuse me as much as you like, that none of the blame of this may fall on you. If, in spite of that, the Archbishop should be guilty of the smallest impertinence toward you, then I beg you and my sister will come straight to me at Vienna, for I give you my word of honor that we can all three live here perfectly well."[1]

In another letter, replying to his father's disapproval of the step he had taken, he says of the Archbishop and his supporters at Salzburg: "Dearest father, no doubt they will try to beguile you by many kind words; but these people are snakes and vipers—all base souls are so—disgustingly proud, and yet always ready to crawl. Do not allow yourself to be misled by flattery. ..... Is it, then, surprising, that at last (irritated to madness by such respectable epithets in the mouth of a Prince, as rogue, rascal, ragamuffin, base fellow), the 'take yourself off' should have been accepted by me in its literal sense? ..... All the edifying things that the Archbishop had said to me in the last three audiences, especially in the last, and the pious epithets this admirable man of God applied to me afresh, had such an effect on my bodily frame, that the same evening, at the opera, I was obliged to go home in the middle of the first Act in order to lie down; for I was very feverish, trembled in every limb, and staggered in the street like a drunken man. ...... Without flying into a passion, for I have too much regard for my health and life to do so (it pains me enough when I am forced to do it), I will now tell you the chief reproach brought against my service. I did not know that I was a valet, and this was my ruin. I ought to have loitered every morning for a couple of hours in the anteroom. Indeed, I was often told that I ought to show myself more; but somehow I never could understand that it was part of my duty

[1] Mozart's Letters (N. Y.: Leypoldt & Holt, 1867), Vol. II., p. 21.

so I only came punctually when the Archbishop summoned me. . . . . . I adjure you, as you wish to see your son enjoy health and happiness, not to write to me any more on the subject, but to bury it in the most profound oblivion; for one word more would suffice to rouse both my spleen and yours. You must yourself own this. Now farewell!" [1]

Mozart was delighted with Vienna when once he felt free from the fetters of his odious attendance at the Archbishop's palace. The sparkle and activity of life there exactly suited his sunshiny and merry temperament. There is no other German town which shows human existence in such bright, gay colors, as does the Austrian capital.

With the first gray of dawn, the busy activity commences. Up in the dormer-chambers, or down below on the ground-floor, blinds here and there begin to be thrown back, and out of the windows peep unkempt heads, or the curly pates of children, probably with still sleepy eyes. Then more windows follow these first pioneers of the day. Soon the house-doors commence to open, while man and maid servants come forth, yawning and stretching, and greeting each other sleepily. Now the milkwomen make their appearance in one-horse-wagons, or with wheelbarrows, and display their clean-scoured cans at the street-corners. With every quarter-hour the liveliness and activity increases. Girls distributing bread from great baskets, and servants receiving it; others wending their way to the butcher-shops or the green-grocer's, occupy the sidewalks. Now the workmen begin to stream in from the suburbs, and the crowd commences to thicken. Young merchants' clerks seeking their dark counting-rooms; children on their way to school; girls going to their work at the factories; gardeners bringing their wares to market; then heavy freight-wagons, and soon lighter vehicles with people travelling or taking their morning ride;—all these crowd, and press, and bustle along the streets. And where the ways are narrow, or the throng of carriages has become entangled, woe to him whose business is urgent, or who feels obliged to hasten! Time and patience he will be sure to lose.

So it goes on until mid-day. Then the scene changes, and a new set of actors appear, presenting a brighter aspect to the looker-on. The elegant world has now finished its morning toilette: fine ladies are ready to show themselves on the street, and the young beaux have had their breakfast at the most fashionable *cafés*. The government officials, with their clerks, are now through with their work; the actors, musicians, and singers are free from their rehearsals; the poets rest for a while from their strivings after immortality; and a throng of gay people streams along the aristocratic quarters, to see and be seen, to hear and be heard, to shine and behold all the splendor.

Ladies of all ages are out walking in their charming morning-costumes, inspecting the new goods and fashions, and gazing into the handsome show-windows, where everything is displayed in the most ingeniously tempting manner. They enter here and there, till the attendant lackey pants under his burden, which yonder secretly-following admirer would most gladly relieve him of, in order to win a thankful smile from his adored one, in return for the sacrifice. Proud dames sail by with their rich costumes; and pretty girls, in jaunty hats and feathers, go tripping past, with sly glances at their own reflection in the long shop-windows, and saucy eyes for the young fellows who turn to look at them. All smiling and all gay, the crowd glitters and shimmers by, like the dancing waves of a silver-foaming brook, over which butterflies are hovering as it kisses its flowery banks. Seems not this smiling Life to lead only over the river of Paradise? Oh this Sphynx! how sweetly she can give us her mocking looks of love!

In front of the principal coffee-houses and places where fine wines are to be found, groups of men are collected, who review the passing troops of ladies, and at the same time plainly display their own biographies in their respective styles of dress and manner. The most important news of the day is here discussed, such as the hoarseness of an opera-singer, the lameness of a favorite horse, or some spicy tale of scandal. Here, too, music and the current literature are criticised, new jokes are related, and the very latest *bon mots* are brought to market—such as every good Viennese has ready for each day in the year, and enjoys the pleasure of seeing them travel quickly from mouth to mouth. In these lounging groups, parties are arranged for the evening, or with equal lightness and carelessness, matters of a lifetime are settled. Other groups collect in the confectioners' shops, where, over an ice or a glass of wine, the serious topic of this or that grisette is exhaustively handled. Even the fair worshippers as they pass out of church are not allowed to go unwatched or unad-mired; and in front of the sacred edifice, or quite as likely within its walls, many a tender rendezvous is consummated.

So passes the afternoon. Then comes dinner; and after a meal which is not apt to be that of an anchorite, the evening darkens, or rather brightens over the city. One by one the streets and shops are lit, till all is brilliancy and splendor. The nearer the time approaches for the theatres to open, the more the gay world puts itself in motion. Crowds of people, freed from the day's toil,—officials whose offices are shut,—soldierly-looking officers, seeking relaxation from their monot-onous duties,—civilians of all ranks press through the streets to their different places of pleasure. Equipages of the nobili-ty and the *haute finance* roll with smooth thunder over the pavement, and through every gate throng in the inhabitants of the suburbs. Workmen, let loose for the evening, some pushing their empty wheelbarrows before them with mechani-cal stolidity, others carrying their heavy tools lightly and jauntily on their great shoulders; innumerable do-nothings, on the look out for adventures; veiled women, on a similar quest; comfortable burghers with short pipes, burning "to-bacconalian" incense under their own noses;—all these, and a hundred other species of the *genus homo*, stream along the thoroughfares, brighter, busier, and noisier than in the day-time.

By-and-by the tide of trampling feet ebbs again; the bur-dens of the day are all borne, the pleasures of the evening all enjoyed, and the honest burgher seeks his hearth, the thea-tres pour their returning streams through all the veins of the great city, the shops are shut up, the doors of the houses are bolted,—then the windows,—and million-eyed Vienna sinks in the arms of sleep. Only into the glittering *salons* of the great, the gay chambers of late revellers, the temples of pleas-ure, and the dens of crime, has sleep no entrance; not till the cock crows does life here also sink to rest, often with sighs, or dreary yawns of weariness, or tears.

"Come!" cried a handsome, jovial-looking man, about half an hour after the closing of the theatre, as he lifted a brimming bumper of champagne, and cast a merry look around the stately company—"Come! one glass to the free-dom of our Mozart, who has so bravely broken his chains, and now is to abide with us, a new man—a new-fledged Viennese!"

And the glasses clinked three times to the health of the honored composer.

The proposer of this toast was no other than the Director of the Leopold theatre at Vienna, the famous and universally popular Schikaneder.

Schikaneder was a note-worthy character. In his youth he had made his way on to the stage, without any training or culture, and by dint of his talent alone had become a good tragic actor. But some years afterward, on his coming to Vienna, he saw plainly that his forte lay in comedy, and soon gained great popularity, not only as a comedian, but as a play-writer. He had another talent also, quite as useful to himself, and that was for pecuniary speculations. As Director of the Prague theatre, and now in the same position in Vienna, he had acquired a large property; at least, the world said so, and it certainly seemed true, for he lived like a prince.

His house vied with the palaces of the wealthiest aristocracy of Vienna in the elegance of its furniture; with the single exception that in those palaces the richness often exceeded the taste, while in the Director's mansion the taste surpassed the richness. Schikaneder was in all respects a jovial and pleasure-loving man, and a *bon vivant* such as could hardly be matched in all Vienna. All the five quarters of the globe were only so many cupboards and cellars for him, whose dainties and choice drinks he knew to the smallest details. Yet it was not for his own gratification alone that he thus ransacked the earth for good things; it was his pride and joy to see his table, as it always was, surrounded by a goodly company of friends and guests. A man with such an epicurean palate could not but have an epicurean heart to correspond; and the present mistress of his affections was the charming singer Cavaglieri, a dark-eyed, black-haired Italian brunette, whose boundless luxury excited public comment as much as her bewitching beauty.

The Cavaglieri sat next her adorer, who had this evening assembled at his house a choice company to an elegant supper in honor of Mozart.

We say a "choice" company, for besides Mozart, the host, the signora, and the poets Bretzner and Stephani, there were also present the three first musicians of the world—Chevalier von Gluck, Joseph Haydn, and the imperial Court-Capell-meister, Salieri.

Gluck, the renowned composer of "Orpheus," "Alceste,"

"Iphigenia," and so many other operas, was at that time
sixty-seven years old; but he was still hale and vigorous, and
looked out cheerfully and brightly upon life. His countenance was not beautiful, but distinguished; and there was
something exceedingly venerable and imposing about him.
The large blue eyes, the full lips, the high and thoughtful
forehead, the hair still dark and thick in spite of his years,
the broad, manly figure, and the self-respect which expressed
itself in his whole appearance, gave a magical charm, and, at
the same time, a tinge of awfulness to the old composer.
But well Gluck knew how to soften this impression by his
kind and courtly manners. Toward Mozart he felt, too, a
sincere respect and honor; while both Gluck and Haydn
had no warmer worshipper than Mozart.

In outward appearance Joseph Haydn, now forty-nine
years old, was very different from Gluck. It was not only
that a youth passed in the bitterest poverty had prematurely
blanched his hair, but the early pressure of life had made
him retire within himself, and stamped a look of almost pain
upon his face. The luxurious life of a sybarite like Schikaneder was utterly contrary to all his strict moral principles,
and only his love and honor for Mozart—a star already so
brilliant in the musical sky—had induced him for once to
take part in a company at the Director's house. But in spite
of all his respect for Mozart, he had already repented his decision a hundred times on this evening. Was not such a
course positively wicked, and must it not lead, sooner or
later, to destruction?

It was a splendid room in which they sat at supper—simple, indeed, as a dining-room always should be, but built
wholly of the yellowish marble which is such a favorite stone
with the Viennese, since the great marble-hall of the Castle
is built of it. It contrasted finely with the pure white of the
alabaster statues which were set against it, and its polished
surface gave back the thousand beams of light which shone
from the chandeliers, and played upon crystal vessels and
silver plate.

The rich deep carpet received the foot so softly, that there
was not the least sound to betray the motions of the atten-
tive servitors, who moved about silently as shadows behind
the chairs of the guests, and only betrayed their bodily reality by the unquestionable realness of the costly edibles and

potables which they handed round on silver salvers, or poured from slender flasks.

Mozart was involuntarily reminded of the Baron von Holbach's cook and kitchen, which had made such an impression on his earliest childhood, as he tasted the "Potage aux querelles," "Anguille, sauce Tartare," "Ris de veau, sauce tomates," "Filets de mouton à la jardinière," "Dindes rôties au cresson," "Beignets souffles," "Crême renversée," &c. And as he thought how many of the years since that childhood had been wasted in the service of the Archbishop, there would be for a moment a savageness in his plying of knife and fork. Ah, Mozart! if thou couldst have had under thy knife that evening all the titled boors and holy knaves whom thou must yet meet in this world, thy supper would have been a long one! But now at last he was free from this particular slavery—free as a bird in the air! And this elegance, and richness, and luxurious pleasure which now surrounded him were extremely agreeable to him. If he could but live such a life, with no other necessity for labor but the enticements of his art!

And where else could such a life be so perfect as in Vienna? The gay capital was at that time the gathering-place for all the virtuosos of Europe. It was the usual residence of Haydn and Gluck, who were to Mozart noble models and friends, rather than rivals. Besides, Vienna offered a splendid climate, and its position was especially favorable for musicians; on one side lay Italy, on the other Bohemia—the very land of music, if there is one on the earth. Then, too, there was an Italian opera there, for whose stage the most famous compositions of the age had been written, and whose poet, Metastasio, was the acknowledged king of libretto-writers. Moreover (and this was the chief attraction for Mozart, who had so long dreamed of opening a new path for German music), a German company was being formed under the direction of Schikaneder, which only needed a proper composer to put itself at once at the head of a new and noble national music.

To complete the charms of Vienna for Mozart, fate had so ordered it that Constanze was now staying there with her mother. Oh! how gladly he would have pitched his tent there, and made the bright capital his home! Only one thing was lacking: it was—money! If he had that, fame

and honor would come of themselves, and he could marry
Constanze, and be—in Paradise!

Such were the sunny dreams which shone in the composer's imagination. Yet, who can solve the mystery of the
human heart? Over this free, frank nature—over this cheerful mind, so quick to open joyfully to even imaginary happiness—there fell many a time, as it were, the phantom-light
of another world,—light which falls on the nearer sunshine
of this world like a shadow, as wan moonbeams fall across
the floor of a lighted chamber. The same Mozart, who could
so completely rejoice in the gay life of Vienna, was often a
heavy-hearted man, who thought earnestly upon death, and
who passed whole nights at his piano, borne up on the wings
of his phantasy into unknown regions, whose secrets death
alone can solve!

But now, in the merry company assembled on this evening
about Mozart, the bright side of life was alone looked upon
or spoken of. Schikaneder sparkled with wit and humor,
and was, without ever losing command of himself, so delightfully comical, that the laughing-muscles of all, even of the
sober-faced Haydn, scarcely found a moment's rest. He was
well supported by Salieri (the Court-Capellmeister, and a
pupil of Gluck's), the two poets, and the charming Cava
glieri; nor did Maestro Mozart hold back at all.

All were rejoiced to see the young and promising composer freed from the clutches of the hated Prince-Bishop of
Salzburg, whose aim had seemed to be to keep his genius
forever from development.

Schikaneder and Bretzner had a fund of rich anecdotes of
the life of His Grace to relate, and Mozart was able to complete them whenever they needed any additions. From him
the talk turned upon other personages of the Viennese aristocracy, and many a small but interesting biography came
to light under the encouragement of the champagne.

It was already after midnight: the Cavaglieri's mirth was
perfectly unrestrained, and all formality and stiffness had
long ago disappeared in the common gayety. Haydn had
slipped away some time before, and Mozart was rubbing his
hands in good-humor and contentment. This state of things
was just what suited Schikaneder, and going up behind Mo
zart's chair he laid both hands on his shoulders, and said:

"So you enjoy yourself with us?"

"Enjoy myself?" answered Mozart, turning his beaming

face half round; "I am happy as a king in Vienna—with such friends—and free!"

"Only one thing is lacking," said Gluck, looking at Mozart with a friendly smile—"to the friends ought to be added one who would be a little more than friend."

"That will not be lacking long," cried Salieri with a laugh, which was not wholly free from a slight tinge of mockery; "they say that love had a hand in divers of the airs in Idomeneus."

"Why should I deny it?" returned Mozart gayly; "they are the best things in the opera, because they have the most truth in them. Who knows but the small god with the eyeglasses will have still more to do with my next opera!"

"Then you have another opera in the works?" asked Salieri quickly, and almost as if the idea struck him disagreeably.

"No!" replied Mozart: "I don't know where the subject is to come from, for it must be a German opera."

"Good!" cried Gluck, Schikaneder, and the two writers. Then said Gluck enthusiastically—

"On and on in the new path! To German music belongs the future!"

Salieri shrugged his shoulders ironically, and said with a forced smile—

"Don't be too confident, my good Sirs; there is only one Chevalier von Gluck, and Italy still remains the fatherland and home of music."

"I must entreat you," interrupted here the Signora, with her irresistible sweetness; "nothing contrary to the agreement! You know you gave me your word that for this whole evening all discussions of music should rest."

"Yes, yes!" said the Director, coming to her support, and filling the glasses anew (for the silent servitors had departed some hours ago). "This evening belongs solely to Bacchus and Mercury, and they are down upon all debate and disagreement. Look at Maestro Mozart, for example—see how well he behaves himself! Do you see his face beam? Let me see—how does the Englishman say?—'The jocund *Mozart sits* tiptoe on the misty mountain-heights.' Isn't he a true Viennese now, by the very looks of him?"

"Why shouldn't he look happy," cried Bretzner, laughing "when his very lodging is in heaven?"

"How so?" asked Gluck.

"Why," continued Bretzner, "the house and street where Mozart lives bear the name of 'The Push into Heaven.'"

"So they do," said Mozart, "and I would give a florin to know why. 'Thereby hangs a tale,' I suppose, to which also the stone tablet over the door points; for on it is cut the figure of a woman who is raising herself into heaven while the devil tries to pull her back."

"That's strange!" cried Schikaneder, laughing, while he lifted his glass to the light and watched the inverted showers of little pearls rising through the champagne; "many a woman has gone over to His Satanic Majesty, but that one should escape his clutches, after once falling into them, is miraculous!"

"Ah ha!" cried the Cavaglieri with a triumphant laugh; "that is a proof that we women keep faith, even with the devil!"

"Yes!" said Bretzner; "especially when you can't break it, as was the case in this instance."

"Then you know the story?" asked several.

"Yes," replied the poet, with a quiet smile.

"Come then!" said the Director; "you are bound to tell it, as penance for a saucy speech."

"Very well," returned Bretzner, not without a side-glance at the Signora, whose lavish extravagance in dress and finery had nearly ruined Schikaneder. "One can learn something from almost everything."

"That's true!" cried Mozart. Then their host popped off another cork, brimmed the glasses with the foaming wine, and Bretzner began:

"In old times there dwelt in Vienna, in the very house where Mozart now lives, a beautiful woman. She was a Juno in form, and a Venus in loveliness; but she was at the same time vain and proud beyond all measure. Her luxury and extravagance were incredible, especially in dress. The livelong day she would sit before her mirror, while the keeping of the house was neglected, and church-going and the holy Mass were altogether despised."

"Then he can't mean me!" interrupted here the Signora, laughing and lifting a threatening finger against the narrator; "for though the luxury in dress may hit me, yet no one can accuse me of neglecting the Mass. But go on!"

"'Tis an account of a veritable occurrence," said Bretzner

with comical seriousness, 'though it happened years and
years ago."

"I know you!" cried the Signora; but Schikaneder held
her rosy mouth shut, and the poet went on:

"Day or night our Junonian Venus had no thought but
how to exceed her rivals in display. To such a pitch did her
pride extend, that soon the purse was entirely emptied. Not
a whit was she humbled by this. One day she was passing
by a picture of the holy Virgin, when her frivolous vanity
led her to mock at the simple garment of the Mother of God,
and she challenged the Virgin to vie with her in splendor of
dress.

"This act of insolent pride cried to Heaven for punish-
ment; and the holy Mary turned away her face from her so
fallen daughter.

"But," continued Bretzner, and his look again wandered
towards where the beautiful Italian sat—"though, as the
Eastern proverb says,

> 'The mills of God grind slowly,
> But they grind exceeding small,'

yet sometimes the wheels fly faster. At midnight there
came a loud knocking on the door of the house of which we
have spoken. Perhaps the fair dame had expected a friend,
or perhaps she was moved by curiosity—a trait which women
are said sometimes to possess. At all events she opened
the door, and lo! an old beggar-woman stood before her.
Harshly the dame began to berate her; but the old crone
raised her crutch, and wielding it like a sceptre, she said with
all the haughtiness and dignity of a queen—'Poor soul! what
are you in comparison with me! and of what value is the
stuff which you wear, by the side of the treasure which I
possess!' and with these words she took out of the basket
which hung on her arm a gown, and held it up for admiration.

"The gown was of the most gorgeous velvet—blood-red,
and flashing with embroidery of gold. And after the gown
followed a girdle, which was clasped with a jewel that
seemed the very sparkle of the morning-star. And with
them the old crone showed veil, and collar, and slippers, of
corresponding costliness.

"Our dame was beside herself with admiration. 'Give

them to me,' she cried, with covetous eyes, ' and I will pay
you whatever you please !'

" The crone gave her a dark look, and said mockingly—' If
you only had anything to pay ! You're at the bottom of
your purse—eh ?'

" ' It is true !' replied the dame, wringing her hands ; ' but
I will give you all I possess which can be turned into gold.
I must have the garments !'

" ' Then I will make a bargain with you,' said the hag.
' Gold is nothing to me : I have enough of it. I will lend
you the things for three days and three nights, on condition
that you will pay me for the use of them whatever shall be
covered by them on the third midnight.' The bargain
seemed to the dame a strange one, but who can always
reason coolly when passion is aroused ? She had only to
change her dress just before the third midnight, and the loan
was paid. So she answered, ' I will do it !' and the thing
was settled.

" For three days and three nights our proud dame shone
in her wonderful dress, and was the envy of princesses and
court-ladies on account of it. No one could discover where
such magnificent fabrics came from. They could find in none
of the shops such velvet or such embroidery.

" But all earthly splendor vanishes like the wine in this
glass !" continued Bretzner, draining his champagne at one
draught. " The three days and three nights were quickly
gone. When now the third midnight was near at hand, the
strange bargain she had made came to the mind of our proud
dame. More and more uncomfortable grew her thoughts.
Darker and darker forebodings flocked around her heart.
The source of the borrowed dress was now evident to her :
it was no earthly skill which had wrought it ! Horror seized
upon her ! Hurriedly she sought to loosen the hellish robes.
But—oh curse of hell !—it was impossible ! She was alone,
and she could not throw off the folds, which clung to her
body as if they were sewed on. Cold sweat ran from her
forehead : she clutched and tore fiercely at it. In vain ! The
dress sat like iron upon her—and the hand of the clock
already was pointing to twelve ! At once her whole life
passed before her soul—its folly—its extravagance—its wicked
pride. She repented—but too late ! Once more she knit
every muscle for a last effort—she would rend the accursed
garment from her form. Impossible ! The woof was woven

in hell, and mocked her efforts. Mad with despair, she ran up and down her chamber, robed like a queen, but cursing like a harlot. Then—it struck the hour of twelve! The door flew open, and the old hag stood before her. How her fiery eyes rolled, and what a diabolical smile drew up her mouth, as laughing in derision she cried: 'You promised me for payment whatever at this hour my garments should cover. It is *you*, my girl! and therefore you are mine!'

"Then a blue flame flickered about the chamber. The hag changed to the Prince of hell, while the blood-red of the velvet and the gold of the embroidery became burning fire, which lapped the body of the horror-stricken woman with hungry tongues. Then the poor soul cried out to her patron Saint, in penitence and despair! And lo! the Saint heard her. Satan had just reached after his victim, when Saint Barbara appeared and gave her a mighty push. The claws of the devil just missed the swooning creature—the cock crowed—she was saved!

"What the rescued woman had vowed to Saint Barbara she performed. As a penitent Magdalen she passed the remainder of her life. Cured of her vanity and pride, she was received in joy and peace among the saved." Bretzner paused for a moment in thought, then he concluded with these words, in an earnest and meaning tone: "To commemorate this event, and for the use and benefit of those vain and frivolous dames whose number in Vienna is said to be considerable, this scene was hewn in stone, and house and street were named 'The Push into Heaven.'"

"And Bretzner received the name of 'the second Socrates!'" cried the Cavaglieri, with a loud laugh. "I believe, by the gods! he wants to turn me into a penitent Magdalen."

"All right!" said Schikaneder, tenderly embracing her— "if Socrates will keep you company! But in spite of the philosopher, you shall have, to-morrow, that splendid robe which you were telling me of, and which was too dear for the Princess Liechtenstein. I will show the proud nobility of Vienna that even a mere artist can have princely taste and princely means!"

"The story has interested me exceedingly," said Mozart. "'Tis very near being a subject for an opera. Even as you related it I heard the trumpet-blasts of hell, when the clock struck midnight. I must remember it for some future use."

"Sinner!" interrupted the Cavaglieri; "music again, so soon?"

"I pray your pardon!" begged Mozart, with mimic penitence, and kissed the hand of the beautiful Italian so fierily, that her southern blood thrilled with it. "Is not your voice music, also?" he said.

So it went on for awhile in the brilliant room, till Mozart and the others began to find their heads getting hot. Gluck remained the coolest of them all; and, at his suggestion, the party now broke up. All took their leave except the Signora, who stood at the top of the steps, with her pretty head leaning on Schikaneder's shoulder, as they bade the guests goodnight.

Gluck's carriage was waiting before the door. The great master invited Mozart and Salieri to take seats in it. The Capellmeister accepted the invitation, but Mozart declined: he felt that his giddy head stood in need of a little walk to cool down its excitement. Bidding adieu to Bretzner and Stephani, whose hearty voices echoed in the empty street, he walked on alone.

It was a night of wonderful beauty, and the yellow moonshine lay softly and silently over the earth. The shops along the streets had long been closed, and the lights in the houses were all extinguished; only Sleep and Death, hand in hand with their still brother. Forgetfulness, seemed to wander about the world, ruling the wide realm of night with their poppy-wreathed sceptres. The perfect rest and peace all about him came to Mozart as a delicious contrast with the riotous evening he had passed. The world of pleasure softly disappeared within him, and a world of quiet seriousness arose in its place. Everything about him was sleeping—was dreaming—and all passions were lulled in slumber; why should not a wondrous dream come upon his own soul?

And as he paced slowly along the street, self-involved, it was to him as if he were dead and his own heart were his coffin. He could feel the death-chill of his own corpse in his bosom. But he feared not; he was filled only with grief that he had done so little—had *been* so little, and that no human being mourned above his bier, over which lay a heavy chain and a crown of thorns. And the shadows of two gigantic forms fell across him and darkened him; and when he strained open his stiffened, half-shut eyes, he saw that the two giants were his friends Gluck and Haydn, and at their feet. lay thousands lost in wondering worship. Then he felt a smile upon his own cold face, not from envy, but from sorrow, because he himself had so hoped and longed to be great —and fate denied it to him.

But what vast, black shadow is this which rises before him, towering to the clouds? And the shadow reaches down to him and opens the coffin, and the stiffness of death yields to its touch, and Mozart grows upward with the shadowy form, up over Haydn and Gluck. And as he now recognizes the shadow, lo! it is Idomeneus, the royal crown gleaming on his brow. And behind him stand yet other shadows, greater still than he, mightier and more beautiful, though unrecognized by Mozart; and the last and mightiest of all lifts a little the gray robe which enwraps his features. Then recoils Amadeus in terror: it is a skull which grins down upon him!

Mozart passed his hand across his forehead. He had reached the end of a dark street, and before him rose, in the dreamy bluish moonshine, the gigantic obelisk of St. Stephen's spire.

Involuntarily he stood still, for at the first instant he scarcely knew whether this was the actual cathedral or the giant shadow which had been a part of his waking dream. Then the light wing-strokes of the cool night-wind thoroughly awakened him. How still, how vast, how lonely stood the majestic building before him! Here, also, a coffin!—the dark colossal coffin of the cathedral nave, entombing the recollections of so many centuries! And here also an enormous finger pointing to the stars—the presaged features of Immortality.

Mozart's eyes followed its ascending shaft slowly upward, as it towered higher and still higher, like the aspiring life of youth; ever striving after completeness, and ever shooting again from its stony buttresses into the air; but ever lonelier, more naked, more earnest,—till, at the top a golden cross, scarcely distinguishable to the eye, glimmers away up in the blue lustre of the moonlight;—like the cross on our grave, which the ghostly hand of fate points out amid the dimness of the future.

Mozart's eyes fell wearily down again, resting for an instant on every buttress and pinnacle. It seemed to him that all those mysterious allegorical figures and images were out of his own life, and that they raised those stony arms for him, and pointing to the star-strewn heavens, whispered lightly: ".Make for thyself undying fame; then the cross upon thy grave may bury itself in the earth—thy memory lives immortal as those stars!" And Mozart answered in his heart: "Even so shall it be! Great Gluck, glorious Haydn, to your height will I attain. More plainly than ever I feel it in this hour—the name of Mozart shall be immortal!"

CHAPTER IV.

KAISER JOSEPH THE SECOND.

MOZART lived now the quiet, unassuming life of a private gentleman and musician in the great capital. Without a position or a salary, he was forced to earn his bread by whatever work was open to such an unobtrusive, sensitive spirit, with only music for a handicraft. No fortunate star seemed to shine over the great but modest composer. No doubt he was very wrong in being great and modest: to be little and conceited hits much nearer the mark in this world. Indeed, fate seems to prefer to bestow good fortune on the small natures, rather than on the children of genius, which is only in accordance with the divine law of compensation,—since the former would be nothing in the world without good fortune, while the latter, through all sorrow and storm, possess the treasures of the ideal world.

So Amadeus gave concerts and private lessons; wrote sonatas on subscription, and worked for music-dealers at so much a page. Frequent invitations to musical entertainments at the houses of the nobility increased his income somewhat by means of the gifts which he brought away, so that he would have been prosperous enough, if he had required no more than what he received. But the young composer unfortunately required a great deal more than he received, for he had become gradually a lover of all the pleasures of a full, free life. This, however, would have been of little consequence comparatively, if he had not so passionately loved his Constanze, and so longed to call her wife. To have at last a home—a home with all its wealth of quiet comfort, had so long been his dream and desire! But the way to gain this blessing is certainly not by having one's wants constantly exceed one's income,—a great truth which Mozart's father and Constanze's mother very well understood.

With the Weber family matters were in this wise: Good father Weber had passed away not long after Aloysia's marriage with Lange. Perhaps this unhappy match was one cause of his early death, for the clear-sighted father's prophecy had been too soon proved true. Lange, who had for a short time reformed, soon fell back, as was to have been expected, into his innate character of frivolity, and pushed his natural giddiness and fickleness to such an extent that after many painful household scenes a separation ensued. Shortly afterward Aloysia accepted an engagement at the Vienna theatre, whither she went, after her father's death, with her mother and the rest of the family. Lange remained at Munich.

The financial condition of the Webers had not at all improved, meantime. There was scarcely property enough remaining after the death of Herr Weber to support the large family in the plainest manner. As for Mozart, we have seen that he needed all he could earn, especially as his father was in such circumstances that from time to time twenty or thirty ducats must be sent to him, for the lightening of his old age.

It was rather a discouraging outlook for an early marriage; and Constanze's mother had gained enough experience during her own life's perplexities and hard turns to make her determined and unyielding in the demand that Mozart should first have a steady and sufficient income before he became her son-in-law. Mozart's father was quite as positive in the same wise counsel. Every letter from Salzburg was full of fatherly exhortations on this point, and of sound practical advice.

But what does passionate love care for sound practical advice? All the more for the difficulties in their way did Constanze and her lover feel bound to each other. The gloom which seemed to shut out the prospect of a happy future, shut them in together all the more completely. Little is love disturbed by poverty. Jean Paul has finely said: "As upon the sea, when it is perfectly still and transparent, one looks down and sees the mirrored heaven rounding up below till it joins with the sky above and makes one hollow sphere, in the centre of which the ship seems hung and floating freely; so Love joins the Actual and the Ideal, Earth and Heaven, till the deep Heaven is all, and there is no more Earth, and the Past and the Future are become the Present. For Love desires nothing but the Now, and that it may prolong itself unchanged; therefore is it inexhaustibly rich, because the Now supplies all the Future's gifts, giving them through the mere presence of the beloved one, and the thoughts on one another. Love keeps the holy constellations of its sky ever above it, even on our rolling earth-ball; for the constellations which the ball conceals at evening, in the East it must bring again!"

So rich and deep a soul as Mozart's needs only hold by itself with invincible will, and the future is already his. Amadeus felt this. When therefore his beloved and now more than ever beautiful Constanze spoke, with tears in her eyes, of the difficulties in their way, he would only smile, and tenderly drawing her to his arms, he would say: "Never fear, darling—my darling! No one knows—not even you—what force I feel in my own soul, what wealth slumbers in my brain and heart. It is an enchanted treasure, whose spell only can be broken by Love. You are mine, and by strategy or storm I will take you. But first let us try to persuade your mother and my father."

But persuasion availed nothing; the cool, steady practical common sense of the old people shook its head sternly, and always answered the bold self-confidence of the young musician with an iron "Wait!"

Then Amadeus resolutely faced the situation, and felt that somewhere must be found a *Pou Sto* from which his lever could and should lift the leaden weight of circumstances; and lo! fate furnished it to his hand.

The age of which we write was a peculiarly interesting and memorable one. It was Germany's new birthday. In society, in politics, in art and science the Winter had broken up, and a bright warm Spring-time was breathing its living breath over the Fatherland. One need only remember the men who were contemporaries then, to appreciate the character of the times: there were Klopstock, Hagedorn, Haller, Kleist, Gleim, Gellert, Rabener, Weisse, Winkelmann, Lessing, Basedow, Adelung, Hölty, Bürger, Herder, Kant, Voss, Wieland, Bach, Händel, Graun, Haydn, Gluck, Mozart, and the radiant morning-stars, Schiller and Goethe,—the former now thirty-three years old, and already famous through his "Robbers,"—the latter crowned as the great poet of the land. And for rulers there were Frederick the Second and Joseph the Second.

"Joseph the Second," says Schlosser in his History of the 18th and 19th Centuries, "tried to effect by means of the Government, just what most monarchies were trying to hinder by means of the Government. He was in opposition to the spirit of the times from exactly a contrary reason to that of other autocrats. He was bent on reforming the whole management of affairs in Austria—the Executive, the Judiciary, the public education, the condition of religion, the laws, and society. But to reform these without the aid of the people, was of course impossible; and the aid of the people Joseph the Second would not accept. His history, therefore, is one long tragedy of a prince who was battling with a heroic will against the existing state of things, without an ally or a comrade to support him."

Among the grand dreams of the Emperor was the plan of founding a new German music, and emancipating the national music from the yoke of the false and artificial Italian school. In this purpose he found an enthusiastic coadjutor in Mozart. To him he explained his plan, and ended by giving the composer a libretto which Bretzner had lately written—"The Elopement from the Seraglio"—with the request that he should immediately write an opera for it.

Mozart was in a fever of joyful excitement at once. He set himself at once to study the libretto on the evening of its reception. His fiery spirit left him no rest. Not only must he at once learn the subject from beginning to end, but that same night the outline of the music must be sketched out in his brain—vaguely and with a flying pencil, it is true, but the outline of the opera must be thought out before sleep was possible. Ah, this everlasting, inexorable unrest—this passion, this unconquerable impulse to incessantly create—it was the demon which even already had begun to haunt him with its evil prophecies.

Everything went swiftly with him. He thought swiftly· his feelings were swiftly aroused, to thrill and quiver long afterward; the blood sped swiftly along his veins, so that at the smallest excitement his heart knocked loudly on his breast; even in eating, drinking, smoking, talking, every motion was quick and sudden. He could scarcely stand still long enough to wash his hands; but would seize the towel and wander up and down the room, knocking one heel against

the other, and composing in his head. Hands and feet were
continually in motion. He must be playing on something—
on his hat, or his watch-chain, or the chairs and tables, as if
they were the piano.' But it was in composing that his
rapidity was most surprising. The thoughts flew, and the
pen drove on to keep pace with them, till he seemed almost
working like a madman. The instant that a musical idea
flashed across him, he grasped it at once in its relations to
what must precede and follow, and with its full harmony.
The melody, the bass, and the parts between, all sounded in
his brain—at first mingled together, then distinguished with
more and more clearness as his soul listened more intently.
The whole score stood forth in his mind at the same moment,
combined and interwoven in accordance with the laws of
counterpoint and modulation, with the parts distributed to
voices and the various instruments of the orchestra, in obedience to a marvellous instinct which could never be deceived
as to the Beautiful.'

We, who only hear music as it has been imperfectly expressed in voice and instrument, as it stammers forth its
burden through human or mechanical mechanism, such as
alone were at hand to translate the message as it came to
the souls of the Masters, can but faintly imagine what that
music must have been as those souls heard it—that tone-
world amid whose unearthly beauty they dwelt perpetually,
and of which their "works," as we know them, are but an
earthly hint and shadow. Walking in that realm, and communing with its diviner creations, it is no wonder that such
spirits as Mozart have ever despised the mortal frame which
they bore about the world. "I have written with my heart's
blood and my bones' marrow!" is the epitaph of all great
men.

The candles were burned down, and the dawn was staring
into the chamber with its cold face, when Amadeus had finished his study of the libretto of the "Entführung aus dem
Serail."

Much of it had exceedingly pleased him, but some parts he
was not satisfied with. The main idea of it almost startled
him with its apparent similarity to his own relations with
Constanze. Every few pages he would spring up, and seating himself at the piano, would strike a few chords, or trace

---

' *Vide* Oulibicheff, Part II., p. 331.   ' Mozart's own statement of it, in a letter.

a melody which had flashed across his brain as he read. At last he had clapped the book together, and cried, "By heavens, this will be something rich! But I must at once get Bretzner and Stephani to alter some of these places, on the spot."

It could hardly be done at once, for when he came to look at his watch, it was four o'clock in the morning.

" 'Tis too early yet!" he said, and blowing out the remnant of candle-end, he threw himself on his bed without undressing. He was too utterly wearied out to lie awake long; but the sleep which came was not refreshing. Black notes swarmed before his eyes in wild dances; fantastic melodies tantalized his ear; and in the midst of them the image of Constanze appeared and reappeared,—no longer calmly and naturally, but confused with grotesque groups of the libretto's characters, and with Osmin's angry grimaces peeping over her shoulder.

Amadeus was therefore glad to awaken early. The two hours of sleep had been enough for him. He rose, and seating himself at his table wrote this note to Bretzner:

"Mon Cher Ami:

"The Emperor gave me yesterday your libretto of the 'Entführung'—never mind how and where. I read it last night, and am delighted with it;—only, the devil may fly away with me if you didn't write the whole thing with special reference to me and my girl of girls. I am in a fever to commence the composition, and your ingenious plot and denouements will be of the greatest help to me. But many things in this world have to be changed (though not deranged); so I want you to take unto yourself Stephani (you can, eh?) and both come at ten o'clock to that celebrated tavern, the Würstl—('tis here still). There will I bespeak a capital lunch eon (with a puncheon), for which I will pay (some day), and we can discuss the whole matter (on an empty platter); and

"I am yours,

"Wolfgang Mozart."

This came near being as sensible a letter as Mozart was ever in the habit of writing when he was in good spirits. He sealed it, and gave it to a boy to deliver. Then he set out to say good-morning at the Weber house, stopping at the Würstl to order breakfast, on the way.

In Vienna, in those days, almost all the houses had a name as much as the children had; and the house where the Webers lived was called the "Auge Gottes." Thither Amadeus now hastened. It was still early, and he rather hoped to find his beloved in her *negligé*, that he might rally her on her late rising; but she was too early for him. Constanze, always trim and neat, as the house was when she ordered it, came to meet him in her pretty morning-dress. She was fresh and charming as a rosebud in her simple gown, which fitted close to her form, after the fashion of that day. Her figure had now rounded out, like her character, into the full, graceful symmetry of blooming maidenhood. The swell of the breast and the white neck were modestly veiled under the snowy chimisette with its muslin ruffles. About the beautiful head, with its faithful eyes, rosy cheeks, delicate nose, and tender mouth, waved the brown hair, slyly escaping wherever it could into numberless little natural curls.

The two radiant natures—one sunshine, the other starlight—greeted each other heartily. Then Constanze asked, in her childlike fashion: "And why so early? Did you want to find out for yourself whether I got up in good season?"

"A good deal so," said Mozart.

"Well, then, know and be ashamed, that I am a good housewife, and am up with the chickens!"

"I am glad to hear that!" said Amadeus, drawing her to him, and pressing a kiss on her forehead; "and I will be sure and reward the virtue when you are my little wife."

"Ah!" sighed the maiden, "who knows whether it will ever come to that! The mother is more and more and *more* determined against our marriage."

"And for heaven's sake, why?"

"Just now because bad men have been telling evil tales to her about you." Then, lifting up her finger in friendly reproof, she added, "And 'tis partly your fault, too, Amadeus!"

Mozart looked at her in surprise, and replied, almost in a tone of pain—

"Is it possible that even you can believe their lies—that you, too, take me for a light-headed spendthrift, because now and then, after hard work, I have a good time with good company?"

"How can you think that?" returned Constanze, with the tears in her true eyes. "Do I not know my Amadeus better!

I know that a man of genius must go his own way, and that a brain-worker cannot live like a collier. I know, too—and oh! Wolfgang, how glad I am to know it!—that in all your jesting, your bantering, your inborn gayety, there is present always a nobility of nature which shuns whatever is unbeautiful or impure. My Amadeus is good and great, yet is there one little something which he lacks."

"And that is—?"

"Prudence!"

Mozart smiled. Then he cried, gayly: "Oh you wise people, with your prudence! Am I wrong then to give you myself, just as I am? It seems to me that in that very thing lies the best proof that I have nothing evil to hide; for only evil-doers need to disguise themselves."

"You persist in not understanding me," said Constanze, with a shake of her head, motioning to him to sit down at her side. "God forbid that I should blame your honorable, open, straightforward way: I love that way as well as you do. No! when I spoke of prudence I only meant that you ought to be more cautious in expressing your opinion about other musicians, and especially in criticising the many Italian singers and composers who are here."

"And have I been incautious?"

"Yes! without intending it at all, you have already made a great many enemies here in Vienna, just by your plain-speaking and your sharp criticisms upon everything which, from your high standpoint in art, has seemed bad or insufficient."

"Ah ha!" cried Amadeus, laughing; "my dear little wife to be, that sounds amazingly like the first curtain-lecture!"

"For shame!" said Constanze, coloring. "'Tis only a warning from a true heart."

"And who has told you that I have made enemies here?"

"Your fatherly friend Duscheck. He is a musician like yourself, and is well acquainted with affairs."

"True; but he is too suspicious."

"He particularly bids you beware of Salieri!"

"Poh! he is one of my best friends."

"Duscheck doesn't think so. He says you mustn't forget that Salieri is an Italian."

"Nonsense!—As if all Italians were knaves!"

"Not so, but they fear you, and your works, and your ideas of a national music.

"Never mind; the best musicians in Vienna are my stanch friends—Gluck, Haydn, Duscheck, Kucharz, Praupner, Kotzeluch, Rösler, Wittassek, and a host more. Ask any one of them, and they will tell you that if I do blame the bad, I gladly recognize the good, no matter where I find it, and that I praise and prize it."

"I know it, Amadeus : can you never believe that I understand you thoroughly? 'Tis no matter what they tell *me*. Sometimes I have even wished that all the world hated you and misunderstood you, for a little while—only for a day, Amadeus—that you might come to me alone, and believe in me forever! No! it is because these slanders poison others' ears. Only yesterday mother repeated her decision, as if it were a religious vow, that we should never be married. And what if your enemies should gain the Emperor against you?"

"Oh ho! the Emperor! What if I should tell you that His Majesty Joseph the Second had just given me a proof of his high estimation of me?" said Amadeus, laughing gleefully over his secret.

"Is it possible!" cried Constanze, in joyful surprise. "And what is it?"

"Why, little heart, it is even this : he is going to establish a German opera here—"

"Oh! that's an old story! Kaiser Joseph is always going to do great things, but—"

"Don't you slander my good Kaiser! He's in earnest this time, and the musicians and singers are already all engaged ; and a certain Wolfgang A. Mozart—look you—is commissioned to write a German opera—a *German* opera, Ma'am—for the opening thereof!"

"Amadeus!" cried Constauze, clapping her hands in delight, and yet with a half suspicion of some hoax about it, as she looked, keenly as a bird, at her beloved: "Do you really mean it?"

"Little skeptic! here is proof for you," returned Mozart, pulling out of his pocket the libretto. "Do you see that? And the best of it is that you and I are both in it."

"How so?"

"Why, do you see? there is Belmonte—that's *me ;* and Constanze, his beloved—that's you. Constanze is captive in a seraglio : *my* little Constanze is captive in the 'Auge Gottes.' There is a ferocious pasha, who holds on to her : while in your case there is a wise but prejudiced mother, and a dittc

father. Just read the words of this solo of Belmonte's—
' *Klopft mein liebevolles Herz,*' etc."

And Mozart, with one arm round Constanze, began to sing
an *aria*, which came to him at that moment—so beautiful,
that he himself was startled at it, and springing up, caught a
sheet of music-paper from the stand and dashed down the
notes at once.

The hour for his appointment with the two poets was now
approaching; leaving Constanze in an unusually jubilant and
hopeful mood over the good news he had brought her, he
bade her a merry good-bye, and hastened to the "Würstl" inn.

There he found three things: first, his two friends Bretzner
and Stephani, who never were behindhand on such occasions;
second, a well-set table with three covers, and as many bottles of champagne; and third, a charming, rosy-cheeked
maid to wait upon them, with whom he always laughed and
chatted—the more, because mine host of the "Würstl," an
old scamp of a fellow, with a paunch like Falstaff, and a
purple nose, invariably made a great ado if any one paid
court to little "Traudel." For her part, Traudel was always
delighted to see the cheery and free-hearted Herr Mozart
open the door of the inn; but the jealous host would long
ago have closed it on him had he not been so valuable a cus-
tomer, and always a great attracter of good company to the
inn.

Meeting the pretty maid in the hall, as he entered, Mozart
threw his hat at a peg, and catching Traudel round the waist,
gave her a hearty smack. Unfortunately the door was ajar
into the room where his friends were sitting with that old
beer-barrel, the innkeeper. The atmosphere of the inn, full
of cookery and tobacco-fumes as it was, was still subject to
acoustic laws, and accordingly the sound of the kiss struck
their ears distinctly.

Mine host was, as we have remarked, a second Othello in
jealousy; and the first object which confronted Mozart as he
entered the room was his elephantine figure (if he could be
said to have any figure), puffing with rage, and his purple
nose all the more fiery because all three of his guests broke
into laughter at his expense.

"Thunder and Moses!" he cried, banging his fist down
upon the table till the dishes rattled with terror—"Can't a
man have a decent maid in the house for fear of yon jackanapes? I believe a confounded musician like this Monsieur

9

Mozart has the very devil in his bones. If I had my way. he should be boiled, roasted, hung and quartered!

Mozart and his friends shouted with laughter. "Bravo! bravo!" cried the former. "He'd make a glorious Osmin!"

"What's that?" cried mine host, more enraged than ever —"what kind of a nickname do you call me? My name is Melzschek, mark you, and not Sosmin!"

"That's it, that's it!" cried Mozart. "You see he wants to bring us to the gallows for having put up with the poor wine and the bad pastry he feeds us with. See what blood-thirsty looks he throws upon us. Man alive! we're not fat capons that you should hunger for us—"

"May be not—may be not!" said the landlord, nodding his bald head savagely, and with a glance at Traudel, who had her apron before her face as if crying, but was shaking with laughter behind it. "Yet I'd like to get your necks under the knife, nevertheless!"

"Of course he would!" said Mozart, turning to his friends and applauding him as if they were at the theatre.

"Yes I would!" and the big fist came down again on the table. "First bled, and then choked, and then hung, and then roasted, boned, and pitched into the Danube!"

"Ah ha!" cried Mozart in sudden triumph. "I've got it now. Out with your paper at once, Bretzner—here's a splen-did *aria* for our Osmin. Write it down quick:

> "Wring his neck and break his bones,
>   Toast him and roast him on red-hot stones,
>   Burn him and turn him, head and heel,
>   Pin him and skin him like an eel!"

And leaping up, Mozart planted himself in front of the land-lord, like a hyena just ready to spring on his prey; and roll-ing his eyes as though he was hungry to taste him, he sang the above to a ferocious air. Bretzner and Stephani shouted their laughter for accompaniment.

Traudel stood in amazement, as if she thought Herr Mozart was in dead earnest to devour her master. But that porten-tous individual himself was a great lover of music, and could not hold out against the comicality of the composer's singing and acting; so he made a virtue of necessity, first grinned, and then joined in the uproarious laughter.

The flight of a champagne-cork, and four brimming and foaming glasses sealed the treaty of peace, which came all the easier to the pacified landlord since Mozart confided to him that the kiss was only a joke, and that he was to be married before a great while. The old fellow was invited to join them at table, and with Traudel to serve them they were all in excellent humor. They went over the libretto together—altered the text here and struck out there; and when the fourth glass of wine was empty, Mozart caught the book out of Stephani's hand, and cried: "By the Seven Stars, I am in just the mood now to compose the duett for the drinking-song! The crabbed Osmin and the cunning Pedrillo, now friends again, are sitting on the floor, Turkish-fashion. They sip the fragrance of their nectar. The old Turk hesitates, lest the shade of Mohammed may be frown-'ng on him; but now he tosses off the liquor. Aha! that smacks well. Once more!" And Mozart sang, waving his champagne-glass in the air, "Vivat Bacchus! long live Bacchus! Bacchus was a gentleman!"

But in *his* ears alone rang at the same time the deafening music of the Janizaries, which was to accompany the duett.

CHAPTER V.

JOSEPH HAYDN.

THE next morning Mozart rose early; and, as soon as he had breakfasted on a cup of coffee and a chip of bread, he set to work in good earnest at the "Entführing." He was seated at a desk near the piano, where the bright sun-shine, slanting in through the window, lay all about his feet; and into its stream of light his pen seemed to be dipped now and then, as his right arm hung over the back of his chair while the left hand supported his chin, as he paused to listen to the music which his joyous imagination conjured forth. Idea after idea came to him, as from some invisible source, and was dashed down with rapid hand on the paper, in all its orchestral completeness. One hour after another went by, and he knew nothing of their flight. The clock struck noon: Mozart heard it not—he went on composing. It struck one: Mozart never thought of its being dinner-time, but went on composing. At last, when it was four o'clock, he was suddenly conscious of being faint. He laid aside his pen, and was aware that he was terribly hungry. But he was near the end of a movement, and must go on till it was finished. So another half-hour went by, when he again threw down his pen.

"There," said he, taking a long and contented breath, as he rose and rubbed his hand across his forehead, which ached with its long concentration; "that is enough for to-day. Now the body shall have its turn. I am almost hungry enough to come to pieces."

And he started to dress himself for going out. Suddenly the tower-clock began to strike: he counted—one, two, three, four!

"Is it possible?" he exclaimed; "four o'clock! Then 'tis no wonder my stomach growled. Where am I to go, though? It is too early for the 'Würstl.' Let's see what there is here." And going to the cupboard in the other room, he took a survey of the contents. A thick crust of bread and half a sausage were the sole occupants of the larder: several empty bottles flanked them, and looked out at him with an expression as melancholy as his own.

"A poor prospect!" said he, taking out what there was, and setting it on the table, where there was scarcely an inch of room uncovered by the manuscript music. "By Jove, I must marry soon, or there'll be no such thing as order in my life."

With this advice to himself, he proceeded to demolish his bread and sausage. But at the second bite, his eye fell on the pages lying about his plate. As he eats, he hums the melodies which he sees. Then he suddenly stops: his eyes shine. A new air has struck him, and laying down his crust, he seizes his pen, and the composition goes on anew. The pen flies: with a dab and a scratch each note is dashed down. His eyes sparkle, the corners of his mouth are drawn up; his brows are now contracted in earnest wrinkles, now arched in joyful excitement. At last he flings down the pen, and springs up—the beautiful air, "To die with my beloved," lies finished before him.

But now Amadeus was so wearied that he must have relaxation. Hastily, as if he feared every moment that the demon of composing would seize him again, he slipped into his coat, and put on his best hat, which began to show signs of some difficulties in the treasury department. He would go and see his friend Haydn, whom he had not met for some time. Little did he think, as he set out for Haydn's house, what dark clouds were now again hiding the life-sky of that much-tried man.

Joseph Haydn, Capellmeister to Prince Esterhazy, was sitting before a writing-desk, in his plain but extremely neat study, absorbed in sorrowful thought. A letter from the Prince, which had just fallen out of his hand, lay open before him. There must be ill tidings in it, for tears were standing in the man's eyes, and while a deep sadness covered his mild face, his hands were folded as though in prayer.

The letter had come upon him like a blow; it read as follows:

"MY DEAR CAPELLMEISTER:

"If it ever was hard for me to take a pen, in order to announce something unpleasant to a man, it is the case to-day.

"You yourself know how much I value you, how thoroughly I appreciate the great services which you have rendered me these many years as Director of my music. Naturally you must have become greatly attached to the position, and yet I find myself obliged to deprive you of it. Weighty reasons, connected with the private relations of my family, compel me to shortly give up all my musicians. Four weeks hence we will have the last grand concert in my palace. It is understood, of course, my dear Haydn, that your salary goes on unchanged till you have found another position for yourself, and I shall always be glad to see you, as a friend of the house.

"You can count upon my influence at all times in your behalf, and I remain,

"Yours most truly,
"ESTERHAZY."

Haydn had been for over twenty years at the head of the fine company of musicians who were supported by the princely munificence of Esterhazy. He had grown to be a part of the establishment;—he had written so much of his best music there; had brought it out with such splendid advantages in the perfection of the instruments and the talent of the performers! Their music had been not only the pride of the

Prince himself, but of all Vienna. He had grown into the
duties of his position there as firmly as the ivy to the wall;
and now that he must leave it, the breaking away tugged at
his very heart-strings.

The event was not wholly unexpected. The Prince had
many times of late talked with him about such a change.
The "private relations of his family," which the letter had
mentioned as a cause, were not, as Haydn knew perfectly
well, so very important. For though the Prince had doubt-
less sustained enormous losses by the extravagance of some
of his relatives, yet his property was so colossal that it was
scarcely lessened by the loss. The truth was, that Kaiser
Joseph had instituted such economical reforms in his own
affairs, as well as in the government, that the high nobility
felt obliged to follow his example. Prince Esterhazy valued
the esteem of his Emperor even more than music, and, therefore, great as was his pride in his " Capelle," and his reverence
for the art itself, he forced himself to decide as we have seen.

Haydn was deeply affected by this event; not because he
would need to be anxious about his future sustenance, even
for a moment—this was secured by the generosity of the
Prince; but it seemed to him that the destruction of his
darling Capelle, with all its associations and its prospects, was
the shattering of his whole fortune.

Soon, however, was the calm meek spirit of the great musician master of the momentary grief. His life, rich in the
"sweet uses of adversity," had been a constant submission
to the decrees of Heaven, and certainly most of its trials—as
he reminded himself now, with childlike gratitude —had
turned into blessings. Why might it not be so in his present
position ? Such was the spirit—thankful for the past, hopeful for the future—with which he always faced his life ; and
the same spirit characterizes his works.

" The expression of cheerfulness, sunny as that of a child,"
says Hoffman, " rules everywhere in Haydn's compositions.
His symphonies lead us into endless green meadows, thronged
with happy human creatures. Youths and maidens float by
in the dance; laughing children, peeping from behind rose-
bushes, cover each other with blossoms. It is a life full of
love, full of quiet enjoyment, in perpetual youth. There is
no shrill tone of suffering or pain, only a sweet sorrow of
longing for the beloved form, which hovers in the far-off
evening-red, nor comes nearer, nor disappears. And so long

as that form still hovers there, the night comes not, foi itself is the eternal evening-red, glowing on mountain and meadow!"

Haydn quickly recovered his self-possession on this occasion. The pain had cut deeply into his heart, but with the words, "The Lord gave, the Lord has taken away, blessed be the name of the Lord!" he was calm again, and was about to reply to the Prince's letter, when Mozart entered the room.

The young man soon saw, in spite of the hearty greeting which his friend gave him, that some misfortune had befallen Haydn, and the latter willingly told him the truth. Mozart's sympathy was heartfelt and warmly given, and he expressed his wonder that the loss could be so patiently borne. Then Haydn smiled kindly, and said:

"That comes easy, my fiery young friend, when one has had life for a schoolmaster."

At that an old wish flamed up in Mozart: "Ah!" cried he, taking both of Haydn's hands in his own, "dear Herr Capellmeister, will you not tell me the story of your life? I have heard so much about you—your greatness as a musician—your noble heart—your self-sacrifice—that I long to know what the school has been which could educate a soul like yours."

As the young man said this Haydn's look rested kindly on his open face, which bore the unmistakable impress of truthfulness and sincere sympathy.

"Yes!" said he, after a moment's pause; "my existence has been indeed a life-school—as it is, of one kind or another, for every creature. I will gladly give you its history, since you are, like me, a musician, and will therefore understand it; for my life has been lived in music, and often I have thought that there is hidden within us much which words cannot express, but which finds its voice in tones."

"And why should we not believe so?" cried Mozart, with kindled face. "A tone—a harmony—is often a glowing kiss of diviner existence,—a kiss which snaps a charm, and discloses the secrets of that inner life which thrills through us and through the universe. Only a poet can comprehend a poet—only a musician can understand a musician."

"That is true!" said Haydn; then leaning back in his chair, and fixing his eyes on the distance, as if to bring back from thence the forms of his far-off home, he began his story:

"Just on the boundary between Hungary and Austria lies

a little hamlet called Rohrau. There, forty-nine years ago, I was born, of parents who were as good as they were poor.

"My father was a cartwright; but like all the Hungarians and Bohemians, he loved music, and was a good player on the violin. My mother, too, God rest her soul! was musical, and played the harp, singing to it with a beautiful voice. You remember the proverb as to the musical character of our land?"

"Certainly," said Mozart; "I heard it when a child: 'In two houses, three fiddles and a dulcimer.'"

"It is correct enough!" continued Haydn, while a gentle smile played round the corners of his mouth. "Therefore I love Hungary and Bohemia so much. Heaven has greatly blessed them in this taste for music. How happy the mass of the people are, in spite of their poverty!—simply because the dear, sweet music helps them bear their burdens, and goldens every hour of rest with a simple and elevating pleasure.

"In spite of all his diligence, in that out-of-the-way village, work often failed my father, and with it the necessaries of life; so he was forced to do what many an other had done—to go out with my mother on Sundays and holidays, and play and sing before the wayside inns. My father played the violin, and my mother sang to the accompaniment of her harp. This was when I was two and three years old, and they often took me with them, for, of course, the poor baby could not be left alone at home. But God's ways are wonderful. One fine Sunday I was sitting at the feet of my parents while they played and sang, when the schoolmaster of the neighboring village happened to be passing by. The music pleased him so much that he stopped to listen, when he noticed me sitting on the grass. I had placed a chip against my neck for a violin, and was fiddling away on it with a willow twig. The best of it was—the old schoolmaster has often told me about it since—that, baby as I was, I had sense enough to stop whenever my father stopped for my mother to sing a solo, and started off again with him on a sixteenth-note. The good schoolmaster remembered me, and when I was five years old he took me into his house and his school, and treated me as his own son. I had lessons, too, on the violin and the trumpet, and in singing.

"Dear old friend!" cried Haydn here, with visible emotion; "long have you been dead and fallen to dust, but in my thankful heart you will live till it shall cease to beat!"

He was silent a little while, till Mozart recalled him from his musings by asking—

"And what happened to you afterward?"

"Afterward?" repeated Haydn. "Oh, yes!—After I had been at Haimburg two years, I got a position as singer in the choir of boys at St. Stephen's church here in Vienna. It was hard to leave my parents, but Heaven had sent them a second child, my brother Michael; and it seemed a splendid thing to come to the great capital and sing in the glorious old cathedral, and learn all the instruments. I remained there till my sixteenth year, studying the principles of music, and learning all I could about various instruments.

"When I was ten years old, I began to compose pieces for sixteen parts. And do you know what I thought about my compositions in those days?"

"What?" asked Mozart.

"Why, I thought," said Hadyn smiling, "that the blacker the paper was, the better the music."[1]

"In my sixteenth year I lost my soprano voice, and with it my place in the choir. With the loss of that place the careless days of childhood were over, and the trials of life began. My situation was a hard one. Without a single protector, without any means whatever, known by no one, I stood alone here in great Vienna. There was nothing for it but to rent a little attic-chamber and eke out my life by teaching.

"It was a bitter beginning," said Haydn, with a look in his eyes as if he still felt pity for the sensitive boy whom he remembered; "yet there was many an hour in which I was perfectly happy in my bare little room. Sitting at my old worm-eaten clavier, I would not have changed places with a king![1] Yes, life is a school for us all; and the lessons which that time taught me were contentedness, modesty, and trust in God. Those three lessons I have to thank for the serenity and cheerfulness of my spirit. But God did not wait till I had learned my tasks, to give me pleasures. I came into possession, during those pinching times, of the first six sonatas of our glorious Emanuel Bach. What a prize they were to me! I never left the clavier till they were all played through

[1] Haydn's own words.

from beginning to end; and any one who knows me can testify that I owe Emanuel Bach a great deal—that I laid hold of his style and studied it carefully.

"At last I was so fortunate as to gain the patronage of the Fräulein von Martinez. She was a friend of Metastasio, and lived at his house. I gave her lessons in singing and upon the clavier, and received my board and lodging at Metastasio's in payment."

"Well!" cried Mozart joyfully, "your fortune was made, then, certainly! Metastasio is so rich, so renowned, and lives so splendidly—"

"That," said Haydn with a smile, "was of little account to me. Yet I am still grateful to the old poet that he gave me a little chamber in the fifth story to shelter my head, and a warm bed to sleep in. I got only sixty florins a year for playing the organ at the convent, and a very scant income from my pupils, who were mostly poor people also, and from my playing in different orchestras; so that many a time in the winter, for lack of wood to burn, I had to lie all day in bed, where I kept hard at work composing."[1]

"But these compositions certainly brought you something?" asked Mozart.

"Oh yes!" said Haydn smiling. "Something—about enough to buy a meal with, for each minuet."

"But—good heavens!" cried Mozart in ever-increasing astonishment, "why did you not publish those beautiful waltzes which are now the rage in every royal and princely *salon ?*"

"Because I found no publisher!" answered Haydn quietly. "I had no name at that time, and knew no one to whom I could dedicate my pieces. They laughed at me—the poor, unknown fellow—when I talked about publishing."

Mozart heaved a sigh, and Haydn calmly went on:

"My being at Metastasio's house was of great advantage to me in one respect: I had an opportunity to learn Italian thoroughly, and to hear a great deal concerning the æsthetics of music, which was very useful to me afterward. There, also, I came to know my ever-memorable old Porpora. Meantime Fräulein von Martinez left Vienna. I lost my board and lodging, therefore, and should have fallen back into my old state of utter destitution but for Heaven's bring-

---

[1] Historical.

ing to my aid another noble man. You have heard of him before, as my father-in-law. He was only a hairdresser, but a royal heart beat under his plain coat. He took me in like his own son, gave me a bed in his house and a seat at his table, and since he was a more practical man than I, looked after the sale of my pieces. When I was eighteen years old I composed my first quartette, which had a good reception."

"And deserved it well!" said Mozart emphatically.

"The success of this quartette incited me to follow it up with similar works. Of course the critics and pedants at once fell ferociously upon my poor name: but little did I mind their attacks; an inner conviction told me that a work loses in taste and expression by a too close and strict obedience to the rules. I therefore went my own way, and followed the inner voice and the impulse of my own spirit. Now was I very happy. I lived and moved in music; and though I often went to bed hungry, and many times even bread failed me (for I had at that time my parents to assist out of my slender income), yet I never ceased to thank God for the precious gift he had lent me in music, which wrapped my whole life in a rosy glow. I gave lessons, wrote waltzes, played the organ, and in the evening I used to go out with a few friends and publish my compositions along the streets. One evening we sang a serenade under the window of the wife of Kurz, the famous comic actor. She was so much pleased with it that Kurz shortly came to me and insisted that I should write an opera for him. I was at that time only nineteen years old, and the undertaking seemed to me almost presumptuous, but I yielded to his urgency and my own ambition, and wrote my first opera—'The Limping Devil.'"

"Which made your fortune!" said Mozart.

"Yes," returned Haydn; "for though it was only performed three times, on account of its satirical character, it brought me to the notice of the noble Prince Esterhazy, who soon put me at the head of his Capelle."

"And there," said Mozart, with beaming eyes, "you wrote those magnificent symphonies and quartettes, which the whole world knows and loves: and in these twenty years you have raised the Capelle to the highest place in European music."

"Only to have to leave it at last!" said Haydn. His face was mild and patient as ever, but the tone of his voice betrayed his sadness. Mozart respected this sadness too much to attempt to lessen it by any commonplaces of comfort. So deep and rich a nature as Haydn's was its own best com forter. Soon, therefore, Amadeus took his leave.

But Haydn sat for a long time silent and motionless. He was looking at the ruins of a palace which he had been a score of years in building. He saw the fallen stones and pillars, each one inscribed with some part of his life—of himself: he saw the past with all its hard places, its bitter disappointments, its mortifications, its great plans and small accomplishment: he saw a fathomless and unknown future opening at his feet. But he did not see the invisible ministering spirits who leaned above him, and hinted comfort to his heart, and caressed him, as they ever do those who have done much, through much tribulation, for the world. He saw them not, but he heard within his soul the soft, sweet preluding of immortal harmonies, and knew not whence they came.

CHAPTER VI.

THE LAST LIGHT.

FOUR weeks passed rapidly by. It was the day on which the last concert was to be given at the palace of Prince Esterhazy, under the leadership of Joseph Haydn.

All the high nobility of Vienna had been invited; for every person who ever was in the habit of visiting the palace, had heard with regret and pain the Prince's intention to break up his Capelle, and they must be present to enjoy this last opportunity of hearing such splendid music. Besides the nobility, there were some of the first artists of the world invited, and among them Metastasio, the Chevalier von Gluck, and Mozart.

The evening came, and the shadows of night settled down upon the great capital; but so much the brighter gleamed the great windows of the Esterhazy palace, which poured a flood of light into the surrounding darkness, and glittered like a fairy castle. The gate and entrance were adorned with evergreens and flowers, and hundreds of blazing lights, till it seemed the portal of a new Paradise, through which streamed the throng of superbly dressed noblemen and ladies.

Inside the palace the splendor was yet more intense. Every room was lustrous with rich furniture and costly art, and a princely taste everywhere had gone hand in hand with the princely magnificence.

Nevertheless, one could not but notice among the thronging guests a certain seriousness, as if the shadow of some impending calamity were thrown over all their gayety and mirth. All about the *salons*, in detached groups here and there, they were talking of the approaching destruction of the Capelle. The concert-hall was not yet thrown open, and as the guests wandered about the palace, or partook of the elegant refreshments which were brought to them by gorgeously-liveried servitors, there was but one common theme of conversation: it was the breaking up of that renowned company of musicians, and the last concert to which they were soon to listen. The name of Haydn was spoken often and regretfully by every one, as they talked. Especially was this true of two stately gentlemen who were lamenting together the close of so brilliant a series of musical feasts. One of them evidently belonged to the highest aristocracy, for his breast was covered with orders. Though the other, who only wore the order of the Golden Spur, seemed not to be of equally high rank, yet the expression of his intellectual face, the proud pose of his head, the stately courtesy of his manner, showed that he was at home in such company, and that he bore in himself a nobility which was firmer based than on the gift of any earthly potentate. The former was Count Zichy, the latter the Chevalier von Gluck.

"It is wrong—by heavens, it is wrong!" said the Count. "If I were the Prince I would cut off half my establishment rather than this Capelle, and especially its conductor, Haydn. He is one of our greatest men!"

"Indeed he is," answered Gluck with enthusiasm. "He is great in the least things as in the largest; always rich and inexhaustible in new musical treasures; always sublime, even when he seems to only smile. He has given our *Quadros* and Symphonies a fulness and roundness which no one before him ever dreamed of."

"And how everything speaks when he sets the orchestra in motion!" said Count Zichy.

"Yes," responded Gluck; "each instrument appears to have an independent soul of its own, which only recognizes its own individuality to blend it at once with all the rest.

With the old composers the mass of the orchestra was frozen
stiff, while only here and there an instrument was thawed
into melody: with Haydn it is all a full free river of harmony."

"It is strange," said the Count, "how simple and natural
all his music seems: one is almost persuaded that each new
thing has been a long time familiar."

"And that," said Gluck, "is one great secret of his hold
on the popular heart. His music tells you perpetually what
you seem always to have known, but are delighted to be reminded of: it surprises you every moment, but it is by its
marvellous naturalness. The child can understand it: the
oldest heart cannot but rejoice to have understood it."

"We are to hear a new symphony of his to-night, are we
not?" asked the Count.

But at this moment the folding-doors of the concert-hall
were thrown open, and the rustling and glittering company
streamed in and took their seats. Prince Esterhazy escorted
the old Princess Colloredo. Mozart stood behind the chair
of his fair pupil, the Countess Rombeck, who had seated herself by the side of the Baroness Waldstetten. Near them
sat the Baron van Swieten and the Chevalier Gluck.

The concert began. In the first part the music was fine,
as it always was, but not remarkable, except for a repressed
expression of sadness, which seemed to pervade the orchestra
as well as the audience. Even the selection of pieces gave
evidence of this mood, which began to be painful. Mozart
could not keep the tears from his eyes. Prince Esterhazy
bit his lips to conceal his own feeling. No one knew what it
had cost him to decide on breaking up the Capelle, which
had for so long been his darling and pride.

But now, at the pause between the parts, an intense concentration of expectancy filled the hall. Every one knew
'hat Haydn had written a new symphony for the second
part of this farewell concert, and all expected something
memorable. The great composer would not take leave of
them in any common manner.

At last the Prince gave a signal, and Haydn, who had
been conversing with Colloredo, advanced to his desk. He
was pale, paler even than ordinary, and the wavering light
which burned in front of him behind a greenish screen gave
something ghostly to his expression. Unmistakable was
the seriousness that lar in his features, which nevertheless

could not extinguish the sweet and mild expression of that noble face.

Now rose the baton of the Capellmeister,—the symphony began,—and every heart in the audience beat loud and fast, as if it too obeyed the silver wand of the master.

Down through the night of earth-life were falling beams of light, and these beams were tones. Melodies glimmered forth, ascending and descending upon these streaming tones like angels. Those who knew and loved the master could hear how the music said, "Even though all things else should leave us, thou, O eternal spirit of music, wilt not leave us! Repulsed, deserted by all other friends, in thee, my art, I find my holiest friend! Praise and thanks to Thee, dear heavenly Father, that Thou hast given it to these earthly children—that Thou to me hast given it—this celestial angel of our life!"

The simple childlike strains touched the hearts even of those who had not that perfect sympathy, which alone could give them the key to Haydn's compositions. To them it was only a glance into a momentary and vanishing Paradise, whose evanescence made them weep, while its beauty still glimmered in their tears.

Prince Esterhazy was touched beyond expression. He was ready to repent his decision. His pride in his Capelle, his love for the art, his reverence for the great composer, all urged him to alter his determination, while the tones of the symphony struck like winged arrows to his heart. It needed all his strength of self-command to make him hold to his purpose.

—But what is this? The drums are silenced. The young man who beat them extinguishes the light before his stand, and noiselessly departs. It was an unprecedented thing in the orchestra. What could it mean?

The music goes on: no one thinks further of the occurrence.

How now? The trumpeters also take their instruments, extinguish their lights, and disappear.

There is a little stir of surprise in the audience. Now one brass instrument after another is hushed, other lights are extinguished, and the performers depart. Still the symphony goes on, but ever softer and fainter! The instruments become fewer—more lights are extinguished—it grows darker and lonelier in the orchestra.

A little shudder creeps over the silent hearers, even though 't is accompanied by a smile at the strangeness of it all. The Prince's eyes are wet. "Haydn!" he murmurs softly, "why pain me so?"

Now the bassoons are dumb, their lights are put out, they disappear. The violoncellos follow them; then the double-bass. And now the first violin alone in the dusky orchestra sobs forth its sorrowing tones. It is the swan-song of the Capelle—the master's farewell! Fainter and farther off dies the wail of the solitary instrument: then it too is silent, its light extinguished, its player has gone.

Now sits the master there alone.

The stillness of death reigns in the hall. One can hear only his own heart beat.

Then Haydn silently laid down the baton which he had wielded so long and worthily, extinguished his light also, bowed his head upon his breast—but at that moment burst forth a storm of applause, such as no concert-hall ever heard before!

"Bravo! Bravo, Haydn!" rang from every mouth. Every pair of hands was madly clapping, and in many eyes the tears stood glittering where tears were little used to come.

Prince Esterhazy had quickly left his seat: all his determinations had been scattered to the winds by the beautiful conclusion of the Farewell Symphony; and, hastening to Haydn, he seized both his hands, and cried—

"Haydn! you shall remain, and the Capelle also!"

Then thundered the applause afresh, and all pressed round the Prince and the composer to congratulate them. Gluck and Mozart reached their honored and now happy friend. And as they clasped hands with Haydn, and the three greatest musicians of their time stood there so united in cordial friendship, the tempest of cheers broke forth for the third time.

CHAPTER VII.

TWO ELOPEMENTS.

MOZART'S opera, "The Elopement from the Seraglio," was now finished; but close about the feet of the master's hopes hissed the old snake of envy, coiling in the dust. Salieri played the same *rôle* which Fioroni did in Milan; and about him as leader clustered the other enemies of Mozart in Vienna, most of them Italians like himself. Salieri, with true Italian cunning, succeeded in wholly concealing his hatred from the object of it. Mozart considered him even yet as one of his best friends.

It was not strange that Mozart made enemies. His daily increasing fame, which now began to be already enhanced by the "Entführung," even before its representation in public, his perfectly frank and fearless way of expressing his opinion; and his criticisms, no matter to whom, or concerning whose works; his open manner of thoroughly liking whomever he liked, and thoroughly disliking whomever he disliked, made lower natures hate him, in spite of all his true goodness of heart.

The Italian musicians in Vienna were hostile to Mozart, because they saw plainly that the new German opera, of which there was so much talk, would be the first blow at the universal sway of the Italian opera. With Mozart once at their head, the Germans would wrest the sceptre from Italian hands. Some of his own countrymen there were, also, who were as bitterly opposed to him through mere envy of his genius, and jealousy of his growing fame.

The result of the intrigues of his enemies at present was only to delay the appearance of his new opera. With a weaker Emperor than Joseph II. to work upon, they might have succeeded in keeping it back altogether. But at last, after several postponements, the "Entführung aus dem Serail" was put upon the stage, with an excellent company of performers, on the 12th of July, 1782.

The band of enemies, under the leadership of Salieri, did their best to ruin the opera, on the first night of its performance. It was the old story of hired hisses and confusion. But the public was not to be deceived. The opera was a brilliant success. Night after night it was given to crowded houses, who night after night made the theatre ring and thunder with *encores* and applause.

Amadeus was delighted; especially as the reception of his new work so far softened his old father's heart, or so far increased his confidence in his son's ability to support a family, that he withdrew his objections to the much plead-for marriage. But that was by no means half the battle. Constanze's mother held firm as a rock by her decision. No marriage was to be heard of till he had a position and a fixed regular salary, sufficient for the support of at least two.

Mozart chafed and raged inwardly at this delay. He had hoped that by this time the new German operatic company would have been formed, and that he would have had a secure position at the head of its orchestra; but as yet there was not a word further about it from the Emperor.

It was late in the evening of a burning-hot midsummer day. Mozart had left the Weber-house in an impatient and angry mood. The mother had reiterated her ultimatum with iron positiveness, and Constanze had parted from him in tears. The night brought no coolness after the sultry day, and the atmosphere was stifling in its stagnant heat. The very darkness added to the sense of closeness in the still air, and seemed as if it would smother one with its thick sweltering folds.

To Mozart it was insupportable. His fairest hopes seemed shattered at his feet, and there was in him that wild unreasoning impulse of vengeful protest, which would have liked to shatter the whole world, and lay it in ruins with those hopes. To his inner irritation was added the outer, and a sense of horrible oppressiveness weighed upon him till he seemed unable to breathe.

It was one of those moments to which every undisciplined heart is liable, no matter how strong or how good it may be by nature, when it wishes almost for a handful of Jove's thunderbolts that it might hurl them at the world, and blot it out of being; or that one of those stars yonder would suddenly grow bigger and bigger, and prove to be a comet that should storm against the earth, and shiver it into a shower of cinders.

It was such a moment to Amadeus. If Constanze had

been by some terrible stroke of fate lost to him forever, he could have borne it, like any true man; but to know that he might have her, that he must and would have her—only not now, but after this eternal waiting and waiting—nearly drove him out of his senses. He walked rapidly away from the house, away from the street, away from the central part of the city—he cared not in what direction or how far. He would gladly have walked away from himself if he could. Heat and rage together drove the sweat, in thick drops, to his forehead, but still he walked furiously on. Suddenly he stopped before a Folks-garden, which was lit up brilliantly, and out of which came the sound of laughter and the merry talking of a crowd of happy people. But it was not the splendor of the lights, nor the gayety of the voices which arrested his footsteps; it was the tones of orchestral music within. They were playing a beautiful waltz which was entirely new to him.

"That is Haydn's!" cried Mozart, after listening a few minutes. "I would bet my head upon it!"

The old Arabian story tells of an iron mountain, whose magnetic power seized upon every vessel that came within a league of it, and drew out all the iron that was in her to itself. No matter how they were secured, bolts, rings, nails, and chains, all darted away to the breast of the great magnet. So it was now with Mozart. At that moment nothing could have been more hateful to him than lights, and chatter, and merriment, yet step by step he entered the garden, and drew nearer to the music. The spirit of Haydn, expressed through those bursts of harmony from the wood and brass—that flickering, dancing, plashing, elfin-sweetness of the violins—was drawing upon every fibre of his nature which corresponded to the clear, childlike, trustful soul of his brother composer. Step by step he approached through trellised arbor and rose-arched lattice, till he stood before the orchestra in the midst of the garden.

Taking a seat at one of the little tables which stood near him, he listened to the swell and fall of the music, nodding his head in time with the conductor's baton. At last, forgetting all his rage and fever, he called for a bottle of wine, and began, under the inspiration of the harmony which thrilled the very air about him, to coolly lay out a certain little plan, whose development was as we shall see.

Just a week afterward, Sophie Weber did a remarkable

thing. She winked to herself behind her mother's back. And not only that, but soon after, finding herself alone in the sitting-room, she jumped up and down clapping her hands, and then danced three times round the room, with a beaming look on her face, which certainly did not betoken any dangerous form of madness. As she paused for breath her mother came in, dressed in her very finest garments, as if for some great feast-day, but with a curious look of bewilderment and doubt on her face.

"I don't understand it!" she said, shaking her head. "Here you have got me to dress up in this foolish style, and I am to go off with you on some mad-cap ride or other, without a vestige of an idea what it all means. Ah, Sophie, I am afraid your old mother is letting you make a fool of her! And where is Constanze all this time?"

Not only had her mother missed Constanze's presence since morning, but the very arrangement of the furniture, and the dust lying thick in the rooms where she always was accustomed to put every suspicion of dust to flight, proved that the little housekeeper had sadly neglected her duties that day. Not only that, but the dinner had been half an hour behindhand, which was like an eclipse in the solar regularity of the Weber household—and had been ill cooked, which was as unusual as if the eclipse had been embellished by an earthquake and two comets. Then again, instead of sitting down with her mother in the afternoon to sew, Constanze had kept out of sight entirely. Frau Weber took note of all this, but she attributed it to the answer which she had given Mozart, and the effects of the "hope deferred" of the young lovers. Now, however, she was beginning to be impatient, and Sophie's mysterious plot to dress her mother in Sunday clothes, and take her away to some unknown place in a carriage, made her still more so.

"What does it all mean?" she asked.

"What does *what* mean, dear mother?" returned Sophie.

"Why, all this disorder in the house, which might as well have had no housekeeper at all for a week past. Nothing is dusted, nothing is arranged, the meals come to the table at the wrong time, the meat is half burnt up, and everything is salted to death, and bungled generally!"

"But, mother dear," said Sophie, caressing her, "can't you be a little patient? You know what a sorrow Constanze has in her heart, and at such times one's mind is on other things."

"It is, eh?" asked the mother, and, in spite of her impatience, a smile played on her face. "You speak as if you knew all about it, little old woman! Only fifteen yet, and you talk about the mind's being on other things!"

"Now, mother!" said Sophie, blushing like a rosebud; "I only supposed it was so."

"Well, well!" said the mother, in a softer tone, "I am sorry for Constanze, and for Amadeus too. He is a good man, but unpractical like all geniuses. If he only had a secure position and a salary—"

"But then he earns so much now, mother!"

"I know, I know—and spends still more! Amadeus hasn't the least idea of the value of money, nor of the needs of a household; and besides, he is so good-natured, that just to please his wife, he would spend a fortune one day for worthless things, and be without bread in the house in a week."

"You are so severe, little mother!"

"I am severe, Sophie, because I have the happiness of my child at heart. I have had an experience with Aloysia which shall never be repeated!—Where is Constanze?"

"Up stairs in her room."

"What is she doing?"

"She has shut herself in, alone."

"I must put a stop to this sudden secrecy. Constanze was always so open!"

"She is crying!" said Sophie, with the tears in her own eyes for sympathy.

Those three words smote the mother-heart so deeply, that she was forced to turn away and pretend to be busy about something the other side of the room, lest Sophie should see how much she was moved. But the shrewd Sophie was not to be deceived. She put both arms round her mother and kissed her cheeks, and said, coaxingly—

"And you'll go with me in the carriage, won't you?"

"But where to?"

"Oh, you will find that out! Just imagine it is Christmas night, and that we have got a little surprise for you!"

"Goosey, goosey!" said the mother, laughing and shaking her head, as she half tried to hold Sophie off. "I am too old for such nonsense. Why can't you tell me?"

"Because one can't tell a *secret,* of course. Now, mother! if you had a *spark* of love for your children—" And the little coaxer so kissed and caressed and besought the good dame, that at last she consented to go whenever the carriage should come for them,—more than half believing that no carriage was to come at all, but that the mystery would be solved by some prank of the children in the house.

At the country-seat of the Baroness von Waldstetten, that evening, there was an unusual stir of preparation. The carriage-way, the steps, the porches, the hall, and several of the rooms were prettily trimmed with flowers and garlands. In the dining-room a supper-table was richly set for nine persons; in one of the rooms a small altar had been erected, seemingly out of flowers alone, on which lay a Bible and a crucifix, while above it hung a silver circlet bearing fourteen burning wax-tapers. Near the altar stood a Catholic priest in his superb robes, to whom the mistress of the house was just giving an imperial document, which was signed by the Landrath von Zetto and the two Barons Thorwart and van Swieten, as witnesses that the affair was legal and correct. At that moment the state carriage of the Baroness rolled up before the door —the steps were let down, and Mozart and his bride alighted.

Constanze was pale, and trembling like an aspen as she leaned on her lover's arm, who had just taken her away from the "Auge Gottes."

It had been done, to be sure, with her knowledge and consent, but only after much entreaty and persuasion, backed by the influence of the kind Baroness von Waldstetten, the motherly friend of Mozart. Constanze had yielded only upon one condition—that her mother's consent should be gained before they were united. Now she lay, weeping with excitement, anxiety, and joy, in the arms of the Baroness.

In the mean time a second carriage had left the Weber-house, bearing Sophie and her mother. The latter had no idea who had preceded them, nor whither they were going. In vain she beset her daughter all the way to explain the mystery. Sophie only answered by kisses and assurances that it was only a little surprise from her children. The mother could only look mystified, watch the streets they were passing through on their way out of the city, and shake her head. She could not but think of the tales of the Thousand and One Nights. Her amazement reached its height when she found that they had reached a handsome country-seat, through whose lofty gate the carriage rolled, and drew up before the door. They were escorted up the flower-strewn steps and into the brilliant drawing-room. Rare perfumes were wafted through the air, and now a soft strain of music fell on the ear.

Frau Weber had no words to express her bewilderment, but only shook her head, and passed her hand across her face as if to see whether she was dreaming or not. Now the music became solemn and full, like church-music; and a melody arose, so reverent, so tender, so beseeching, that the good dame felt it suddenly warm about her heart. Then a folding-door was opened. She stood blinded.

A flood of light streamed from above the altar, before which stood the priest. And the beams of light seemed to thrill and vibrate to the sweet tones till they mingled with each other in the air.

But what is this? That pair standing before the altar—is not that pale, trembling maiden, clothed in a simple snow-white dress, with a myrtle-wreath upon her hair, Constanze—Constanze, who, almost swooning, droops her head on the shoulder of Amadeus?

Frau Weber rubs her eyes. It cannot be—Constanze is at home, shut up in her chamber. How could she come hither? What mean these preparations?

The next instant Constanze and Amadeus are at the mother's feet, and the dear sweet voice, which she has loved from its first wail in the world till now it is a beautiful woman's voice, is pleading with her.

"Mother! dear, true mother, give us your blessing! Let us, before God's holy altar, become man and wife. We are one already by our love, let us be so to the world!"

Frau Weber saw clearly enough now how matters stood. "An elopement, is it?" she muttered, with a little effort, apparently, to be severe and unyielding. "Are they trying to force me to consent?"

Then the Baroness approached the perplexed mother, and explained how all had happened, and besought her not to stand in the way of the young people's happiness. Amadeus seemed like her own son, she said; and she had helped him in this little plot, because she knew it was for the welfare of all that the lovers should be married at once. Baron von Thorwart, who was a sort of godfather to the Weber children, and the trusted adviser of their mother, added his entreaties. And when at last the venerable priest came forward and reminded her in a low earnest voice, " What God hath joined together, let no man put asunder !" she could no longer hesitate.

" In God's name, then," she cried out, " take each other, my children ; and may He give you His blessing and make you happy !"

Then she laid her trembling hands on their heads, and bowed her own above them in a moment's silent prayer.

After the marriage-ceremony, the happy little company sat down to the elegant supper which the hospitable Baroness had provided for them. There was mirth and music, talk and song and jest, and the happiness of the young pair brimmed over and filled the older hearts with gladness also.

Till late in the night the guests remained together : then one after another departed. Sophie and her mother were the last to say good-night. And then the husband and wife were conducted to the bridal-chamber, which had been richly prepared to receive them in one of the wings of the mansion.

The moon was just setting in the west, and threw a wan light around the silent house. It was like the glimmering Past of their lives. And above, the stars shone, and in the east new constellations were rising, like the dim and infinite Future. But Past and Future were alike unseen by them. And as they sank into each other's arms, there swelled forth upon the night-wind, from the park below, a strain of ravishing music. It was a serenade from a company of his friends, playing one of Mozart's most beautiful symphonies.

PART V.

NOONDAY.

CHAPTER I.

SHADOWS AND LIGHT.

"STANZERL! little woman, kiss me good-bye!" cried Mozart to his dearly-loved wife. "I must go and see the Abbate: the idea of the new opera won't let me rest!" and throwing an arm about Constanze, he pressed a kiss on her cheek, another on her fresh lips, and ran out.

She had been his wife now for five years. Their marriage was in 1782, and the world now dated its documents 1787. They had been very happy years to them, so far as their relations to each other were concerned. They were, if possible, more truly lovers now than on their marriage-day. And the great secret of their happiness was, that they understood each other. Constanze recognized the nobleness of her husband, and revered his genius; and it was by her clear-eyed appreciation and comprehension of his plans, his thoughts, his trials, that she comforted and strengthened him for his work, day by day. At the same time, she knew well his weaknesses and his sins; knew them, not to find fault, but to find help for him against them.

Since his marriage, Mozart had worked harder than ever. His unfortunate custom of composing at night clung to him still, and had become an inveterate habit. The mornings were passed in bed. At ten o'clock he began his day's work of giving lessons; for the pot must boil when one has wife and children, whatever becomes of Art. It was no light task to go the rounds of his pupils in Vienna, taking often a good part of the afternoon, and the whole of his patience and freshness. But the pupils were necessary to his existence; for

Kaiser Joseph, thanks to the intrigues of Mozart's enemies, left him still unprovided with a situation.

When, tired out with teaching, with conducting, with filling orders for new dance-music, with orchestral classes, and so on, his nervous system was prostrated, and he longed for rest and refreshment, the overstrung nerves usually found only an apparent renewal in fresh excitement. Intense stimulation followed intense strain. Wine, punch, mad-cap merriment were invoked to repair the ravages of labor, often till into the morning; while poor Constanze, who watched this course with the calm clear eyes of an intelligent woman, saw but too plainly how it encroached more and more on the health of her husband. Often he saw it himself; and at such times a deep melancholy would overcome him, which grew sometimes into a dark premonition of early death.

Sometimes, when the young wife had vainly warned and besought him to live more reasonably, and Mozart had notwithstanding been led away by his friends and by his own heart's thirst for pleasure, even to the extent of dissipating the whole night long, and spending more than he could at all afford to, there would be painful household scenes. But reasonableness and love always were victors. Mozart could not bear to see a trace of tears in Constanze's eyes. The lightest pain which touched her heart made him unhappy till she was comforted. Many a time, cut to the heart by her grief, he would curse his bad habits up and down, and promise better—yes, often would promise far more than his wife asked of him.

Through light and shade the true little wife always kept a good heart and a cheery face; and was full of pranks and irresistible comicalities if she succeeded, to her joy, in keeping her husband at home by her side through the evening. With Constanze and Music, his would have been a singularly happy life had it not been for two things—his enemies, and the constant anxiety about sustenance. He was so good-natured and free-hearted, that he continually made the latter trouble greater than it need have been, by spending and giving as though he had a great treasury at his back, and then toiling like a giant to make up for it. Many a night he worked without a penny of pay, or any expectation of pay,—merely for the benefit of some acquaintance who wanted a piece of music of this sort or that. And for his friends the same thing continually happened. He would spend hours in the service of any poor travelling *virtuoso* who chanced to call upon him for assistance, composing music for their concerts, and giving them bed and board with no thought of remuneration. Base men who knew his generous heart constantly intruded upon him, *used* him, and then deserted him. Yet Mozart never lost his faith in human nature. Like an innocent and inexperienced child, he took it for granted that. every man was as noble as he himself was. Even when he had been shamefully imposed upon and basely betrayed, his indignation lasted but for a moment, and all was forgotten.

His enemies had increased in number, for in these five years he had composed many great works. And for every work of his creation there arose a group of enemies, wrought upon by envy, jealousy, or fear. He had written, besides a host of smaller pieces, an oratorio, "Davidde Penitente;" a sort of comic opera entitled the "Stage Manager;" and the fine opera, "Le Nozze de Figaro" (The Marriage of Figaro), which was the best thing he had yet done. It was brought out in Vienna, but was a failure; while at the same time a far weaker opera of Martin's, "La Cosa Rara," was a brilliant success.

The cause of "Figaro's" failure was—the snake in the grass again. Salieri—the little natty court Capellmeister, whom Mozart always jestingly called *Monsieur Bonbonnière*, because he was continually nibbling sugar-plums wherever he went—had been at work. He and his comrades bribed this singer and cajoled that one, bought up part of the orchestra and threatened the remainder, till the whole Italian opera-troupe agreed to render the new work as badly as they could. They were only too faithful to their agreement; and so murdered the music, that at the end of the second Act' Mozart hurried into the Emperor's private box, and begged him to interfere in his behalf. But the indignation of the composer and the reproof of the Emperor were equally powerless. The best passages of the opera were made farcical; and it was not till many years afterward that the work recovered from this blow in Vienna. The affair made Mozart vow never to write another opera for Vienna.

But Vienna is not the world. "Figaro" found its way to Prague, and was enthusiastically received in that city. Bondini was at the head of a fine Italian opera-troupe there, and

---

" **Figaro**" was originally in four acts. though now generally given in two.

by them the "Figaro" was successfully given almost the whole winter long. Delighted by this reception of his work, and cordially invited by Count Joseph von Thun, Mozart visited Prague. He was welcomed with the utmost cordiality. His appearance at one of the presentations of his opera was the signal for a tempest of applause from the whole house. Bondini at once urged him to write a new opera for the Prague boards; and Mozart, rejoicing at the opportunity, hastened back to Vienna to find a suitable libretto, which in those days was the chief point of difficulty with a composer: in our times it seems to be of less importance than the pretty painting and gilding of the scenery.

So it came about that, as we said at the beginning of the chapter, Mozart kissed his wife good-bye, and went out in search of a libretto.

The Abbate da Ponte (Abt Ponte), was the successor of Metastasio as court-poet. He had written several famous librettos already—among others that of Salieri's opera, "The Danaides," and that of Mozart's "Figaro." As good luck would have it, he had a new one already sketched out, which exactly suited the composer. Its subject was the history of the famous "Don Juan," and it was entitled "*Don Giovanni osia il Dissoluto Punito.*"

CHAPTER II.

THE MYSTERIOUS FLOWERS.

MOZART loved nature so well, and took such delight in the enjoyment of its charms, that every summer he hired a little country-house in the neighborhood of the city. It was a costly luxury, but he could not live without it: it seemed so to him, at least. When he could sit in his study, with the long windows into the garden thrown open, and the rich odor of the flowers came streaming in on the fresh morning-air that filled the room, how easily he could compose It was in this pleasant place that he now set to work with the utmost enthusiasm on his new opera of "Don Giovanni."

It was his custom to rise every morning at five o'clock,

usually from the lounge where he had thrown himself down after half the night spent in writing, and take a ride on horseback. It was an expensive habit; but he worked hard, and needed both the exercise and the refreshing breath of the morning. Before he left the house, he always would slip into his wife's bedchamber, and leave a light kiss on her sleeping forehead; then he would write a little note in pencil, and lay it on the stand by the bedside, that Constanze might find it there when she waked. The note was generally something like this: "Good-morning, dear little wife! I hope you have had a good sleep and pleasant dreams. I shall be back in two hours. Behave yourself like a good little girl, and don't run away from—your husband."

It needed this perfect affection between them to make their life a pleasant one in their present circumstances. If they had loved and trusted each other less, or understood each other less completely, the practical difficulties of their existence would have pressed heavily upon them. Mozart was constantly harassed by debts: Constanze was daily anxious about her husband's habits of extravagance and of late hours. Too many florins went in suppers and wines for boon companions: too many evenings were worse than wasted with gay company in the city. If he had been less pushed by work, and less tormented by debt, this would not have been; and it was Constanze's comfort, as well as her sorrow, to know that these faults were only the ruinous recoil of a terribly over-strained bow.

But now a strange thing happened. Every morning when Mozart entered his study, he found lying upon his desk by the side of his music-paper, a fresh bouquet of flowers; and the remarkable part of it was, that they were the same kinds of flowers each morning. The bouquet was invariably composed of rose-laurel and pomegranate blossoms.

The first few times Mozart laid them aside, after enjoying them for a moment, and thought no more of it, for his head was full of "Don Juan." He supposed that Constanze had laid them on his desk. But when the thing had been repeated for several days, he mentioned it to his wife, and found that neither she nor any of the household knew anything about it.

The next morning there lay the bouquet again in the same place, made up, as before, of rose-laurel and pomegranate blossoms. Neither of these grew in his little garden, so it was evidently from some one who did not live in the house. But how came it on his desk? The man and the maid both were reliable, and both swore that they never had put it there, or known anything whatever about it. It could not have been thrown in through the window, evidently, for in that case it would not be found lying in the same spot beside his music-paper, each time.

Here was an adventure, certainly. The bouquet must have some hidden meaning. Suddenly Amadeus recollected a little Italian Dictionary of Flowers which he had brought from the Uslinghi house in Rome when a boy, and with whose abstruse lore he had amused himself when there. He took it down from a corner of his bookcase, and blowing the dust off the top, turned to the word "pomegranate." It meant, "One kiss from thy lips, and I am happy!" Then he turned to "rose-laurel." Its language was, "Faithful unto death!"

Ah ha! So it was a woman in love with him, was it? Mozart was not the man to make such a discovery with indifference, especially just now when his whole nature was excited with musical creation. His imagination at once painted for him a bewitching picture of a beautiful woman, languishing in passionate love. The romance and mystery of the affair had a charm for him. The female characters of his opera, with which his brain was busy night and day, became flesh and blood to him at once, and it seemed as if the round white arm of "Donna Anna" was beckoning to him from his paper. He threw down the pen; he could compose no more that morning. He ordered his horse to be saddled at once. Then slipping into Constanze's room, he looked fondly at the dear sleeping face, left a kiss on her brow, laid a note for her on the stand to tell her he would be longer gone than usual to-day, and left the chamber on tiptoe.

He had to smile at himself as he got on his horse and rode away. He had kissed Constanze with the sincerest affection, yet here was this mysterious love-affair running away with his imagination. He was too honorable to think of concealing it from his wife, and yet too much interested not to determine that very night, if possible, to solve the riddle. So he dismissed the paradox from his mind with the thought— "I will tell Stanzerl all about it at dinner-time. She will laugh at the absurdity of the thing!"

At the dinner-table, sure enough, he told his wife that the bouquet had appeared again on his desk, and that he was certain, from the meaning of the flowers, that some woman had been silly enough to fall in love with him. Constanze laughed with him at the occurrence, but in her secret heart she made a resolution. It was, that she would outwit her rival by showing Amadeus double love, double attention, double cheerfulness, that he might not be led away from her even in his imagination.

It was a noble determination and bravely carried out. She dressed herself with extraordinary care that afternoon. It seemed to Amadeus that she never had looked so beautiful before. She was full of wit and gayety, as they sat together at the tea-table, and her ways were so winsome, and her caressing love so irresistible, that Mozart sat with her all the evening till long after his usual hour for work.

It was nearly midnight. Constanze had gone to bed an hour ago, and Amadeus was pacing up and down his study, composing in his head. The night was wonderfully beautiful. It brought back to his recollection the softness and loveliness of the nights in Italy. The heavens were full of stars, and a balmy odor arose from the flower-beds in the garden. Like wavering butterflies hovered before his mind the memories of his youth—the nights at Rome with Giuditta—the nights at Naples by the side of the proud Bernasconi. Where now was the little companion of his boyhood in that happy Roman life?

Instinctively he raised his eyes to the heavens, as if he would ask the stars. But the eternal stars glittered on, cold and still. What cared they, the eternities, for the fate of poor dust-born creatures? The heart might leap for joy, or break with pain, they remained there silent, stern, unmoved, and solemnly followed their immeasurable paths. Not from them could any answer come, nor any sympathy. But Amadeus felt that he must have something to share the rush of feelings which came over him.

He threw the window wide open to let in the air and fragrance, and took his violin from its case. Half unconsciously he breathed forth, in tender tones, the emotions of his soul. And the tones melted into the same melodies which he used to play seventeen years before, in Uslinghi's garden in Rome. But there was no Giuditta here to crown him with flower-wreaths as of old. Perhaps the beautiful Italian was no longer living—certainly she was no more a child, no more his faithful friend.

Still he played on. And now he perceives a thunder-storm
building its black cloud-towers in the west, and the tempera-
ture is changing. It becomes more sultry every moment,
and not a breath of wind stirs the air. Mozart throws open
his clothes and bares his breast, that the night may cool his
feverish blood; and as he does so, he sees Giuditta's amulet,
the little golden cross, glimmer in the starlight. He looks
at it long in silence. Twice already it has spoken to him a
warning;—once when he was erring in his love; once when
Cannabich told him, that unless he ceased to toil all night,
he would never see forty years. The first time the warning
was needed; was the second to be also fulfilled? He put
the little cross to his lips reverently, and hid it again on his
heart.

Then tremble again the strings of his instrument, and
fainter melodies breathe forth into the night, which gathers
thicker and blacker around, as the storm moves slowly up
the sky and blots out one constellation after another.

Hark! was not that a light rustling sound in the garden?
Was this the bringer of the mysterious flowers?

Quick as a flash Amadeus slipped silently out into the
garden. A little way from the house, and directly opposite
the window through which the bouquet must have found its
nightly entrance to his study, stood a little covered garden-
house. It served commonly as a shelter for the gardener's
tools, though Amadeus often took his siesta on an old sofa
which stood in it. There was a door at the front and back,
and a window on each side; so it was just the place to listen.
Mozart therefore hastened thither on tiptoe down the garden-
walk. It had become pitch-dark. There was no longer a star
visible in the cloud-roofed sky, and as a distant thunder-peal
muttered in the west, the first big rain-drops began to patter
here and there.

Just as Mozart was silently entering the door of the garden-
house, some one as noiselessly stepped out of it.

"Ah ha!" he whispered, as he clasped his arm round a
form which was not to be recognized in the darkness. "Have
I caught the mouse at last? Now we shall see—"

But the words died on his lips, for putting his other hand
on his prisoner, he felt a woman's form. He could feel that
her dress was of fine material; her hair was fragrant of some
faint perfume, her motion, as she turned away from him, betokened gracefulr ess, and her figure betrayed youth.

"Who are you, little caged bird?" whispered Amadeus.

The prisoned one answered not, though Amadeus thought he heard a repressed titter. "A good sign," thought he—"she enjoys her captivity!" Now he began to catechize her. But she made no reply, while mean time the rain poured down outside in torrents, and the thunder roared and rattled overhead.

Mozart asked no more questions; he had all he could do to overmaster the struggles of the lovely form which he held fast in his arms. His blood was kindled, his pulse beat, his limbs trembled, and now, instead of questions, he gave her kisses, which fell on burning cheeks. And—oh bliss!—now began the captive to cease her struggles, till at last she returns the kiss of the passionate maestro.

But at that moment Mozart drew back as if a thunderbolt had struck him, while a peal of laughter rang out from the prisoner. In the sudden illumination of a flash of lighting Mozart had recognized—his wife.

"For God's sake," stammered he in amazement, "how in the world, little wife, did you come *here* at *this* time?"

"May I ask the same question of my husband?" returned Constanze, but in so merry and frank a tone, that Amadeus breathed easier.

"Why," said he, "I was trying to find out who it is that brings me the bouquet!"

"Excellent!" replied Constanze; "for exactly that reason I was here too. I wanted to make things easier for my dear husband and his unknown admirer. I thought if I could only learn her name I would invite her to visit us, and then he could take his choice between us."

"Constanze!" protested Mozart.

"And," she continued gayly, putting both arms round her husband, "do you think I am so vain as to suppose that the victory would be on my side?"

"My dear, dear little Stanzerl—" began Mozart, in a pleading voice.

"Though a certain great musician and composer did say, the other morning, in a scribbled little treasure of a note, that I was a good wife—"

"Yes, that you are!" cried Mozart; "so good and so faithful that you shame your husband."

But now it was Constanze's turn to stop his mouth, which she contrived to do in a way which we will not undertake to describe.　It was still very dark, and the rain continued to pour down, but the thunder now rumbled farther off. Mozart drew his little wife down by his side on the sofa. Chatting and laughing, they no longer heeded the storm. When, after a long time, they left the garden-house, the storm had passed, and the first light of the morning glimmered over the world, which sent up its incense of vapor and odor, like a vast altar to the Eternal.

CHAPTER III.

SORCERY.

THE next morning the accustomed bunch of flowers lay in its place on Mozart's desk. It must have been put there while he and Constanze were in the garden-house. But neither of them thought of any further investigation into the mystery.　Amadeus was deep in his opera, and his wife was quietly busy in making preparations for their journey to Prague; for "Don Giovanni" being now nearly half finished, the remainder was to be done in Bohemia, whither they would go in a few days.

There was at this time a fresh sensation in Vienna.　It was a new Italian singer, Signora Mandini, who had raised an extraordinary *furore* among the highest circles, as well of the musicians as the nobility.　Not only her voice but her dazzling beauty had taken the capital by storm.　She was the very image of a noble Roman woman;—large and splendidly proportioned, with eyes dark and starry as midnight, out of whose dusky depths shone boundless possibilities of passion; with fine, abundant hair, a boldly-chiselled aquiline nose, and sensitive full lips.　Her skin had the tint of a southern clime; her form was voluptuously moulded, yet lithe as a panther, and there was a force and energy in her movements which impressed every one.　Signora Mandini was independently wealthy, for she had made a brilliant *débût* in Italy, and she had there turned the richness of her voice into more substantial riches.　Everything about the Prima-donna delighted the inhabitants of the gay capital, except her unapproachableness, which was anything but pleasant to her admirers. The proud Roman kept them all, young and old, noblemen and artists, at a respectful distance.

The Signora had received an invitation for this evening to the house of Prince Gallizin, and Mozart was among the other invited guests, since the Prince was one of his stanchest friends among the nobility. He was curious to see the new singer, for of late he had heard her praises on every side.

When he entered the house he found the company more numerous and splendid than usual, for the Emperor was expected, and in fact they only awaited his arrival to commence the musical portion of the evening. It was not to be a formal concert, for Joseph the Second, much as he loved music, had no patience with such. At his request they were to hear only a few of the most eminent artists, besides Signora Mandini.

Impatiently they were expecting the Emperor, when she herself, almost at the same moment with His Majesty, entered the room. Mozart was astonished. What a glorious woman was that!—a woman such as he never had seen, but such as he had pictured his " Donna Anna" in his fairest and boldest dreams. She wore a black satin dress, richly trimmed with black lace, its low corsage revealing the rounded shoulders and full bosom, on which a necklace of pearls rose and fell. Her face, in which there seemed to Mozart something strangely familiar, betokened a constantly repressed overflow of life, which spoke from every feature. Mozart tried in vain to recall where and when he had ever seen that face before. But he was too distant from her to see her clearly, and must wait for a nearer scrutiny.

Soon after their arrival, the Emperor approached her, and, after a few moments' conversation, requested her to sing, which she gladly consented to do.

"And who shall accompany you ?" asked Kaiser Joseph.

"Is not Maestro Mozart here ?" inquired the Signora, in the softest Italian, which was her only language.

"Certainly," answered Prince Gallizin, and gave an attendant a sign to summon the composer.

No one had noticed that, at her question concerning the maestro, a flitting color passed over the face of the beautiful Roman.

The Emperor now took the seat which had been prepared for him, the rest of the company arranged themselves about the instrument, and Mozart approached. But a hot plush flew to his face as he saw that the Signora wore in her bosom a bunch of flowers such as he had found each morning on his desk. In the centre of it were blossoms of rose-laurel and pomegranate. He knew not what to think or to say. And when the Signora greeted him almost reverently, and asked if the great master would deign to accompany her in that beautiful *aria* which he had written for the Bernasconi, and when he caught something mysteriously familiar in the voice and in the passionate look, then Mozart lost his wits entirely, and every thing around him seemed unreal. He had been bewitched by some sorcerer, who was peopling the room about him with ghosts and shadows.

The Mandini remained perfectly calm and self-possessed, only the little smile about her mouth seemed to be increased by his perplexity. It was all a thing of a few moments; for the Emperor and all the company were waiting for them. Mozart seated himself at the piano, and with the first chord which his nervous hands struck from the keys, he was himself again. He played with his usual perfect skill, and the Mandini sang gloriously. Again and again the Emperor asked them for one more piece, and each time their performance was more delightful. Each of them seemed determined to excel the other in their perfect rendering of the music. Never had the audience heard anything finer; and when they had ended, all agreed with the Emperor's judgment, that the impression should not be weakened by any other music that night.

Mozart would gladly have had a few words with the Signora in private, that he might solve the mystery of the bouquet and of the familiar look in her face. But shortly after her singing she had disappeared, and Mozart cared no longer to remain.

Lost in deep thought, he descended the marble steps into the hall. So absorbed was he with his own reflections that he took no notice when a servant in livery motioned to the street as soon as he appeared, and a carriage drove up before the door. Accustomed as he was to go and return from such *soirées* in a carriage, he quietly allowed himself to be shown to a seat. The door was shut, and the horses started at full speed.

Not till the carriage stopped, and he perceived on alighting that he stood before a strange house, did he come to his senses.

"How is this?" he cried; "where have you taken me to? Don't you know where I live, any longer?"

But instead of the familiar livery of the Prince's servants, a stranger silently but respectfully held open for him a little gate.

"Well!" cried Mozart; "has everybody gone mad to night? I suppose you mistook me for your master."

"No!" answered the servant, in Italian. "Will your Excellency please to enter?"

"What Excellency? I am Capellmeister Mozart!"

The servant nodded assent—"Maestro Mozart."

"And whose household are you of?"

The Italian put his hand in his breast and reached out to Mozart the well-known bunch of flowers.

"Signora Mandini?" asked he in astonishment.

"Si, Signore."

"And you are a servant of the Signora?"

"Si, Signore."

"Perhaps you have carried such bouquets before?"

The servant nodded assent.

"To whom?"

"To Maestro Mozart."

"And what have you brought me here for? Who is Signora Mandini?" cried Amadeus, hardly knowing whether he was awake or dreaming.

But the Italian made a deprecatory gesture, as if he dared not answer further. Then he said, respectfully—

"Follow me, Maestro, and you will understand."

Mozart mechanically obeyed, as if still in the sorcerer's power. Only one thought was clear to him, and that was one which made him almost giddy: it was the beautiful Mandini who had sent him those morning messengers of love!

But, how came the Mandini to know him so soon after coming to Vienna? For she had hardly been there two days before the flower-bunches began to be laid upon his desk—those eloquent blossoms! "One kiss from thy lips, and I am happy!" and, "Faithful unto death!"

Mozart followed rapidly the Italian, who led the way through a long and dimly-lighted passage. They were apparently coming out somewhere in the rear of a great building. At last he stopped, opened a door, and motioned to Mozart to enter.

It was a large deserted room, whose damp and mouldering atmosphere betokened that it had been for a long time un-used. The tapestry was torn in many places and covered with thick dust : the furniture was old and worn.

Mozart started in surprise.

"What am I to do here?" he asked his guide, almost sternly.

"Nothing, Maestro," answered he quietly. "Go on a little farther : in the third apartment you will find your destina-tion."

"Shall I find the Signora there?"

"Si, Signore."

But what was his amazement when now he entered the third apartment !

"Am I dreaming, or awake?" he cried out, passing one hand over his brow; for he found himself in a wild grotto. It was artificially arranged, as he saw at once, with ramifica-tions in several directions. A dusky twilight increased the mystery of its appearance.

This grotto, also, seemed familiar to him. As he peered into its dim recesses, a wonderful dawn brightened in his soul, ever clearer and clearer !

"It is she !" he cried out with almost childish pleasure— "It is she ! There stands the altar with the statue of Saint Cecilia ! and there the mossy bank on which I sat with Giu-ditta !"

Scarcely had he spoken the name, when, putting his hand in perplexity to his forehead, and staring into vacancy with wide-open eyes, he suddenly saw through the veil of mystery. The image of the lovely Giuditta mingled in his imagination with that of the Mandini.

"By all the saints !" he cried, smiting his hands together, "it *was* her form, her mouth, her eyes—it was her very self !"

At that instant a voice began a song. It was the same melody which had wakened him so joyfully from his dreams in the grotto seventeen years before ! He cried out exult-antly—"Giuditta !" And she lay in his arms—his first love, his guardian angel, the beautiful Roman; but now a ripe mature woman—the glorious Mandini herself !

CHAPTER IV.

THE THREE LIONS.

A HUGE lumbering coach, covered with dust, and piled with baggage, drew up before the door of the "Three Lions" inn, at Prague. The big bell over the entrance, tugged at by the stout arm of the "Boots," rang out a loud signal, in response to which there hastened down the steps two porters and a plump little landlord, with twinkling black eyes and a fresh fat face. No sooner had the latter let down the steps of the coach than he cried out joyfully—

"By the holy Saint Nepomuck! 'Tis Herr von Mozart!"

"Yes, here I am again," replied Amadeus, leaping out, with a merry face, and shaking hands heartily with the landlord. "And lest I should be too disorderly, I've brought my wife with me this time."

"Good! good!" cried mine host, and reached both hands out to Constanze with such hearty good-nature, that she took them laughing. "You are welcome, Madam. As for Herr von Mozart, I needn't tell him whether he's welcome or not. He knows well enough that all Prague is glad to see him— yes, and all Bohemia, for that matter!"

"And now can you give us a couple of rooms?" asked Mozart, clapping the landlord on the shoulder. "I promised Duscheck to finish my opera in his pleasant summer-house, but I don't like to overrun him for quite so long, and we'll stay with you for the first week."

"You do me honor," said the landlord, much pleased; but—," and he rubbed his ear in perplexity.

"Well, what's the matter?" asked Mozart, as he helped Constanze out of the coach.

"Why didn't the Herr von Mozart write beforehand?"

"Your Lions' den isn't full of Daniels, is it?"

"Oh no! But the best rooms are engaged for some time ahead."

"To whom?"

"That I don't know. They are coming to-day."

"But these mysterious guests haven't engaged the whole house, have they?"

"No—"

"Well, then, old friend, let us have a couple of rooms at once."

"If they are only clean," added Constanze, "we shall do very well, I don't doubt."

"That takes a stone off my heart!" cried the host, and his friendly face lit up again; "for if the Herr von Mozart and his beautiful wife had been angry, I should have—"

"Bolted three bottles of wine and a capon!" said Amadeus, laughing.

Then they followed the landlord, as he trotted on ahead to their apartments. They were on the first floor of the inn, and next to the so-called state apartments, which, as we have seen, were already engaged. On the left side was a pretty little bedroom for Madam Mozart: then a large parlor; and opening from this, a study and bedroom for the Herr, her husband. The latter room was connected by a door with the state apartments, but against the door stood a table, and it was bolted on the other side. Every thing wore an aspect of neatness and good taste, and in each of the bedrooms hung a picture of the ubiquitous St. Nepomuck, without which no good Bohemian could enjoy a sound sleep.

Mozart was more than contented with the rooms. The arrangement just suited him.

"Only," said he, "we must have a piano in here; but Bondini will see to that."

Frau Mozart was equally well pleased, but she at once began to make some silent and troubled calculations as to the probable cost of such extensive lodgings. For a week they could have got along well enough with two rooms. But she had not the heart to lessen the friendly landlord's respect for them, by suggesting that these rooms would be too expensive for their purse.

The sharp little eyes of mine host spied out the economical housewife, however, in Constanze's anxious countenance, and shrewdly inferred the state of affairs. Little as he favored economy in his guests, this was an exception. The lord of the Lions could once in a while afford to be generous. So rubbing his hands contentedly, he said, with a beaming face—

"Most honored Madam, I feel ready to cut my head off that I can't give you my best rooms; but these—"

"Are abundantly good enough," said Constanze. "Two rooms would have answered for us."

"Impossible!" exclaimed mine host, bowing his bald head delightedly. "It couldn't be thought of! I know how the Herr von Mozart must live, from the last time he was here. He'll be up and down, composing all night long, and needs his own chamber therefore. Ladies mustn't be disturbed by such goings on.. And as for the parlor—oh, you'll have visitors enough, you may be sure! And besides," added he in a whisper, but with such overflowing good-nature that Constanze could not be vexed at him—"besides, dear Madam, I take into account the honor which such guests do me; and you shall pay no more for this suite than for two rooms in the second story!"

Just then the big bell announced a second coach before the door. It was a handsome equipage, drawn by six fine horses, but the windows were closely shut. The landlord and porters went out to receive the travellers, and a footman in livery got down from behind the carriage. But instead of letting down the steps and opening the door, he asked the landlord—

"Can speak Italian?"

"Bah!" he replied; "we are in Prague. Speak either German or Bohemian!"

The Italian shook his head, and taking a note from his breast-pocket, handed it to the landlord. The contents produced an immediate change of expression in the now beaming face of the plump host. The note was in the handwriting of a well-known banker of Vienna, and these were the occupants of his state apartments.

"Will it please their Excellencies to alight?" he asked, with a respectful bow.

"Si, Signore!" replied the Italian, as he opened the carriage-door.

The landlord and his satellites opened their eyes wide with curiosity to see who were within; but they got small satisfaction, for there stepped quickly out a tall lady clothed in black and thickly veiled, followed by a veiled maid, and both hastened into the inn with the Italian servant, to take possession of their apartments.

"And who is your mistress?" asked the host, curiously when the servant came back to see to the baggage.

The Italian seemed not to hear the question.

"My good friend," repeated mine host with some dignity, "may I have the pleasure of knowing the name of your mistress?"

"Si, Signore!" said the Italian quietly.

"Who is she?"

"Si, Signore!"

"What the devil!" cried the landlord, in anger; "dcn't you hear me? I want to know your mistress's name and rank!"

"Si, Signore!"

Mine host of the Lions lost all patience. Good-natured as he was, he would have liked to give this yellow-visaged knave in livery a sound box on the ear. But he manfully restrained himself, and turned away with the disgusted exclamation—

"He is an ass!"

"Si, Signore!" replied the Italian, and calmly went on unpacking the luggage.

Meantime Mozart and his wife had gone to call upon the Impressario Bondini, director of the Prague opera. But he was, unfortunately, out.

"Then we will go and see Capellmeister Strobach," said Amadeus, turning to Constanze; "and you will find him a splendid man."

But the Herr Capellmeister also was out.

"Then," said Mozart, cheerfully taking Constanze's arm in his again, "we will go and find Kucharz, the orchestra-conductor."

But bad luck seemed to attend their visits: Kucharz was away with Bondini!

"The fates seem to have determined," said Amadeus, laughing, "that, like some great potentates, we shall remain *incognito* to-day. All right! Then I shall show my Stanzerl the town."

Constanze was glad enough to exchange the dreaded calls for a walk, as her limbs were stiff with riding so long in the coach; and besides, she wanted to see the fine city which her husband had described to her so often.

Arm in arm they wandered through the streets, while the twilight gradually came down upon the land and threw its veil over the town, which looked still more impressive in the dim light, with its forty-eight churches, fifteen cloisters, nine synagogues, fifty-four public squares, and sixty-eight palaces.

By the time they had returned from visiting the famous bridge, with its many statues, and the costly tomb where St. Nepomuck lies in his solid silver coffin, it was dark, and they sought the "Three Lions."

"Stanzerl!" exclaimed Mozart, as they drew near the inn, "there is somebody in our rooms; I see lights there and shadows moving!"

"It is probably the maid putting things in order for the night," replied Constanze.

When they approached the gate they saw a servant, who had been watching for them apparently, turn and run up the steps.

"The old Lions' den," said Mozart gayly, "seems to have acquired a taste for mysteries to-day."

As they entered the hall, they stood still in surprise. On each side of their parlor-door stood a servant with a light, which threw its beams on wreaths of foliage and flowers above the entrance. There stood the little chubby landlord, his face lit up like a full moon, and his black eyes twinkling with delight; and as he rubbed his hands and hopped from one foot to the other, he cried gleefully—

"Welcome, Herr von Mozart! welcome to our good town of Prague!"

Then the door was flung open, and a chorus of merry voices shouted, "Welcome to Prague!"

Mozart recognized them all immediately; and, carried away with pleasure at the surprise, he embraced Bondini and his little wife, then Strobach, Kucharz, the basso Luigi Bassi, and half a dozen others.

In the middle of their parlor a table had been set, and now was awaiting them with a fine supper. Flanking each plate was a flask of wine, and the dishes were prettily trimmed with flowers. Mozart no sooner caught sight of these bountiful preparations, than he clapped his hands and gave a little shout of jubilation. "We will make a night of it!" he cried.

Constanze was not so well pleased. Much as she enjoyed this cordial reception of her husband, and cordially as she sympathized in his enjoyment of it, her wise little head at once began to figure up the cost of such a supper, with its tall flasks of choice wine. Amadeus had been obliged to borrow money in order to come to Prague at all, and how long would it take for such entertainments as this to use up in advance all the proceeds of the new opera! But mine host of the "Lions" was again her good angel. Ostensibly by accident, he took occasion to let drop the fact that it was all at Bondini's expense, and that Mozart's "Figaro" had made Bondini quite a rich man.

Constanze was much relieved to hear this, and all her natural gayety at once came back to her; and soon she and Bondini's sprightly little wife were having a great frolic in ornamenting her bedroom.

The supper was excellent, the wine of prime quality, and the company wide-awake with life and good-humor. Mozart was brimming with wit and fun, and only regretted the absence of his good friend Duscheck, who happened to be out of town.

The conversation soon fell upon his new work, and Luigi Bassi, for whom Mozart intended the *rôle* of "Don Juan," was eager to know what the name of the opera was to be, and its character. But Mozart gayly replied, holding out his glass for Bondini to fill with the foaming champagne—

"Never you mind, Bassi! the devil will get hold of you soon enough—only wait!"

"Maestro!" cried Bondini, with comical pathos, "you don't mean to bring the Old Serpent on to the boards?"

"I sha'n't tell you!" answered Amadeus. "But I've got a libretto—*such* a libretto! Abt Ponte wrote it for nobody but me, he said; because no one else had courage enough for it. It is a daring, fiery thing—you shall see! In 'Idomeneus' and 'Figaro' I did not snit myself. You know how it would be if the spring-time ought to come, and would be glad to come, but could not;—on all the bushes and trees sit millions of buds, but they are shut up, waiting; then suddenly comes a shower—the thunder calls out, 'Flowers to the front!'—a warm May-rain streams down, and everything breaks into bloom! The devil take me if that was not just my case when 'he little Abbate handed me the libretto!"

"And who takes the principal *rôle?*" asked Bassi.

"You, Luigi!" said Mozart. "You are the hero, and the devil will get you, sure enough!"

After a little more urging and a little more champagne, the secret pressed too hard for outlet; so taking a schedule of the parts of "Don Giovanni" from his pocket-book, he handed them to Bondini and Bassi for inspection. But to his surprise the *basso* did not seem wholly pleased with his part.

"It is fine—very fine!" he replied, when questioned by Amadeus; "but, my dear Maestro, these *arias* are a little too plain and easy for me."

"Do you think so?" asked the composer, smiling.

"Yes; -and too short—are they not, Maestro? Why not write me a real long hard *aria;* or give me one which you have already written; won't you?"

"Not I!" said Mozart, with a mocking smile, and shaking his head. "These airs are not very long, that is true; but they are just exactly as long as they should be. As for their difficulty, I think you will find your hands full if you sing them as they should be sung."

Bassi's face lengthened perceptibly, and he replied ironically, "Do you think so?"

Then Mozart sprang up and opened the piano, which had been brought in during his walk with Constanze, and called out to the singer: "Come, try this air for instance—*Fin chan dal vino calda la testa!*"

He struck the first chord, and the *basso* began the *aria,* rather unwillingly.

"Softly, softly!" cried Mozart, laughing, and stopping him after the first two measures. "Not so furiously over stock and stone! Can't you wait for the end of my music, you love it so well? If I write *presto,* must you needs sing it *prestissimo* —and have you no respect at all for *piano* and *forte?*"

Every one laughed except Luigi himself; and Mozart continued, with a serio-comic earnestness—

"Who do you suppose is singing this *aria*—eh? It isn't a tipsy Dutch burgher, but a Spanish cavalier, whose mind is on his lady-love rather than his liquor, and whose song is to help him win her. Come, now! toss off a glass of champagne, think of your mistress once, and then—hark! How it begins to hum in your ears, in the lightest, airiest *tempo; piano—piano! crescendo—forte—piano!* till at last every thing rings with it in a *fortissimo!* That's the way I want it done!"

And Bassi, inspired by the enthusiasm of the great master, drained a glass of champagne, stole a kiss from the fair Saporitti, and sang the solo with such effect that the whole company shouted their applause.

"What do you think now?" asked Mozart, turning round with a beaming face, after he had put Bassi through his solo three times.

"Maestro!" said the singer, almost with reverence, "I will do the best that is in me to sing it as it deserves to be sung."

The gayety was kept up to a late hour. Even Constanze, urged on by Bondini's little wife, became quite riotous, and almost equalled that merry soul in her unrestrained wit and laughter. Mozart himself seemed wholly given over to the wildest puns and a reckless profusion of rhymes,—always the surest sign with him of complete enjoyment. Not till midnight did the company separate, with a great shaking of hands, kisses, and laughter.

When all had departed, Amadeus accompanied his wife to her bedroom. He was so excited, and they both had so many things to say, that he threw himself into an easy-chair while she disrobed. They chatted for a long time, till Amadeus stopped her mouth with a kiss, bade her good-night, and went to his own room.

But in such a nature as Mozart's the tossing waves are not easily calmed down, when once aroused. He could neither write nor sleep as yet; so he went to the window, and stood there gazing out into the starlight, while he drummed on the window-panes with his fingers, as if he were at the piano. A confusion of thoughts whirled through his brain.

What a bright day he had passed! And with to-day's experiences mingled those of his whole past life;—his brilliant boyhood—his romantic youth—the meeting again with Giuditta, which linked together the past and the present in such a wonderful chain!

Had she not confessed to him that, from the first moment of seeing him, she had given him her heart? Had she not told him how it was her love for him, and the hope of thus meeting him again, that induced her to go upon the stage — that it was this hope which alone had urged her on, through every toil and difficulty, till she could stand, where she now stood, as Prima-donna—that this passionate hope had driven her from her beloved Italy, far over the Alps into the cold clime of Germany?

And he? He confessed to himself that he had loved her passionately—that he loved her still! Not with the same love which he felt for Constanze—that was something holier, nobler, less tainted with the love of self and of pleasure : that was love, respect, and reverence, all in one! But he knew in his soul that he still felt for Giuditta the same strange overmastering passion as of old.

He was almost giddy with his thronging recollections and the conflicting thoughts that filled his brain. Still his fingers went on drumming upon the window-panes, so loudly and fiercely that the glass was near being shattered. Wherefore? Only because something rang in his soul that sounded like reproof. This passion—*need* it be overmastering? Had he not honor, and the will of a man? Then the melody hummed itself at his ears—"*Fin chan dal vino calda la testa,*" and he thought, "What is life worth unless one taste the cup of its pleasures?" As many a time before, the dark presage of an early death passed over him like the shadow of a mighty wing; and, as out of the grave, he seemed to hear a voice that said: "Woe to thee, fool! if thou pluck not the blossoms speedily! The dead and empty hours will be jeering ghosts to mock and dance about thy coffin!"

Suddenly there was the click and tinkle of broken glass— he had drummed the pane till it flew in pieces, while he whistled between his teeth the "*Fin chal dal vino.*"

At the same instant a warm breath touched his cheek. He turned swiftly around, a soft arm was clasped about him, and with a whispered "Amadeo!" the beautiful head of the Mandini sank upon his breast.

He knew no longer where or who he was—the air was in a dizzy whirl of fantastic spirits—the walls, the shivered glass, the furniture, eddied about him, mingled with a swarm of mocking goblins. Was it the ghost of Don Juan that was avenging itself upon him? He knew not, for his senses were reeling under the burning kisses of Giuditta.

When he came to himself and looked around him, every thing was in its proper position in the room, except the table which had stood against the door leading into the state apartments. That had been moved to one side.

CHAPTER V.

PASSION AND LOVE.

DUSCHECK had returned to Prague, and would not hear of Mozart's remaining any longer at the "Three Lions." So he removed at once to his friend's spacious mansion, to stay until his opera was finished. Mine host of the inn was very much cast down at losing his honored guest, but it had been the experience of his life that the brightest birds always flew away soonest, and he was philosophically resigned to the loss. What was his surprise and consternation, however, when, the very next day after the departure of the Mozarts, the mysterious occupant of his state apartments left the inn also, her maid rewarding the good-nature and attentiveness of their host so far as to explain to him that her mistress had hired a country-seat in the vicinity of the town.

It was too much for the good landlord's philosophy; he could only shake his round head, and lean on alternate shoulders against the doorway, in a state of bewilderment. It would have been too much for his good-nature also, except for the generous roll of shining ducats which the veiled lady had given him to console his disappointment at her departure. Her gift had amounted to five times his dues, and the solid new gold pieces had the effect to save his trust in human nature from utter ruin.

Mozart was delightfully situated at his old friend's house. Besides the pleasant rooms which were assigned to himself and Constanze in one of the wings of the mansion, Duscheck had fitted up a pretty summer-house, which stood at the end of the garden, for his use as a study. He had here his writing-desk and the fine piano which Bondini provided for him, as well as a bed where he might sleep whenever he was over-weary at his nightly labor. The door and the two long windows of his little music-house opened into the pretty garden, which was kept in fairy-like beauty, and was delicious with all manner of sweet shrubs and flowers. Here, breathing the balm-breath of nature, inspired alternately by the golden flood of sunshine that poured in at the long window, and by tl e starlight that held all the earth in silent enchantment beneath it, he devoted much of the night and a good part of each day to " Don Giovanni."

All about him, strewing the desk and floor, were his manuscripts; sheets of music-paper half filled, beginnings of unfinished *arias*, fragmentary bits of orchestral parts, dashed down and abandoned—a chaos to any eye but his own. Carefully laid in a drawer, however, were the finished portions of the opera, to which was added, day after day, a fresh sheet or a succession of such, as the work went on.

No one ever entered this summer-house but Mozart himself; not even Constanze, for she knew well that her orderly hand would only bring disorder into that apparent confusion of papers, and her presence while her husband was at work, however it might delight him, could not but slacken the composer's flying pen. " No one?" Yes, there was one exception.

The early evening, after tea, Mozart always gave up to his wife and the household of his old friend Duscheck. Either they sat in the pleasant drawing-room and chatted or sang together, or Constanze would entice her husband out for a walk in the quiet streets, where the bustle of the day was ended, and the gayety of the night had not yet begun.

Every evening at this time, as soon as it was dusk, a little gate in the rear of Duscheck's garden was carefully opened, and a man's form, lithe and subtile in its motions as only an Italian could be, slipped stealthily across the garden, and entered the summer-house. Seating himself at Mozart's desk, and drawing a little dark-lantern from beneath his cloak, he threw its circle of light upon a sheet of music-paper which he spread before him. Then opening the drawer where lay the finished leaves of " Don Giovanni," he hurriedly took out the pages which had been latest written, and swiftly copied them note for note. After a rapid comparison of his copy with the original manuscript, the latter was carefully replaced, the drawer shut, and the wary form noiselessly disappeared. Night after night this was repeated. Little did Mozart dream, as the opera drew near completion, that some one besides himself had a copy of the music. How would his heart have beat if he had known who was sharing his thoughts and emotions as, day by day, they crystallized into the music of " Don Giovanni !"

Meanwhile the veiled guest, whose sudden departure from

the inn had given such a shock to the chubby landlord's comfortable philosophy of life, was established in a pretty country-seat near Prague. It was a small but elegantly furnished house, built in the Italian style, and with gardens and conservatories which recalled as far as possible the luxuriant life of the South.

It was the afternoon of a bright autumn day. The sun was setting red and fiery, as if it already were battling with the approaching winter, and its last level rays blazed on the glass roofs of the conservatories behind the little country-seat, and burned on the ripening oranges that hung inside. In the drawing-room the Mandini was pacing up and down like a caged leopard.

"I am nearly wild with loneliness and this tedious life!" she exclaimed, in Italian.

"Yes, it is always tedious and lonely here!" answered her maid, in the same tongue. "Till lately we could at least count the falling leaves for amusement, but now, the Madonna preserve us! the trees stand there cold and naked, stretching out their dry arms in despair toward the gray heavens!— Ah! Signora, how beautiful our Italy is!"

"It is beautiful, Antonia," said the Mandini, "only where the Beloved is!"

"Then let us take him to Rome with us!" cried the maid, with a deep sigh; "for there Paradise is, for you, and we can forever leave this wearisome, cold Germany!"

Giuditta turned from the window where she had been standing. Her eyes were moist, but under their drooping lids burned a smouldering fire, and her voice was thick and tremulous with passion, as she replied:

"Have I not told you often enough, Antonia, that you must never speak to me of Italy?"

"And wherefore, Signora? Is it not home?"

"Because my love for Italy is the rival of my love for Amadeo! You know it, Antonia! You know what it cost me to break away from my fatherland. But the longing after my Beloved—my life's star—my Art's high-priest—was stronger even than the cords that bound me to our Italy, the beautiful! I could not resist that deeper longing; I must see Amadeo again—must be near him—must have his music in my heart and on my lips. It has been accomplished—I am happy—but the wound still burns. Need you keep it always open?"

"Ah, Signora!" said Antonia, bitterly; "I am not so happy as to have a German lover."

"I understand the taunt," replied Giuditta, haughtily.

"It is easy for the Signora," went on Antonia,—"the Mandini, who in Rome, in Naples, in Milan, had princes at her feet,—who was worshipped by men like the fiery young Marquis Calabritta, or the rich and powerful Cardinal Cosmi,—who—"

"Who remained cold as the snow to each and all of them!" interrupted the Signora; "and came to Germany to find a friend,—not so young and fiery as the handsome Marquis—not so rich and powerful as the Cardinal,—who is no prince and no Italian; but is he to whom the Mandini is indebted for all she is and all she has, and who towers above all mortal men in his creative genius!"

"Yet 'tis the man, not the composer, that you love!" said Antonia, overawed by the passionate tone of her mistress.

"I love both in Maestro Amadeo; yes, I worship Art in him, its master," said the Signora. "It was his music that reached out its arms across the Alps, and drew me to follow him. But you do not understand me. Let us leave the subject."

And Signora Mandini seated herself at the piano, and sang that recitative of Donna Anna's in the first Act of "Don Giovanni," "*Padre! caro Padre!*" and her rich and passionate voice seemed seeking to calm her wild unrest by its expression in tones.

It was in truth not the man alone that Giuditta loved in Mozart, it was the artist and the art. Soon after his departure from Italy her parents had both died, and her thoughts, ever fixed steadily on Amadeus, her one love in the wide earth, turned naturally to music. To enter his world, the realm of tones, was her only hope of meeting him again, or of joining her life to his—even invisibly and afar off, if it must needs be so. With unwearied diligence she set herself to the study of her art. Year after year she toiled, alone, without encouragement, without any human aid, save the inspiration of Mozart's compositions and her passionate love and longing to climb nearer to him up the heights on which he was sitting crowned.

After years of labor, of poverty, of discouragement, of God knows what temptations and trials, she made her way to the first place on the Italian stage. Under the assumed name of Mandini she surpassed every rival singer, and won

her laurels as the acknowledged prima-donna of Italy. But
't was a lonely and barren victory so long as the Alps lay
between her and her beloved master, towering up to part
them like the fate which must forever separate their lives.
Enemies beset her path at every step in her fatherland.
A splendid woman, ravishing all Italy as well by her voice
as her voluptuous beauty, yet whose heart, like hers, was cold
as ice to all around her, and only burned steadily upward in
its own absorbing worship, could not but have enemies.
The presumptuous love that was constantly offered her by
artists and nobility, repulsed and scorned as it always was,
turned to the bitterest hatred.

Here at last, in Bohemia, she lived in perfect retirement
and *incognito ;* near enough her beloved to know his daily
life, to watch him when he little suspected her vicinity, to
live upon the breath of his music as he created it, day after
day. She had known that he was married, long before she
left Italy ; but this scarcely separated them farther than they
already seemed before, to her ;—she, the forgotten, unthought
of, lonely Roman girl ; he, the great master, upon the far-off
throne of his art. And when at last they met again, in
Vienna, and she fell upon his breast, and knew that he gave
her passion as of old, she knew as well—and oh, how bitterly !—
that his love he could no longer give.

Giuditta was no saint : she would have braved earth and
hell to have Amadeus wholly to herself. She sometimes
hated Constanze with a burning, pitiless hatred, that would
gladly have burst in upon them in their chamber and stabbed
her in his arms. Yet neither was Giuditta a fiend : she could
pity as well as hate ; she could put her own will under her
feet, as well as that of others. She would not have broken
Constanze's heart, even to hold Amadeus in her arms ; nor
would she tempt the husband to be a liar and a betrayer in
his own household. He had been given to another : her life
had been destined to be barren of his love ; and she bent
before the decree, if not submissively, yet with a proud
loyalty to the fate which issued it.

Her passion was earthly, but her art was divine ; and the
love that was half worship of the art and half burning desire
for its master, laid hold, therefore, both of earth and heaven.
Had it been all heavenly, Giuditta would have held herself
forever aloof from a man to whose honor her very presence
was a temptation. As it was, she felt that she could not

live unless she sometimes met him face to face, and touched him, and for a moment held his eyes in her own.

And Amadeus—? He was very busy with his opera—his thoughts were deep in the concluding Act of "Don Giovanni." Yet he was not ignorant of what was in the Mandini, or what was in himself. When he met her, the present was whirled away as upon the rush of a flooded river; he was young again in Italy, and life was all rose-bloom, and upon his breast lay a beautiful Roman girl—it was Giuditta! He reasoned thus: Was the heart so narrow that it must hold but one? Could he not have a friend as well as a wife? Had not this Italian woman been the one friend of his boyhood, the guardian-angel of his youth? Above all, did not her passionate love, her long devotion, deserve anything in return? Yes! It would be dastardly to treat as an enemy one who held him almost as a god! She should be his friend. It was the eternal boyhood in him which claimed her still. Constance was his wife: *that* he would never forget!

Amadeus was sitting in his little summer-house, this evening. "Don Giovanni" was finished, excepting the overture; and the master, his great work now done, sat improvising at the piano, expressing his happiness in wild and changeful music. His themes were all from the new opera, for his brain was still ringing with it; but he handled them in fantastic variations, mingling the airs, and weaving them into new fancies as the humor took him. There was no light in the room, except the moonbeams that shone all about him and lay white on the keys of the piano. It was a mild evening, one of those dreamy delicious nights that only come in early autumn, when the moonlight is dim and the wind is only a succession of languid sighs. The door of the summer-house was wide open: everything was still and silent, even in the mansion at the other end of the garden, for Constanze and the Duschecks had gone to a concert together.

While Amadeus played on, his imagination was busy with the characters of his opera, as he tossed its music to and fro under his rapid fingers. He felt their presence all about him in the room. Had he not heard them enter at the door behind him, when the wind softly rustled the leaves; and seen their flitting forms, as now and then the shadow of a moving bough stirred on the floor? It would scarcely have startled him to hear their voices mingle with the tones of the piano.

Suddenly, from a swift tangle of capricious chords, he struck into that *duettino* in the third Act of " Don Giovanni," *La ci darem la mano*, humming the part in his light sweet tenor, when—hark!   Soft and tremulous as a song-bird's throat, arose in the room the answering part of Zerlina— *Vorrei, e non vorrei mi tremaun poco il cor.*   Amadeus ceased not, but his fingers grew colder than the keys on which they fell, and his heart beat thick and fast with awe. The voice went on, richer and fuller now, till again he took up the tenor in his clear tones; and still he played the accompaniment ever lighter and more *staccato*, as though he were striking it upon the white moonlight rather than the keys beneath.   And then the two voices went on together through the duett—hers tremulous with passion, his almost shrill, though so faint, as if an icicle pendent in the burning sunlight—till they ceased in the final repetition of " *Andiam!*" " *Andiam!*"

She had flung herself down at his side, sobbing, with one arm across his knees, and her beautiful head bowed down against him.   His hands left not the cold keys—they dared not: still they sought out faintest harmonies.   At last she turned her face up toward his own, her dark eyes glittering with tears in the moonlight.

"Amadeo!" her lips said, rather than her voice.   " *Maestro—*"

" Giuditta !" he answered, looking down at the proud imploring face, and a shiver passed through his limbs.

" I knew it was finished," she went on.   " You did not think I was stealing it page by page!   And I could live no longer without seeing you.   It has been so long!   Amadeo, I should have died without your music !"

" Say not so, child !"

" Ha !" she said, with a wild laugh, " 'Say not so !'   'Tis the cool German in you that spoke that.   The heart beats calmer here, and perhaps one dies not so easily as in our fiery Italy.   And yet, Amadeo, you are so much an Italian !"

"Do you think so ?"

" Do you not love Italy ?"

" Yes, 'tis a glorious land !"

" Shall you never go back there ?"

" How gladly would I !" replied Amadeus, and the fervent tone betrayed how deeply he felt it.

"Oh, *Maestro !*" cried Giuditta, springing up with a sud

den throb of hope in her heart, "come back, then, with me !"

"And my wife—?" asked Amadeus, slowly and earnestly, his hands still wandering among the keys.

"Why must you remind me?" she answered, and her face again sank in her hands. Then flinging one fierce arm about his neck, she turned his face upward, and pressed kiss after kiss upon his brow, his eyes, his mouth. For an instant his brain reeled, but his hands left not the cold keys, and with one mighty effort he held his will firmly as in a giant's grip.

"Giuditta !" he said ; and this time the low, thrilling tone smote her with awe, and her hands again covered her face.

"Child ! for God's sake leave me, spare me—spare yourself ! We have our Art—give thanks to Heaven that this is left to bind our lives together."

"You love me not !" broke in Giuditta. "You never loved me !"

Amadeus took one trembling hand from the piano, and as though it had been the hand of another man, he reached it to his breast, and took out the little golden cross and held it up in the moonlight. Then replacing it reverently, he began playing again—softly, lightly, as if it were the dripping dew, freezing as it fell.

There was a faint rustle as of some one departing—a smothered sob that came back from the midst of the garden, such a sound as must haunt one forever—and all was again still.

The tones of the piano were hushed also. The master had crossed his arms on the instrument before him, and his head was bowed upon them, silent and motionless.

An hour afterward—a thousand years it seemed to him— Amadeus felt a gentle arm put over his shoulder, a cool soft cheek lay upon his own, and the fresh lips kissed him which he knew so well.

"Oh, Stanzerl—darling little wife !" he cried, springing up joyfully, and taking her in his arms.

"I thought I might come to-night, for I knew the opera was all done," said Constanze.

"Yes, it is over, thank God !" said Amadeus. "I am very, very glad you came !"

"I came in as still as I could, to see if you were asleep Were you dreaming of me ?"

"I was dreaming—I always dream : God grant that I may always find you when I wake !"

CHAPTER VI.

THE GRAND REHEARSAL.

THE day had arrived for the first grand rehearsal of Don Giovanni. Mozart was in extraordinary spirits. As soon as he was awake in the morning, he commenced to sing the different parts; and as he dressed himself, he walked about, knocking his heels together, and seeing the whole opera produced in his head. At breakfast he was full of gayety, and treated Constanze to a great entertainment of nonsense and rhymes. He improvised an imaginary account, in doggerel, of the mishaps which would attend the rehearsal: how Donna Anna would have a terrible cold, and little Madam Bondini the toothache, and Bassi would stamp off the stage in dudgeon, and the first violin would be half a tone below the pitch, and the *adagios* would all go *prestissimo*, till at last the company should be driven mad and fling the composer out of the theatre, neck and heels.

But in reality, these or other similar terrors of a Capellmeister before rehearsal disturbed Mozart very little. He knew the excellence of the Prague orchestra, composed as it was of distinguished artists, and that every one of the singers was as much bound up in the success of the opera, and as enthusiastic about it, as he was himself.

As he entered the theatre, beaming faces met him on all sides, and for each he had a jest or a friendly word. Bondini embraced him heartily, and in return therefor Mozart gave a kiss to the Director's sprightly little wife.

"Little woman!" he said to her at the same time, "I believe there couldn't be found on the earth a more perfect Zerlina than you, in looks and action."

The overture had not yet been written, so the rehearsal must begin with Signore Ponziani's solo, "*Notte e giorno faticar*," as Leporello.

The baton of the maestro descended, and the music began.

"Where are you going?" asked the box-keeper, at that moment, of a veiled woman who was advancing behind the outer row of seats toward the side of the theatre. She made no answer, but pointed toward the curtained box next the stage.

The man now recognized her. It was the same lady, clothed in black, who so often engaged this box, especially at Mozart's concerts, or when the "Figaro" was given. He had received positive instructions to admit no one to the rehearsal, and he was about to announce this respectfully to the lady, when he felt something slip into his hand. Instinctively he held it up to the lamp-light, which flickered dimly in the rear of the theatre, and lo! it was a shining ducat.

Neither of them spoke a word further, but they understood each other so well that the door of the box was immediately opened, very softly and carefully, and the veiled lady noiselessly entered unseen by any one.

The rehearsal meanwhile went on, much to Mozart's satisfaction, and to the delight of the performers. Mozart himself was everywhere;—now in the orchestra, and now on the stage; at one moment conducting, at the next arranging or altering the scenery. In the ball-scene, where Bassi—who was otherwise an inimitable Don Giovanni—did not dance to suit him, he stepped into the circle himself, and, to the amusement of everybody, danced the minuet with Zerlina, and with such an elegant grace, that they gave him a round of hearty applause.[1]

So it went on to that splendid *finale* of the first Act, which is a masterpiece, not only of the composer's art, but the poet's. The successive situations unfold naturally out of one another; jest and earnest, comic and tragic are woven together, yet without the least appearance of effort or confusion. One is persuaded that the characters are grouped there, not on account of the audience, but out of their own necessary relations. At the close the scenery and arrangement are interesting, even aside from the music. There are three rooms opening into each other, each containing a band, and these bands play at the same time a minuet, a contradance, and a waltz. You hear and see that a carousal is going on. In one place sits a group drinking wine: here is a tender couple making love in pantomime; there a company of card-players. Among them all go pairs of dancers, jostling the lackeys, who are bringing in refreshments to loud calls of "*Caffe! ciocolate! sorbetti! confetti!*"

[1] Historical.

11*

Look! How amorously Don Juan approaches little Zerlina, while Leporello neatly puts the churl of a bridegroom to one side! Then Don Juan and Zerlina disappear.

Immediately a cry is heard from behind the scenes:

" *Gente ajuto !*"

The three bands and the dancers at once stop, while the orchestra, which has been silent during the ball, dashes into an *Allegro assai* in $\frac{4}{4}$ time. But now as the cry of Zerlina again rises above the menacing unison, " *Ora grida da quel lato !*" a loud "Stop!" rings from Mozart's lips, as he raps the desk with his baton. All are silent.

"Bondini, little woman!" he calls out to where Don Juan and Zerlina stand in the side-scenes, "the cry for help was not right."

"Not right?" repeated the little dame, sticking her laughing face out.

"No!"

"Why not?"

"'Twas too late, and not loud enough."

"Very well!" said she; "I will do it better, then!"

"Good!" cried Mozart. "Now then, friends, once more from the *Allegro*.

The music went on again; but at the same point "rap, rap, rap!" fell the baton, and all stopped.

"Wasn't it right that time?" asked Zerlina wonderingly, and with such a comical face that even the conductor had to laugh.

"No!" he replied. "Cry out once alone."

The little dame obeyed. All burst out laughing.

"It won't do!" said Amadeus. "Louder!"

"That's right. Now—*Da capo !*"

The orchestra started off again, but again the inexorable rap of the baton halted them. This time Zerlina's face was not so cheerful.

"My dear child," said Mozart, ruffling his hair, "it won't do yet!"

"But what of it?" asked she, a little vexed. "Is it so much matter about the cry?"

"Certainly it is: try it once more. Now then—*Da capo !*"

Again the orchestra commenced, and again Mozart stopped them. Then stepping from his platform on to the stage as if out of patience, he placed himself behind the pretty little

woman, and over her shoulder gave the signal to begin once
nore. When the moment came for Zerlina to utter her cry
for help, he suddenly embraced her with such force and boldness that she gave a terrified shriek with the utmost naturalness.

"Bravo, bravo! That's the way to do it!" cried he to the
startled singer, who stood with one hand pressed against her
beating heart, while a shout of laughter broke from the rest.'

Madam Bondini herself could no longer keep a sober face.
" You are a horrible man!" she exclaimed, striking him
lightly on the too daring fingers. " How could you frighten
a body so!"

" My dear creature, that's a study from nature!"

" I sha'n't be Zerlina any longer!" cried she, trying to put
on a pout.

" Oh, yes you will," said Mozart; " and an angelic one too!
Come—*la ci darem la mano*, Signorella Bondini!" and he
looked at her so frankly with his handsome merry face that
she could not but obey him. Then he stepped down into
the orchestra again.

"*Allegro assai*, four-four, *E* flat major!" rang out his
word of command, as he raised the conductor's baton.

This time it went excellently, and without checking them
Mozart cried—

" Bravo! Bravo!"

Soon the violins tremble, hesitate, pause. Then as the baton
quickens its beat they flash into triplets, and the mighty
storm of the chorus begins—" *Trema, trema scellerato!*"

—The first Act is finished; and the word passes from mouth
to mouth on the stage and in the orchestra: "Splendid!"—
" Beautiful!"—" Glorious!" and it seemed to Mozart as if the
ghost of an audience applauded from the empty house, or
from the boxes.

It took a little time for the musicians and singers to get
over their enthusiasm before the second Act could be com
menced. Soon, however, all hastened to their places again,
for everybody was now delighted to have a part in the opera
and proud of the opportunity to do their best with such ex-
quisite music. Even the grisly troop of devils rubbed their
hands with excitement and pleasure, as they moved about
behind the side-scenes, in their hideous black and red tights

¹ Historical.

embellished with horns and tail, awaiting the moment when they should seize Don Juan.

As the rehearsal again went on, one of the devils jogs his neighbor with his elbow, offers him a pinch of snuff, and asks—

"Nepomuck, how do you like it ?"

"It's splendid !" he replied, disposing of the snuff with a long-drawn sniff through his masked nose. "I never heard such music in my life."

"How it scares a man, now and then !" said the first devil.

"Yes, but when it isn't angry it hits one's heart so ! Ah, wasn't that last beautiful !—Crispin !"

"Well ?"

"I'd be a devil for nothing, just to hear the music—wouldn't you ?"

"Yes; but hold your tongue now—I want to listen."

And the two devils sat down on a mossy bank in the back of the arbor where Mosetto had been concealed, and listened as solemnly as if they were in church.

Everything went well; and at last it came to the scene in the churchyard.

On both sides of the stage are monuments and urns with inscriptions and emblems: here and there is a thicket of cypress and willow. A ruined wall, crumbling into decay, is visible through the trees. In the background stands the statue of Don Pedro, the stony outlines of horse and man sharply defined in the moonlight.

The impression was fine. Even Mozart was surprised. Bondini, who stood on the left wing of the stage, noticed the composer's satisfaction, and cried—

"Is that right, Maestro ?"

"It is beautiful !" he answered—"just as I had imagined it."

Then a new idea seemed to strike him, and he called out—

"Gentlemen trombones ! In order to increase the awful effect of the two *adagios* which the man in stone yonder has to speak, won't you please to post yourselves behind the statue ?"

"Good !" said old Master Stradetzky, as with the two other trombone players he took up the position assigned.

Then the baton waved on again. At the second *adagio* of the ghost, " *Ribaldo, audace, lascia ai morti la pace !*" Mo-art exclaimed, "Wrong!" and rapped for silence. "The trombones are out—*Da capo!*"

The movement began again. But at the same point the leader stopped them: "Wrong! the trombones are out again!"

Then stepping on to the stage, Mozart patiently showed Stradetzky, who was a good player though a little obstinate, how it should go.

But now, at the third repetition of the same mistake, Mozart lost his temper, and, stamping with his foot, he cried—

"Why the devil can't you blow that right, Stradetzky!"

The old musician was angry also now, and said gruffly—

"I can blow all that can be got out of a trombone, but what *you* have written there the devil couldn't play, and you couldn't teach him to play it!"

Any other conductor than Mozart would have broken loose at him for this, but he only laughed. Then he said, good-humoredly—

"Heaven preserve me from any such pupil! If I have written what the trombone can't do, then I must write something else, that's all!"

And turning to the manager, he called for pen and paper, and altered the place, giving the accompaniment to two oboes, two clarinets, and two bassoons.[1]

Now it went excellently.

At last came the moment for the devils to rush out; but they were to be disappointed devils after all. Scarcely had they made their appearance, brandishing torches of red fire, when Mozart cried out desperately—

"For God's sake, take these creatures away!"

"Why," said Bondini, coming forward, "it says, 'Here Don Juan is seized by the devil!'"

"Of course!"

"Well, then—?"

"But it makes the thing too atrocious."

"How is he to be seized, then?"

"Bah!" said Mozart, "he is man enough to go to the devil when he is called!"[2]

"But—?"

"The chorus of furies must sing underneath the stage, which will be much more awful." And so it was done.

[1] Historical.   [2] Mozart's own words.

When the rehearsal was over, the enthusiasm among the performers was intense; and there was a confused buzz of admiring exclamations and plaudits as they prepared to leave the theatre. In the midst of it Mozart could hardly persuade himself that he did not hear a ghostly clapping of hands and a light "Bravo! Bravo!" from invisible lips in the empty seats and boxes.

As he turned to go out, he nearly ran over a small man in black and red tights. It was one of the devils, who had removed his mask, and stood looking at the maestro with a mournful visage

"Well!" said Mozart, "you don't mean to seize me, do you, in revenge for not getting hold of Don Juan?"

"N-n-no!" stammered the devil; "certainly not, but—can't we play then at all in the opera?"

"Oh, it's your wages, is it?" And he felt after his purse.

"No!" he exclaimed; "the devil take the few pennies. I mean we don't care about *them*, poor as we are; but we can't hear the music any more!"

"Yes," broke in Crispin, emerging from the shadow of the side-scenes, and removing his horns and tail as he came. "Herr von Mozart, you will pardon my speaking to you, but," and the tears stood in the poor fellow's eyes, "I shall be remembering that music when I die!"

Then Mozart's eyes grew suddenly moist, also. It was the sweetest praise which he had heard to-day. Shaking both their hands cordially, he said:

"At every performance of Don Giovanni, while I am in Prague, you shall have free admittance. Only come to my house always the day before."

And the devils departed rejoicing.

CHAPTER VII.

VENICE, the ancient city, the pearl of Italy, every one knows; but only those who have lived in Prague are acquainted with "Little Venice."

It is an island in the Moldau, and belonged, at the time of which we write, to a company of sharpshooters of Prague. On certain days, all through the summer, they held meetings here, and shot at a target for prizes. They had, moreover, excellent music on such occasions, so that "Little Venice" was a favorite place of resort for all pleasure-loving people. Half the island was given up to green grass and shrubbery, ending in a little thicket which made a cool lounging-place on hot summer-days. At the other end of the island was the shot-house, from which a long alley, between tall trees, led down to the target on the bank of the river.

In the great room of the shot-house, which was really "Little Venice," but gave its name to the whole island, hung upon the walls hundreds of painted targets, perforated with the bullets of past prize-matches. There was Venus rising from the sea-foam; but there was a hole through her girdle. Next her was that favorite character of those times, Harlequin, with his nose shot away. Farther on was Diana, descending upon clouds to Endymion; but the murderous lead had taken her on the wing, and an eye was gone. In fact, nothing had remained sacred to these "Freischützen," as they called themselves. "Free-shots" indeed they seemed to have been. There were Roman emperors, and Greek goddesses; Delilah, with a bullet-hole through her shears; and Judas the betrayer, who had received a shot through the bottom of his eye, which did not at all add to the amiability of that feature's expression.

The "Free-shots" were extremely proud of these trophies of victory, and every good burgher of Prague fancied that his wine tasted a little better in that room than anywhere else.

During the summer, "Little Venice" was always lively and

gay with company, but the warm summer days were now past, and autumn had come.

It was one of the last days of October, bright but cool, and there was only one guest to be seen. He was a man in a gray overcoat, with large figured buttons, in black silk hose and buckled shoes, and with the inevitable cue at the back of his handsome head. He was pacing up and down the long alley, evidently buried in absorbing thought.

He seemed to be a strange fellow, for now his gaze was fixed on the ground, and then his head would be suddenly raised, and his great beautiful eyes would distend and darkle, as if mighty ideas were flashing through his brain. As one watched him, it would appear as if he were drinking in the sunshine and all the bright aspects of nature, and working them into new forms in his own spirit; yet a keen observer might have seen that the man neither saw nor heard any thing about him. His mind was busy with another world, a diviner region, in which his face showed that he saw unspeak able beauty.

A beggar spoke to him. Without looking at him, he put his hand in his pocket, and gave the fellow a piece of money. The beggar looked surprised and delighted, and glanced in astonishment from the gift to the giver; for he held a bright thaler in his hand. "H'm!" he muttered. "That's a fool. I must try him again!" So he limped to the opposite end of the alley, and begged of the abstracted man again. And again the man put his hand in his pocket and gave him something. The gift must have been a considerable one, for the beggar chuckled and limped away.

But the man saw him not. Always brighter his eyes shone, and his face beamed more joyfully, as with a livelier motion of the hand he beat time to an invisible music.

"'Tis done!" he spoke aloud to himself, stopping in his walk; "done to the last note! But—if I only had it written down! I hate the horribly tedious, mechanical work of writing it."

He went a few steps farther, stopped again, and rubbed his forehead, as though it ached with the long concentration upon some intense labor. Then he said, smiling gayly to himself: "Poh! what matters it? I've got six or eight days yet, and, thank heaven, my memory will hold fast to every note of it!"

And the man, who of course was no other than Mozart, walked back to the shot-house.

Six days after this walk in "Little Venice," Mozart was sitting in his room when Bondini entered. The Impressario's face, usually so calm and good-humored, betrayed by its look of anxiety that something lay heavy on his heart. Frankly and straight-forward as ever, Mozart asked what was the matter.

"My dear Maestro!" answered Bondini, "I should think you would know what the matter was!"

"I?"

"Who else?"

"Is it about the opera?

"Yes."

"Why, I thought the rehearsal went capitally!"

"Couldn't have been better!"

"And to-morrow evening the curtain rises."

"Yes, at six o'clock!" and the look of anxiety on Bondini's face deepened into despair at the thought.

"Well, what's the matter then?" asked Mozart. "Weren't the tickets all sold in advance a week ago? What more could a Director ask?"

"Nothing; only, the opera can't be given to-morrow!"

"Can't be given?" cried Mozart, staring at Bondini with great eyes. "What's the reason it can't be given?"

Bondini only spread his hands wide apart, and gasped.

"Is Saporitti sick?"

"No."

"Your little wife?"

The Director shook his head.

"In the devil's name, then, who is? Bassi? Lolli? Baglioni?—"

"Nobody's sick!" said Bondini.

"See here, my friend"— and Mozart began to get angry— "if you don't want to drive me mad, tell me what the matter is! Has the police got its nose into the affair, at the last minute?"

"Oh, bah! The police! Is it possible you don't *know* what the matter is? Do you mean to say that *you* don't know why I can't give it to-morrow—this 'Don Juan,' for which all Prague has been waiting impatiently, for which every seat was sold a week ago?"

" No, I don't !" said Mozart.

" Well !" exclaimed the astonished Bondini; " if a man wasn't ready to cry over it, he could laugh himself to death ! It's nothing—nothing at all ! only—you haven't written the overture yet !"

" Is that all ?" said Mozart. " Oh, there's time enough for that !"

Bondini was thunderstruck; at last he stammered, " For the overture to a work like ' Don Giovanni ?'"

Amadeus smiled archly, then going up to Bondini, he laid both hands on the Director's shoulders, looked him in the eyes, and asked—

" Do you suppose, my friend, that I would, with my own hand, ruin the best work of my life by a bad overture ?"

" No !" cried Bondini; " certainly not."

" Well, then, set your mind at rest."

" But, Maestro, the parts will have to be all copied."

" Tell the copyist to be here at seven o'clock to-morrow morning."

" And the rehearsal—?"

" Oh, this doubting Thomas !" cried Mozart, laughing aloud; " he doesn't know his own orchestra.　I tell you, Bondini, *my* Prague orchestra plays at sight !"

" You have an enormous faith !" returned the Director, still looking troubled.　" Everything depends on the overture; if that goes wrong—"

" Now, Bondini !" exclaimed Mozart, coaxingly; " just you trust to me and your orchestra !"

" Well, all right !　But if it goes straight, I shall hand you over to the Inquisition."

" What for ?"

" As a sorcerer !"

" Only see that the copyist is here at seven, and we shall need no sorcery.　I will commence the overture at once. Good-bye !"

Bondini hurried away, somewhat encouraged, as he saw the composer seat himself at his desk, take out his music-paper, and dip his pen in the deep inkstand.

Scarcely was he out of the house, when Duscheck entered the room.

" Mozart !" he exclaimed, " I have had the horses harnessed, and Constanze and my wife are already in the carriage.　It is a splendid day, and there won't be many more such this year. Come along!"

Amadeus jumped up as if Duscheck had been an electric shock, seized his hat with one hand and poked at his necktie with the other, and in two minutes was seated by the side of his wife, and the horses were off. When they came back the short November afternoon had already darkened into evening; and through its darkness they saw from afar all the windows of the Duscheck mansion illuminated as for some grand festivity.

Mozart was the first to notice it—

"What has broken loose at home?" he exclaimed in astonishment.

"You'll soon see!" replied Duscheck.

But what was Mozart's surprise on reaching the house and alighting, to find himself surrounded by a group of his best friends, who had prepared a little feast in honor of the completion of "Don Giovanni."

It was a delightful company. Bondini was there with his little madcap of a wife, as well as all the members of the opera-troupe, except Saporitti, who—to the sorrow of everybody—had a headache, and had remained at home as a precaution against being ill the next day. She had set her heart on appearing in the opera, and was as pleased with her *rôle* as a child. The headache was reported as slight; so the company soon forgot the anxiety which its announcement at first excited.

The evening and a good part of the night flew away in unrestrained merriment and gayety, and at last they sat down to a fine supper. Everybody was in excellent spirits, but Mozart exceeded them all, laughing, joking, and reeling off endless strings of comical verse.

"Fill your glasses!" cried Duscheck. "Here is to the success of 'Don Giovanni!'"

The glasses clinked, and the toast was drunk with the greatest enthusiasm. Then said Bondini—

"It's very well for you to drink to the success of the opera; but if you had suffered the anxiety and despair which I have for the last few days, till this forenoon in fact—"

"How so?" asked Duscheck, while Mozart went on laughing and bantering with little Madam Bondini, not hearing what the others were saying.

"'How so?'" returned the Director. "I will tell you. Till this forenoon our good maestro hadn't written a stroke of the overture!"

"What!" exclaimed several voices at once. "And is it done already?"

"Certainly!" said Bondini quietly; "for when I left him he had gone to work on it. The opera couldn't possibly have been given otherwise."

At that moment Mozart turned his merry face toward them.

"Well!" cried Bondini; "how did you get along with the overture this forenoon?"

"With—"

"The overture!"

Mozart turned pale. Everybody started, and a universal expression of dismay went from face to face.

Amadeus pulled out his watch—it was almost midnight!'

"It is, eh!" said he, thoughtfully. "Then I've got no more time to loose. In ten minutes it will strike twelve, and at seven the copyists are to come. Some hours yet! Good-night, gentlemen: good-night, ladies—I kiss your hands! Stanzerl, bring a glass of punch with you to keep me awake. And now, may all the good spirits stand by me!"

Mozart hastened to his room, where pen and paper were lying as he had dropped them in the forenoon. The company broke up in great anxiety, and with gloomy forebodings of the morrow. For the opera could not be given without an overture, and what mortal could in a few hours of the night write one that would be worthy of the "Don Giovanni!"

Bondini was in perfect despair, and only his wife kept up her courage and confidence.

Meantime Mozart had seated himself. Just as he was on the point of diving into his work, he caught sight of Constanze's face, which was full of deep sorrow.

"Stanzerl!" said he, in a gentle voice—"my treasure! come here and let me whisper something in your ear."

"But, Wolferl," she replied imploringly, as if expecting some new prank, "won't you please begin?"

"Come here!" repeated her husband; "put your little ear down here a second."

Constanze obeyed. Amadeus gave the soft cheek a kiss, then whispered lightly—

    Historical.

"You needn't be a bit anxious, dear heart. It's all finished long ago!"

"How? where?" she exclaimed, her face lighting up.

"Here," said Amadeus, laughing, and pointing to his forehead. "I finished the overture a week ago, and put it all away safely in my skull; only I was too lazy to do the horrid work of writing it down. It will all be on paper by the time the copyist comes, and my Stanzerl will be satisfied with it. I think the world will, too!"

"If it has all stayed there where you put it," said Constanze a little dubiously.

"Ah, ha!" cried Amadeus, laughing, and beginning to write at the same time. "If I could carry Allegri's *Miserere* home with me when a youngster, without dropping a note, I think I can carry an overture of my own for a week. Now then, Stanzerl, sit down here by me, and tell me a story out of the 'Arabian Nights'—Aladdin's Lamp, or something—so that I sha'n't go to sleep."

"Shall I tell you about Noureddin-Ali and Bedreddin Hassan?"

"All right!" And Constanze set the glass of punch before him, took her knitting-work, seated herself by his side, and began:

"There was once in Egypt a very just and merciful Sultan. His bravery made him the terror of all his neighbors. He loved the poor, and shielded the orphans, and protected his people from the oppressions of the rich. Now the Vizier of this Sultan was a wise and keen-sighted man, who was learned in all arts and sciences. The Sultau had two sons, and the name of the elder was Schemseddin-Ali, and that of the younger was Noureddin-Ali."

So it went on for three hours. Mozart wrote rapidly; but uow weariness began to overcome him, and at last his yawns and nods grew more and more frequent, till sleep could no longer be fought off. Constanze clapped him on the shoulder, and said—

"Dear, it won't go; you are too tired. Come! Sleep an hour. I will keep awake and call you."

Mozart rubbed his forehead and eyes. "Well," he exclaimed, drowsily, "I'll take your advice; but be sure you wake me up after an hour."

And he lay down on the sofa. "You are a good little wife," he whispered; then kissed her once, and was asleep.

Constanze sat by his side and went on knitting. She thought on the times of her first love—the Christmas night when she had sent her dear friend the little pocket-book; the fatal consequences which had followed upon this gift; and then the hour when it had, after long trial, made her happy at last.

And as she thought over the past, image after image of her whole life arose before her. How many pleasant hours at the side of her husband; and ah, how many sorrowful and anxious ones! Then she fell to thinking of the new opera, and how much renown it would bring Amadeus, and what a change it would make in their life.

She sighed deeply; then put down her work in her lap, and looked at the slumberer, and thought—"Ah, if there might only be no more worrying about money!"

Then again she sank into dreams, which linked from one to another, on and on; but now they were bright fancies,—she was dreaming of a beautiful future.

The hour had passed. She put out her hand and opened her lips to wake her husband, but he was sleeping so quietly! "It will be time enough if I let him sleep one more little hour," she thought. "His genius makes things easy for him which would be impossible to others. Sleep on, dear soul! in an hour you can go to work again."

So she took up her knitting once more, and went back to her dreams.

At last the clock struck five.

There was no more time to lose—Constanze must wake her husband. He rubbed his eyes, sprang up and looked at his watch.

"Five!" he exclaimed, threatening her laughingly with his finger. "That was contrary to the agreement."

"But you were having such a good sleep!"

"Well, it will do yet," he answered. "But now, dear child, go you to bed. You look utterly tired out."

Constanze obeyed, and Mozart went at his work with fresh strength. Two hours afterward the copyist entered. It was seven o'clock, and the overture to "Don Giovanni"—that masterpiece of Mozart's creations—lay finished before him![1]

---

[1] Historical in every particular.

CHAPTER VIIL

DON GIOVANNI.

ONDINI had slept as little as Mozart. Not only his credit as Director was at stake, since all Prague had been for weeks awaiting this first presentation of "Don Giovanni," but his whole future hung on its success or failure. For it was Bondini's last chance. Once before, the Prague theatre, and he at the head of it, had been at the last gasp when Mozart's "Figaro," drawing a packed house night after night through the past winter, had paid his debts and given him a new lease of life. And now had arrived another ebb in his finances. The enormous outlay for new scenery, costumes, singers, etc., had emptied the chest entirely. If the new opera was damned, it would leave him hopelessly in debt: if it succeeded, as he had hoped, he was a made man, and the theatre saved.

And now his whole fate might be settled against him by a bad overture, hastily thrown together in a few hours. Was it not enough to give a poor Director a sleepless night, when he knew that the overture was only just being commenced, and that in any case it must be played without a rehearsal?

Instead of sweet sleep, a horde of demons seemed perched on the pillows of Bondini. No sooner did his eyes close than he heard in his unhappy head, between waking and sleeping, a horribly bad overture going on. Devils were playing the different instruments, and Stradetzky was pumping out such villainous noises from his trombone that the audience stopped its ears and ran for life.

Bondini started up. Thank heaven! it was only a half-awake dream!

"Curse it!" he muttered, and lay down on the other side, nvying the slumber of his wife, who quietly slept beside nim, and whose pretty little red-cheeked face, in the glimmer of the night-lamp, looked like a rosebud half buried in the snow of the pillows. Scarcely had he shut his eyes again, when an impish form leaned over his head from behind him and handed him, with a derisive grin a perfumed note.

Every Director knows what such a perfumed note on the eve of a new opera has to say. The sweat stood on Bondini's forehead. He tore it open—Saporitti was sick!

"Fire and fury!" cried he, and sat up in bed again; "the opera can't be given—Saporitti is sick!"

"For Heaven's sake!" murmured his wife, partially waking up; "what's the matter now? Go to sleep!"

"Oh, yes, certainly!" replied Bondini, with angry irony, and yet glad that he had only dreamed.

Then he turned over again. But this time he could not shut his eyes; for before his mind came the bills which he had got to pay for the new stage-machinery, costumes, decorations, etc. Long columns of figures came trooping up to him: an endless army of them, some with long legs and some with short ones, the naughts rolling over and over, the fives pacing solemnly backward, and the sevens with one arm stretched out and shaking their fists at him. Suddenly there rose up from among them the statue of the horseman in the opera, ghostly white, and pointing with one awful hand to a gigantic seven, which had grown upward before him and was threatening him with its long arm extended. He thought he must utter the name of the figure to exorcise it; but, struggle as he would, he could not articulate the word. At last, with a mighty effort, he burst out wildly with, "*Seven!*" and sat bolt-upright again in bed, trembling in every limb.

"'It's heaven,'" said his charming little spouse, half asleep. "I am glad you think so!" and slept again.

So it went on. The clock struck two—three—four—five: but no peaceful slumber for the Director. Now it was a horse in the orchestra; and now, a singer coming on half-dressed. And now the curtain sticks fast when partly drawn up, and cannot be budged: he must move it—or, tear it down. There! and with a convulsive tug he had pulled the bed-clothes nearly off the bed.

"Bondini!" exclaimed his wife, indignantly, as she turned over and went to sleep again. "You are excited; you drank too—much—punch."

But the Director could endure it no longer. He got up and dressed himself, and went out of the house. He had arranged with the copyist, who was to go to Mozart at seven o'clock, that on his way back to where he and the other copyists were to do their work, he would meet him at a certain street corner, in order to lose no time, and learn the result of the composer's labors.

Wrapped in his cloak, Bondini hurried to the appointed corner. It was only six o'clock, and still dark, and a cold fog enveloped the city. What could be more uncomfortable than to walk through the silent streets of a city on such a chilly, foggy November morning, with an empty stomach and an anxious heart? Arrived at the corner, there was nothing for it but to wait and shiver.

It was all still. But what is that? Was that another cloaked form approaching through the fog?

"Confound it!" muttered Bondini through his teeth. "What would people say to find me standing here at this hour? What if my wife should hear of it!"

But the other man seemed just as desirous to escape attention, for he, too, slipped into a hiding-place. Both stood there in separate nooks, shivering till their teeth chattered.

It was now quarter of seven, and growing lighter. A voice said, half aloud, "Is that you, Bondini?"

"Strobach?" replied the Director, and the two friends came out of their corners and shook hands.

It was in truth the Capellmeister, who was also in a fever about the overture.

"I am on red-hot coals!" said Strobach.

"And I on ice!" answered Bondini. "This fog is infernal. There comes somebody!"

"Kucharz!" said the Capellmeister.

"The devil!" exclaimed Bondini. "Couldn't *you* sleep, either?"

"I am responsible for the orchestra, you know," he answered.

It struck seven o'clock.

"Only ten minutes more," said Bondini.

They waited anxiously without speaking a word. Now they heard the sound of footsteps coming on a run. It was the copyist, emerging through the fog. All hastened to meet him.

"It—was—ready!" he panted, out of breath. "Here—it is."

Bondini, Strobach, and Kucharz fell upon the manuscript like bandits, and devoured it with their eyes.

"Astounding! It is witchcraft!" they exclaimed. But the copyist gave them no further time for examining the notes. He must hurry, or it would not be copied in season.

"Double pay!" cried Bondini after the .nan, who canght the manuscript and started down the street. "You are all to have double pay, remember, if you get it done."

"All right!" came back from the depths of the fog.

In the afternoon before dark, people began to stream along the streets of Prague toward the theatre. The doors were not yet opened, and the throng before the building every instant thickened. It looked like a hive of bees, at the door of which the queen-bee has settled, and the swarm is heaped all about her.

The crowd talked and joked in joyful expectancy. They pressed and squeezed, pushed and shoved, to get a standing-place nearer the closed doors. It was an opera going on outside before the real opera had opened.

The aristocratic portion of the audience had not yet shown itself, but the parquet and galleries would evidently be filled the instant the doors were opened. And all this packed mass of humanity was growing more and more excited as the time approached. They had heard marvellous reports about this new opera of the great Wolfgang A. Mozart, the darling of Prague. Even the story of the overture had got abroad, and added its interest to the universal suspense.

At ten in the morning Bondini had hastened to the house of Signora Saporitti, to inquire after her health. She was somewhat better than yesterday, but had still considerable fever and a bad pulse. Bondini was in despair again; but Saporitti comforted him with the assurance that she would sing even if she was half dead.

This assurance was small comfort, however: a half-dead prima-donna was a very questionable piece of property for the first night of a new opera, on whose success was hanging the fate of the whole theatre.

But what was to be done? Better so, than not at all.

Bondini strode up and down the dark stage, where, by the feeble light of a few lamps, they were arranging the last decorations.

The Director was pale, and his forehead was puckered up like a pan of cream half skimmed. He was waiting in the greatest anxiety for the return of the two messengers whom he had sent to Saporitti and the copyists.

At last came the latter one.

"Now, then!" cried Bondini with feverish impatience. "Have you got the orchestra parts? Are they ready?"

They soon will be, Herr Impressario! The men are scratching as if they would write their fingers off; but—"

"What in the name of all the devils is the trouble?"

"The *Andante* is nothing but sixteenth and thirty-second notes!"

"Good heavens!" cried Bondini, wringing his hands. "What's to be done? The doors are being opened, and the overture not yet *copied*—let alone looked at or rehearsed!"

Up and down the stage he went again with long strides, and such desperation in his looks, that the unhappy messenger got out of the way with all speed.

"Is the Capellmeister there yet?" cried Bondini now.

"Oh yes, Herr Impressario!" replied the retreating messenger.

"Send him here then!"

"Oh yes, Herr—"

"*Quick!*"

Strobach entered. "Dear Capellmeister," said the Director in a trembling voice, "do you know—"

"I know," he replied; "but we have an hour yet—"

"And if the damned copyists are not ready *then?*"

"We'll take the overture to 'Idomeneus!'"

"Yes, and bungle the whole opera! Oh, by all the saints, I'm a ruined man!"

Just then the second messenger rushed in, white and out of breath.

Bondini made for him like a tiger, seized him by both shoulders, shook him, and cried out so furiously, "Now then! how is it with Saporitti?" that the man's legs trembled under him, and he lost the power of speech for a full minute.

"Out with it, you scoundrel!" thundered the Manager.

"Will she be here?" asked Strobach, more mildly.

"N-n-no!" stuttered the man. "She was all ready to get into the carriage, when she fainted away in her maid's arms—"

"Fainted *away?*"

"Yes, and lies so now!"

But at that, Bondini was swooning himself, and Strobach had to help him to a chair.

"Water!" cried the Capellmeister, as all the theatre-people came running up; "and no noise, lest the public hear it!"

At that moment the Director's little wife hurried in. She

was in the dressing-room when she heard what had happened, and had rushed out with her toilette only half made. She had therefore a curiously amphibious appearance, the lower half being "Zerlina," and the upper half her own pretty self, wrapped in a shawl. Others of the group were in a similar condition, so that as Bondini came to himself his eyes opened on a comical and interesting display.

"Come, my dear," said the upper half of Zerlina, which was his wife, "aren't you better now?

"Oh—ah—eh?—the devil!" muttered the Director, recovering.

"Courage!" said Strobach. "We'll see what we can do."

"*Do?*" exclaimed Bondini, in the wildest despair; "when there is no Donna Anna?—The wisest thing we can do is to go hang ourselves!"

"Oh no, dear man," said his wife, coaxingly.

"But we can't give the opera!"

"Why not?" asked at that moment a woman's musical voice, in the purest Italian.

All looked round in surprise, and saw a noble-looking woman, richly dressed in black, standing beside them. In her beautiful face lay a certain expression of confidence—yes, of triumph. Her large dark eyes were all aflame with eagerness. The low corsage and bare arms betrayed a finely-moulded and voluptuous form: indeed, there could not have been a more perfect Donna Anna.

Their astonishment was so great, that, for a moment, no one found words to answer the Signora's question. At last, Bondini stammered, with savage irony—

"Have you then, perchance, a Donna Anna in your pocket somewhere?"

"Not in my pocket," said the Signora, smiling proudly; "but I can furnish a Donna Anna for you!"

"In the shape of—?"

"Myself!"

The Director shook his head despondently. Then said he, with the bitterest sarcasm—

"Oh, of course, this being the first presentation of a new opera, just finished, you have the whole *rôle* in your head?"

"There is no time for questions, Herr Impressoni. Every minute is precious. I hear the public already becoming impatient. Enough for you that I know the part. As you see, my figure is almost the same as that of Saporitti, so there will be no trouble about the costumes."

"But—but—"

"Would you know my name as security?"

"It *would* be desirable, Signora; otherwise I cannot—"

"Very well," she replied; "but no one else must know it. Nor must Maestro Mozart know that I have undertaken the *rôle* of Donna Anna."

Then stooping down to Bondini, who still sat in his chair as if paralyzed, she whispered at his ear—"Mandini!"

Scarcely had that name left her lips, when the Director leaped up as if he had been sitting on a torpedo. Joy beamed from every feature. He struck his hands wildly against his knees, and almost danced round her, while he exclaimed—

"And you know the part?"

"I do!"

"We are saved, then! Signora, you are our preserving angel. God bless you!" Then he called out to the rest of the company. "Quick! quick! we've lost time enough already. The opera is all right—on with your dresses—make everything fly!"

Bondini had forgotten the overture in the excitement of the last few minutes. But now he remembered it again, and messenger after messenger was sent, only to return with the reply: "Not quite ready!"

It was quarter to six: the orchestra parts not finished.

It struck six. Still they waited in vain.

Bondini looked as if he could have taken the part of the ghost of Don Pedro excellently well. Sitting in his chair, more dead than alive, he beckoned to Mozart, who had just come in from a walk, and was congratulating himself on having just hit the hour for beginning, as he was to conduct the opera.

"Mozart," groaned the Director, "what time is it?"

"Just six."

"Time to begin the overture then!"

"Yes, and only hear how impatient the audience is. You mustn't wait a minute, my dear Bondini! I am as happy as a king! But what's the matter with you? Are you sick? Has anything happened?"

"No!" groaned the Director. "That's just what's the matter—nothing has happened!"

" I don't understand."

" Why, the orchestra-parts of the overture are not copied yet !"

"Thunder and lightning !" exclaimed Mozart; "I don't see how that can be."

" *I* do," replied Bondini reproachfully; but at that instant they hear a double tumult—the cries and noises of impatience in the audience, and a jubilant exclamation from the orchestra Capellmeister Strobach sprang up the little steps, and announced—

"It has come ! it has come !"

"Thank God !" cried Mozart, and hastened down into the orchestra-room.

The parts of the overture had been brought in with the ink still wet and covered with sand.[1] Then Mozart turned to the musicians, and said—

"Gentlemen ! you will have to play this overture at first sight. It was impossible to have a rehearsal; but I know that I have thorough artists before me, and I am not afraid. We will take our places at once, if you please." And they hastened into the orchestra.

A moment afterward Mozart entered and stepped on to the conductor's platform. He was received with a thunder of applause from the densely-packed house, which the handsomely-dressed and graceful composer acknowledged by a profound bow. His heart was beating high with pleasure, and his blue eyes were lit up and sparkling.

He delayed not an instant, but lifted the silver-tipped baton, and—as with the thunder and trumpet-peals of the last judgment—arose the first chords of the solemn *Andante.*

An atmosphere of trembling awe gathers around the majestic music. Half-notes, echoed in horror-breathing octaves, rise up on all sides, like the faces of ghosts, which cast a long, dull glare at the terrified beholder and disappear, to make way for other fearful shapes. Hark ! how the thunder rolls beneath us ! How the voice of the wounded victim moans ! How the phantom answers, and stretches forth a black gigantic arm out of the earth to grasp the betrayer ! Then the wind-instruments, in their culminating masses of harmony, denote the death-struggle, and the last convulsions of life quiver in the *tremolo* of the violins.

[1] Historical.—Nissen, p. 512.

The vast audience listens, breathless and awe-stricken · while the orchestra glows with enthusiasm.

And now the *Allegro* introduces the hearer into the life of "Don Juan."

The *D sharp* of the violins clashing with the *D* of the bass gives utterance to the fiendish hostility of "Giovanni" toward the human race. The fierce wolf comes stealthily crouching toward the fold; with one spring he has seized the lamb, and the trumpets greet the successful robber with a blast of hellish triumph. Then the intelligence of the crime is spread—the alarm is sounded—they assemble themselves to avenge the wrong. And now arises that succession of magically-interwoven passages, which makes this overture a work as unique in its sphere as the opera is in its own.

As the overture ceased and passed into the Introduction, a storm of applause rent the air. The house shook with "*Bravo's,*" for both Mozart and the orchestra. Both had done wonders, and the whole audience by this time had learned that the overture had been played *prima vista.*

Mozart's face beamed with delight, and a little smile played across it as he turned to Strobach, and said softly without checking his baton or missing the time—

"Wasn't I right about the overture?"

"Perfectly! I am amazed!"

"There were two or three notes dropped under the desks, but on the whole it went excellently!"[1]

The curtain rolled up, and the opera began.

Leporello sang his "*Notte e giorno faticar*" finely, and the audience had begun to applaud him, when—!

The whole opera had nearly been thrown into confusion, for Mozart stared as if demented. The baton nearly slipped from his fingers! Impossible! Incredible! Is it witchcraft? Giuditta Mandini as Donna Anna!

Through the whole theatre there is a visible stir.

"Who is that?"

"Who is this splendid woman?"

"What does it mean?"

But in a moment every whisper was dumb, for such tones they had never heard before.

Mozart had quickly recovered himself, informed by Strobach in a whisper of the facts of the case. One thought filled

---

[1] Mozart's very words.

his brain—she had saved the evening; and a wild gratitude and admiration for her daring deed fired his blood, and raised his excitement to the highest pitch.

She sang gloriously, for that hour was the crowning triumph of her life! As she came forward, half attired, in a white *déshabillé* which revealed her beautiful shoulders and arms, with her dark wealth of hair streaming about her—and then as her rich voice rang out above the clamorous instruments— it was a ravishing effect! Bassi filled the part of "Don Giovanni" superbly. There was not a soul upon the stage, or in the orchestra, or among the audience, who was not carried away by the common enthusiasm. Another such opera-night the world has never seen.

—When it was over, and the tempest of applause had subsided as the audience poured out of the theatre, and the congratulations and excited greetings were all done, Mozart looked around for the preserver of the evening. But the Mandini had disappeared.

"Don Giovanni" was the key with which the great composer unlocked the temple of everlasting renown. It was the culminating point of his life. With Mozart it was now high noon.

PART VI.

CHAPTER I.

TWILIGHT.

IT was the year of the storm.

For a long time the clouds had been massing along the horizon, darker and gloomier, till their gilded summits rose piling and toppling upward toward the zenith. The atmosphere grew more and more still, sultry, and oppressive; menacing thunder began to mutter and groan, and now and then a lightning-flash blazed its zigzag path against the darkness. Men's hearts felt the presentiment of coming woe, and trembled. Then the tempest broke, in its fury of fire and blood. It was the French Revolution.

Near the end of June, 1791, the news spread over Europe of the flight and capture of Louis XVI. of France. It was startling news, wherever it fell: but in few places was it heard with such horror as in the Austrian capital; for the unhappy queen, Marie Antoinette, was the darling daughter of Maria Theresa and the beloved sister of their Emperor.

Joseph II. had ended his long strife with the world in 1790, one year before, and his brother Leopold had ascended the stormy throne of Austria.

It was four years since the opening-night of "Don Giovanni," the success of which opera had made the fortune of Bondiui, the proprietor and manager of the Prague theatre · and the Mozarts were now living again in Vienna.

It was growing late, one summer evening, and Constanze Mozart was sitting solitary and alone in her chamber;—alone for Amadeus had not yet come home, though the clock had struck ten; alone, for of the five children which Heaven had sent her—two girls and three boys—only one remained, and he, the little seven-years-old Karl, was long ago asleep in his own little bed. But toward the end of the next month Constanze hoped to be again a mother; and the beautiful thought was all the fairer to her woman's heart, because the hand of fate seemed now to be laid heavily upon her.

The table stood ready for tea, but the meal had remained untouched; and Constanze sat resting her arm on the table, and supporting her head on her hand. The candles were burning low. Her work had fallen on her lap, and she looked fixedly before her as though her mind was far away.

How few of all the bright hopes of her life had as yet fulfilled themselves! She had been happy with her husband, who loved her now as he did on their marriage-day, who treated her with all the reverent tenderness of a lover; but this noble, affectionate husband, this diligent worker, this mighty genius, this morning-star in the musical heavens of Germany—oh, how was it with him? Harassed by debts, injured by enemies, disappointed by princes and emperor, his life was one ceaseless struggle for an honorable sustenance.

From his greatest works he had gained nothing in Vienna. "Don Giovanni" had shared the fate of "Figaro." It was brought out, thanks to Salieri's treacherous intrigues, in a slovenly and bungling manner, while at the same time an opera of Salieri's own, "Axur," was presented with all possible advantages of splendid scenery and artistic performance. Notwithstanding that his fame had gone far and wide, and that he was recognized to be, as Haydn himself called him, "the greatest musician of Europe," he had to return to the old treadmill. By giving lessons, even to children, by writing dances for balls, by musical "jobs" of this or that trivial sort, he was forced to eke out a scanty subsistence for his family.

Bondini was made a rich man by "Don Giovanni." Mozart got but a hundred ducats for it! And of this sum, after paying his debts and travelling expenses, there was almost nothing left on his return to Vienna. Soon Care again reached out her skeleton finger over his head. Away, now, with the masterpieces of art! Clip the bold wings of the soaring spirit! What, man! wouldst see thy wife and children suffer and starve? Give the world such work as it will pay for!

So it was no longer the call of his guiding genius which he heard; but such calls as these instead: "Maestro, I want some songs for my daughter, to these words which I have here."—"I would like an Italian *aria* for my wife."—"I must have a trumpet-piece for my cavalry company."—"Good-morning, Master Mozart. I want half-a-dozen minuets; but you must have them ready by to-morrow night, for the ball at Prince X's!"—"Write me a sonata for my christening-day party. You shall five ducats and supper!"

Shame on thee, ungrateful world! Hide thy face and weep, as Constanze now is weeping in her lonely room.

Harder and closer pressed his creditors, and Mozart wrote, out of pure need, an opera for the Italian theatre in Vienna, "*Cosi Fan Tutte, osia la Scuola degli Amanti.*" But the libretto was wretched, and the opera failed.

Then Kaiser Joseph died, and with him sank Constanze's last hope, for he had honored her husband, and never ceased to promise him great things. In the hope of making something by a few concerts, and at least getting rid of his creditors for a short time, he went to Frankfort, where the Electors were assembled to choose a new sovereign.

Here he found honor and respect, and a little money besides; but the curse of a debtor is, that no sooner is a little money acquired than it goes for the old debts, and nothing remains but to make new ones.

Constanze sighed as in her review of the years since their happy journey to Prague, she came to that time. Then rising, she went to her cabinet and opened a drawer, and took out a bundle of letters which Amadeus had written her then. She sat down again, unfolded one of the letters, and read:

"Frankfort-on-the-Maine, Sept. 29th, 1790

"My sweet, darling, beloved Wife:

"We are this moment arrived—one o'clock in the forenoon. So we have only been six days on the road. We took up our quarters at the inn in the suburb Sachsenhausen, delighted beyond measure to have secured a room. We had a capital dinner at Ratisbon, divine music, English cheer, and splendid Moselle. We breakfasted at Nürnberg, an ugly town. In Würzburg we refreshed our precious selves with coffee. A grand, fine city. The charges were everywhere very moderate; but at the third station from here the landlord thought fit to cheat us famously. I anxiously look forward to news of you, of your health, of our affairs, etc.

I am quite determined to do the best I can for myself here and shall then be heartily glad to return to you. What a delightful life we shall lead! I will work, and work in such a manner that I may never again be placed by unforeseen events in so distressing a position."[1]

And in another letter, written one day later, she reads:

"I am happy as a child when I think of returning again to you. If people could see into my heart, I should almost feel ashamed—all there is cold, cold as ice. Were you with me, I should possibly take more pleasure in the kindness of those I meet here; but all seems to me so empty. Adieu, my love!
"I am ever your loving
"MOZART."

"P. S.—While writing the last page, many a tear has fallen on it. But now let us be merry. Look! swarms of kisses are flying about. Quick! catch some. I have caught three that are delicious. Adieu, my dearest, sweetest wife! Be careful of your health, and do not go into town on foot. Write to me how you like your new quarters. Adieu! I send you a million kisses."[2]

Constanze's eyes were full of tears as she folded up the letters, and thought: "Ah, this forced cheerfulness! As always, he jests with a broken heart, to conceal from me and from himself that he is unhappy. Lest it may grieve me, he wears a mask over the pain!"

Then, holding the bundle of letters lovingly clasped in her hands, she fell again into a mournful train of recollections.

There was a deathly stillness around her, unbroken except by the weary ticking of the clock. Suddenly Constanze lifted her head and listened. She had heard a slight noise in the street, close by the house.

"That must be he!" she exclaimed joyfully; and her heart beat so fast and loud that she pressed one hand upon it.

But the noise ceased.

"No," said she, sorrowfully; "it was not he. He promised to come at nine; and now"—she looked at the clock—"it is half-past ten."

Then a long silence. Constanze's thoughts became more

anxious and troubled. Could anything have happened to him? Or had he only stopped to play billiards, as he did so often?

"Poor man!" she said to herself; "after working so hard, and being so worried, no wonder he likes to stay at his favorite game. And the doctor says the exercise is just the thing for him too!"

Another half-hour, and still he came not. "Oh, why should I try to deceive myself!" she thought, as the tears chased each other down her cheeks. "He never plays so late as this: he has gone to the inn with some roystering company, to forget the weariness of his brain and the trouble of his heart in forbidden pleasures! And when he comes home, the strained nerves will be set to work again till daybreak; and already his health is so undermined that he faints away over his desk. O God! spare him to me; let him not ruin himself, O Heavenly Father!" And throwing herself down by her chair, she buried her face in her hands, and sobbed like a child.

Suddenly she heard another noise at the door, she thought. Raising her head, she listened intently: it was only the wind at the shutter. But as she still listened to make sure of it, there came the sound of steps along the pavement, and a clear tenor voice sang the serenade from "Don Giovanni"—"Look and listen at the window!"

"That is he!" cried Constanze; and she sprang up, forgetting to wipe her tears away, but with a smile beaming through them, and hastened to meet her husband.

Mozart greeted her in the happiest humor, and caught her almost wildly in his arms. But, whether it was the tobacco-smoke which clung to his clothes and his hair, or a sudden recollection of her condition, that made her turn away a little from the too stormy embrace, Amadeus noticed it, and stepped back as if hurt.

"You appear to be very indifferent about my coming home," said he, in a tone which betrayed some irritation.

"Oh, Amadeus!" exclaimed Constanze, astonished. "If you only knew how I have longed for you ever since nine o'clock!"

"Have I come too late, then?"

"You promised to be home by nine!" replied Constanze mildly. "I thought we were going to have such a pleasant evening. See, the tea-table is all set, but everything is cold now

"Why didn't you take your tea at the proper time, and go to bed? You knew—"

"I will tell you why I could not go to bed, Amadeus," and great drops sprang to her eyes at his question: "I was troubled about you—I could not sleep."

"Am I a child, then?" asked Mozart, impatiently.

But now he noticed for the first time that her eyes were swollen with weeping. It was always like a dagger-stroke in his heart to see his wife's eyes bear traces of tears. His great, true love for her rushed back to his consciousness, and he caught her in his arms again, crying—

"Stanzerl! forgive me! I was too vexed and worn out to-day, and a little angry besides; and—"

But how quickly real affection forgives!

"You betook yourself to the Würstl?" asked his wife, smiling, as Amadeus drew her down at his side on the sofa."

"Yes!" he exclaimed, as if vexed with himself. "I let myself be led by the devil, and went again to that cursed Würstl! You know, Stanzerl, how gay and merry everything is there. There's a company of roaring young fellows, keen and quick as lightning, full of wit and anecdotes and life—it makes a man forget his cares, for a few hours at least. Oh, you ought to have heard Schönmeyer![1] He was running over with the funniest new songs. Heaven knows where he gets them all; but they give me many an idea. And then there's that comical dog, Hassener, who has a ridiculous story about every man, woman, and child in Vienna!"

"Yes!" replied Constanze; "it's all very pleasant, but you know it costs ever so much; for I would bet that you furnished the supper, in your generous fashion, for the party."

"But, Stanzerl—"

"Wasn't it so?"

"Yes, child, but they make the evening so bright and gay—"

"Ah; but, Amadeus, it only increases your debts, and makes the days dark and troubled to pay for it. And your health, my darling! it is slipping away while you stay with such company. They can stand it—they are used to such a life, to revelling and carousing; but it is killing you. Your organization is finer and more delicate; and while they are sleeping all day to make up for rioting all night, your restless

---

[1] A buffo opera-singer.

brain rushes into work. Remember the weakness which so
often comes over you, now-a-days!"

Mozart was silent, for the truth of her words sank deep
into his heart. Then said he, after a little pause:

"You are right. I know it; and I promise you, on my
word, I will never again spend the evening out."

Constanze smiled. "Don't say that!" said she, softly,
putting her arm round her husband's neck. "Mustn't pull
up the wheat with the tares!¹ You shall go out many a time
to see friends, and to unbend your mind; only, stay not so
long, and—avoid the Würstl. The company may be ever so
gay; but it is unworthy of you, and betrays you into evil."

"Constanze!" exclaimed Mozart, "it has cost me a cursed
sum of money to-night, I admit; but I swear to you—"

"What is that you have brought me?" interrupted his
wife.

"Little mouse! it is a *bonbonnière*, full of the finest bonbons.
They came from the new confectioner's where we were looking into the window the other day. I knew you wanted
some of those chocolate-creams."

Constanze thanked him with a kiss, but there was a little
hurt in her heart; for she thought how ill he could afford to
buy her any unnecessary luxuries, and that every such ex-
penditure, however trifling, was paid for by his own life's
blood.

"And now," said Mozart, after they had sat and chatted
nearly an hour, "you must hurry to bed."

"And you—?" asked Constanze in alarm.

"I must work awhile."

This was just the answer which she feared.

"Dear Wolferl," said she, imploringly, "I beg of you, by
everything that is dear to you, come to bed. It is long
past midnight!"

"I can't yet!" he replied; "I feel just right for composing
now."

"And your health—? Oh, Wolferl!"

"Bah!" said Mozart, laughing; "I am used to it. Besides
I've promised that cantata, 'God watching over us,' for to-
morrow night. So you see, Stanzerl, it must be done."

Constanze answered only with a deep sigh. In truth, it
must be done. How easily and pleasantly Amadeus might

¹ The German phrase is, "Mustn't pour out the baby when you empty the bath
tub."—Tr.

have written the cantata after tea, if he had only come home earlier! Yet it was her husband, her great composer, her beloved; she would not say a syllable to make his work harder for him.

And Constanze went slowly and sorrowfully to her rest, as she had done so many, many nights before. As she folded her hands and bowed her head by her bedside for prayer there rose the swell of grand chords from the other room, and Mozart sang, half aloud—

"God, watching over us, slumbers not nor sleeps!"

Ah, how the quiet, trustful tones crept into her heart, and loosed the bands of grief till the tears came! She wept long. Then, as it grew brighter in the purified atmosphere of her spirit, she folded her hands again and prayed, "Lord, abide with us, for it is toward evening, and the day is far spent."

CHAPTER II.

THE PRESENTIMENT.

MOZART sat in his study, and at his side stood his most intimate friend, Abt Stadler,[1] a noble form, clad in the simple garb of the Church.

Both were looking at the libretto of "Die Zauberflöte," a new opera, which Mozart had engaged to write for Schikaneder, and the text of which had just been sent him by the Director.

Stadler and Mozart again and again shook their heads as they went through the libretto, which had been written by Schikaneder himself.

At last Amadeus exclaimed, half in jest and half in anger—

"This will be pretty work,—tickling the asses' long ears again!"

"No, Mozart! throw the book away; it isn't worthy of you!"

---

[1] Abt Maximilian Stadler, born 1748, and therefore eight years older than Mozart. He was a distinguished organist and composer of sacred music, and a firm friend of Mozart from boyhood. He wrote a fine oratorio, "The Recovery of Jerusalem," a noble requiem, many psalms, etc.

"But, dear friend, you forget that I have promised to write an opera to suit the times and the popular taste. Schikaneder came to me the other day, half crazy with his troubles. He is over head and ears in debt, just on the verge of bank· ruptcy; and says I alone can save him. A comic opera that should hit the public fancy would set the man on his feet again."

"Schikaneder!" replied Stadler, in disgust. "Why, he spends more money in a day than you or I would in a week. He and Signora Cavaglieri live like Barmecides!"

"Yes, I know he lives luxuriously; but he is really in a desperate condition, and I believe the man will cut his own throat if I don't write him a comic opera!"

"But," remonstrated Stadler, "how are you going to do it? It is square in the face of your nature and tastes!"

Mozart leaned back in his chair, put one arm across his head, and with his frank face smiling at Abt, he said:

"Maxerl, it is not your nature to live in the water; but if you stood on the bank, and saw a man drowning, and knew you could save him, would you hesitate to jump in because the water wasn't your element?"

"No!" said Abt, as if ashamed. "You are right. If only this man were worthy of the sacrifice which you make for him!"

"But would you stop to ask whether the drowning man's life were worth saving?"

"Noble friend!" replied Abt, "I cannot answer you."

"It takes courage, I admit," said Amadeus. "Here, for instance, I am to set a dozen quadrupeds dancing by blowing a flute; and here is a grand duett between a bird-catcher and his wife, the inspiring words of which are, "Pa-pa-pa-pa-pa," and so on; and may the devil take the accursed thing! But my word is given, and I am in for it. Well, triviality has the victory in this world! Why not make myself famous by a right asinine work, that shall forever overtop my other creations? Long live Vienna and its noble taste!"

"You are growing bitter!"

"No, that is the humor of the thing. What is it Lange used to be always roaring out of Shakspeare—'Go, doff the lion's hide, and hang a calf-skin on those recreant limbs!'"

Abt Stadler stopped in his pacing up and down the room.

"Do you know," said he, turning to his friend, "how that libretto appears to me?"

" How ?"

"As the product of a diseased brain, a mind that has gone crazy."

" Well, Schikaneder indeed seemed half out of his wits when he came to me the other day. It may be so."

" You see," continued Abt, " there is no connection between the incidents, nor between the characters; no chain of reason from beginning to end. It is all like a confused dream, or a lunatic's fancies."

Abt Stadler continued pacing slowly up and down the room, while Mozart sat with wide-open eyes gazing out into vacancy. His friend was lost in thought, and took no notice of a strange change that was taking place in Mozart's face.

The veins on his forehead were swollen, and he rested his head on one clenched hand,—half secretly, as if he feared to betray his pain to his friend. His eyes were distended, and his lip was bitten between his teeth. One would have said, to look at him, that he was suffering some unendurable bodily agony.

Suddenly Stadler caught sight of his friend's countenance, which seemed to have grown ten years older in the last ten minutes.

"Dear Wolfcrl!" he exclaimed, standing still in horror, "what is it? Are you ill?"

" It is nothing," said Mozart.

"What pains you so? Tell me, old friend!"

" It is nothing," repeated Mozart; " only a devil which catches me at times, but passes away if I am left alone a little while."

Stadler was silent a moment. He had seen Amadeus at such moments before, but never when he appeared to suffer so. Constanze, too, had spoken with him of the increasing frequency of such attacks. At last, he said—

"I will not press myself into your confidence. I will not trouble you, old friend; but if you will let me, I will stay with you for a little while."

"Yes, stay," said Mozart, smiling mournfully. " God knows how much longer we shall be able to be together !"

Stadler made as if he did not hear the last words. Seating himself at Mozart's piano, he seemed idling with the keys.

There was a deep silence in the room. All at once arose from the instrument harmonies which seemed the praise-songs of the angels in heaven,—so mild and soft, so ineffably sweet, so divinely tender, that Mozart's soul trembled beneath them. It was his own *Ave verum*, which Abt was playing with a master-hand. Imploringly breathed the tones that prayer—

> "Ave verum corpus natum
> De Maria virgine,
> Vere passum immolatum
> In cruce pro homine.
> Cujus latus perforatum
> Unda fluxit sanguine.
> Esto nobis prægustatum
> In mortis examine."

"Yes," whispered Mozart; "be our comfort in the hour of death!" And the ice which had held his heart was melted. He rose, and going to his friend he laid a hand upon his shoulder, and said:

"Maxerl! you shall know my secret: but you must swear not to reveal it to Constanze."

"Wherefore?" asked Abt; "is she not your true wife, who gladly shares every sorrow of your soul?"

"'Tis for just that reason!" said Mozart. "She has enough to bear already. She loves me so tenderly, that I would not for all the world lay a new sorrow on her heart."

"Well!" replied Stadler. "Be it as you say. I promise."

"Know, then, that I am soon to die."

"Wolferl! what an idea!"

"Even so, for I am poisoned!"

"My dear old friend!" said Stadler, "forgive me—but how came such an insane notion in your brain?"

"It is no notion," said Mozart in a tone of the deepest conviction.

"Then tell me what reason you have for thinking so."

"I feel it! I know it!"

There was a long pause. Then Stadler said:

"Mozart!"

"Well?"

"Do you know what it is to poison a man?"

"Yes, I know. It is to do a murder."

"And dares Mozart, the least suspicious, the noblest of men, accuse a brother, a fellow-creature, of such a crime?"

"No! I know whence the poison comes; but my lips will never disclose it. Enough of this. I should not have told you, Maxerl, but you saw my pain. It seems sometimes as if the icy hand of Death were already at my heart, and the blood boils in my brain. Then I know that my days are numbered, and to leave Stanzerl and the children in want, to leave them on the cold Earth alone, seems horrible. I do not fear death;—oh, Maxerl! it is easy, when one has grown familiar with the thought.—I have done what I could; and I know that when I am gone, this music I have written will live on, delighting and purifying the hearts of men."

He was silent, and great tears stood in his eyes.—When, half an hour afterward, his friend Albrechtsberger and his favorite scholar Süssmayer entered the room, there was no trace of what had passed, in Mozart. But Stadler's face showed the marks of recent suffering. He could not shake off the feeling that the great master's prophecy was true.

CHAPTER III.

THE VIOLET.

IT was a room in Schikaneder's splendid mansion. He had been consulting with his confidential servant, Chigot, as to the best means of putting off his creditors, and keeping his expensive establishment above-water. Chigot stood at this moment near the door, deferentially awaiting his master's further speech. He was a small man, growing gray and a little bald, with a sly, dry, silent face, suggestive of endless craft and a fathomless depth of secrecy. Schikaneder sat in a luxurious stuffed easy-chair, clothed in an elegant crimson silk dressing-robe, with one of the heavy tassels of which he was daintily playing, with the long white fingers of one hand, while the other languidly held the delicate handle of a cup of chocolate, that stood on a silver-footed little table at his side.

"What in the world has become of Mozart!" he now exclaimed impatiently. "I appointed nine o'clock for him, and here it is quarter of ten. I am getting tired of waiting. Is there anybody in the anteroom?"

"Oh, yes!" answered Chigot, with a submissive bow; 'a very pretty maid."

"What does she want?"

"To ask the Herr Director for admission to the chorus of the Leopold Theatre."

"And you say she is pretty?"

"She is quite beautiful."

"Let her come in, Chigot."

Chigot abased himself in a low bow; and as he turned to go, he said in a low voice, smiling like a satyr—

"'Tis a rare morsel—would do for the house, perhaps!"

"Old sinner!" exclaimed Schikaneder, laughing.

Chigot turned again, with his hand on the door-knob, and said—

"But what would the Signora say?"

"Bah!" replied his master. "It's easy to quiet her. She is a woman!"

"And for that very reason—"

Schikaneder shook his head. "A woman," he continued, carelessly, "is like a guitar. Both are incomplete instruments, but both are pleasant and seductive; very easily got out of tune, but also very easily put in tune again by a little skill. I will see to the tuning!" and he laughed cynically as his old servant slipped out of the room.

A few seconds afterward the visitor came in. It was indeed a lovely girl;—not so much beautiful, as trim and pretty. Her frank and honest eyes looked bashful and embarrassed at the handsome and powerful lord of the Leopold Theatre. Over her sweet face, with its sensitive little mouth and timid glance, lay the expression of maidenly innocence. Yet her young heart must have had sorrows to bear, for this was betrayed in a certain look of patient sadness,—a look which would have won the respectful awe of a less profane spirit than Schikaneder.

But the man of the world was utterly a stranger to either respect or awe; life had long ago uprooted them from his heart. He saw only the outward appearance—the soft face, the slender figure, the pretty hands and feet, and the dress so tidy, yet so poor.

She could not have been more than sixteen years old, and was evidently in want; perhaps so stricken with poverty as to be desperate, and then—so much the better, thought the Director.

"Come nearer, my child!" he said to the girl, who was overawed by the elegance of everything about her, and remained near the door.

She obeyed him tremblingly.

"What is your wish?"

"I wanted," she stammered, coloring, "to ask Herr von Schikaneder to take me into the chorus at the theatre."

"Well," answered the Director, enjoying the embarrassment of the poor child; "have you the requisite voice and musical training?"

"I have taken lessons a good while," she replied, timidly; "and they say my voice is good."

"We will try it," said he, getting up and going to the piano. "What is your voice?"

"Soprano."

"Sing these notes."

Her voice proved to be nothing extraordinary: it was fresh, clear, and of pure quality, but too weak for the stage. The Director said this, not softly, but in a harsh and indifferent tone, as if he would sell his compliance with her request at as high a price as possible.

At that moment Mozart entered the room with a roll of music under his arm. Schikaneder muttered a curse between his teeth, but turned about with a hearty greeting.

"Excuse me a moment," he said, "till I am done with this little visitor. The good child," and he took her by the chin and lifted up her face, "wants to enter the chorus for the opera, but her voice is too weak."

Both Mozart and Schikaneder now looked at the maiden. The former was surprised at the innocence and loveliness of her appearance: the latter saw with secret joy two great tears come into her eyes.

"Herr von Schikaneder!" she stammered, imploringly, "do not cast me off—I have a sick mother!"

Schikaneder shrugged his shoulders:

"So it is only through distress that you come?" said he. "You forget that the theatre is not an almshouse."

"I thought," said she, coloring deeply, "that I might, perhaps, through my voice, take care of mother."

"Are you, then, so unfortunate?" asked Mozart, now with a voice of pitying mildness.

The poor child answered only with a flood of tears. Amadeus, who had laid down his hat and music, sought to com-

fort her. Schikaneder threw himself down in his easy-chair
again, and said—

"Be quiet, child. Perhaps you will do better as an actress
than a singer. We must see about it. Come here again this
evening, and you shall recite something before me, and if I
find that you correspond to my wishes and purpose, I will
take care of you."

At these words the pretty little face brightened up as if
a sunbeam had flown over it; but so much the darker grew
the expression of Mozart's countenance. The peculiar tone
of Schikaneder's voice had not escaped him. Could he—but
no, his friend could not be capable of such sacrilege! Amadeus reproved himself for having even suspected him of it.

The maiden was opening the door to depart.

"This evening, remember," called out the Director once
more. "And take time enough, for I want to have you try
a long *rôle*, and see whether you can do it properly."

"As your honor commands," said she, with a trembling
obeisance, and disappeared.

There was at the same moment a triumphant smile on Schikaneder's face, as he rubbed his hands, and said half aloud,
"Chigot was right!"

Mozart felt as though a dagger had struck him: he had
not heard the words, but he saw the smile. His friend seemed
to him now as a fiend incarnate; and yet, might it not be
that he misjudged him? At all events, his own cheerfulness
was all gone, and disgust and anger had taken its place; for,
whatever spots there had been on Mozart's life, innocence
had always been as sacred to him as the honor of a sister.

"Now then, Mozart," said Schikaneder from his easy-chair,
"what have you brought to-day that is new?"

"Papageno's song."

"Ah ha!" said the Director, joyfully. "My grand scene
in the first Act—'The catcher of the birds am I, and always
laughing, hi, hi, hi!'"

"Yes!" answered Mozart, ironically; "that's a fine thought
for music—'hi, hi, hi!'"

"'Thought!'" exclaimed Schikaneder, laughing. "Is a
libretto a philosophical treatise? All the public wants is to
amuse itself by seeing and hearing."

Mozart's mind was full of the little maiden, and he did not
feel like discussion. So he sat down silently at the piano
put the notes before him, and played and sang the song in

question. It was good, but not the one which we have now in the opera. This was more deeply handled, and though comical, yet in a higher style.

"It won't do, Mozart," said Schikaneder. " 'Tisn't ridiculous enough."

"What?"

"Papageno is something of a clown, and must—"

"Then write a clown's song yourself, to suit you!"

"But, my friend—?"

"I know what I am doing. It is unworthy—"

"Nothing is unworthy which helps to our end."

"Fine principle!"

"Practical principle!" replied Schikaneder, calmly. "Whoever would offer the ideal to men, or point out a new path for them, or put before their dull eyes the beautiful, the noble, the sublime, in their purity and greatness, may count with certainty on receiving, instead of praise and recognition, kicks and curses. What is it that the crowd want? They want their senses tickled, only their senses. They want to enjoy, and to do it without the trouble of thinking. They can't understand the highest; and what they don't understand they curse and ridicule. Unhappily, 'tis much easier to curse a thing than to appreciate it, so they curse away in the name of God."

Mozart's face wore a grim look of anger. He recognized a great truth in the Director's words—a truth which his own experience with "Figaro" and "Don Giovanni" had sadly taught him; but to hear from those frivolous lips a truth which had cut into his own heart so deeply, was doubly irritating.

"What the devil do I care!" he exclaimed, and his eyes flashed with scornful rage. "Shall I do as the half-artists do—merely snatch after popular applause? Do you think there's nothing in the world to work for except the chink of ducats, and the clapping of horny hands in the theatre?"

"Mozart," said Schikaneder, with all the oily suavity of his nature, "what was it you promised me?"

"To write an opera, but not to scrawl one!"

"An opera to suit the popular taste!" repeated the Manager slowly and meaningly.

"And be damned!" cried Mozart, enraged; and springing away from the piano, he fairly danced up and down before Schikaneder, and sang in shrill derision: "The catcher of the birds am I, and always laughing, hi, hi, hi!"

But scarcely had his voice fallen on Schikaneder's ear, when he leaped up, and clapping Mozart on the shoulder, cried—

"That's capital! That's just the thing! Just as I wanted it."

Amadeus was himself surprised. An idea had come to him in his anger which was not so bad. He must needs seat himself at the table straightway, and write down the new air. While he was hurriedly doing it, Schikaneder slyly took the first song from the piano and hid it away among some music-books.

When Amadeus had finished, the Director looked at it and then said:

"Mozart, this popular opera will do more for your fame than all the rest of your works. The critics will find enough in it that is scientific, and the masses will be delighted with it."

"Oh yes!" said Amadeus bitterly; "the masses will be whistling it, no doubt—"

"And the name of Mozart will be spread all over the world by it. Friend, rely on this prophecy of a practical man: the 'Magic Flute' will make you famous just as sure as my name is Schikaneder! And now, what else have you got written?"

Then Mozart sat down again at the piano and played that inimitable chorus of the priests— *O Isis and Osiris.* And as he played on and on, the expression of anger on his face yielded more and more to his natural look, till his features were lit up with that exaltation—that mysterious calmness— that heavenly harmony, bright with cheerfulness, yet solemn and sublime—to which this music has given immortal expression.

Even Schikaneder was enraptured with it. "It is grand!" he cried. "That *Soon will be worthy of us*, is glorious. You have caught my idea exactly!"

"Indeed!" said Mozart with a deep irony, which the Manager did not notice, for he was thinking only of the effect which the chorus would produce.

Schikaneder now pressed Mozart to stay to dinner with him, promising him an elegant *déjeûner à la fourchette.* But Mozart was in no mood for it. The occurrence which had met him on his arrival had built up a wall of ice between him and the unprincipled Director. He therefore declined the invitation, and frostily took his leave.

On the way home a multitude of thoughts thronged his

brain. He longed to warn the poor maiden of her danger, and to give her such aid as he might be able to; but he had no idea of her name, or where she lived. He at last determined to watch for her in the evening, and intercept her on her way to Schikaneder's house. But still his good heart kept saying to him over and over, that perhaps he was doing the Director injustice by such a suspicion of his motives. So he reached home; and going at once to his room, he threw himself down on the sofa and supported his head in both hands.

Then came over him that strange melancholy which now so often seized him. Long he brooded over the dark shadows that palled his heart. Suddenly he got up, took a piece of music-paper and hastily wrote down some notes. Then seating himself at his piano, he played and sang this little song of Goethe's, to which he had written a beautifully tender *motif* and refrain:

> " A violet in the meadow stood,
> Unseen, bent down in lowlihood—
> It was a darling violet !
> Soon came a shepherd-maiden there,
> With tripping step and blithesome air
> So fair, so fair !
> And sang a carol sweet.

> " ' Ah !' thought the violet, ' for the power
> To bloom as Nature's fairest flower,
> But for one moment only !
> To be by that dear maiden blest,
> And plucked, and pillowed on her breast,
> Though 'twere, though 'twere
> But one, one moment fleet.'

> " Alas ! the maiden nearer drew,
> Nor saw the violet where it grew,
> And crushed the little blossom !
> It died, but it rejoiced—' I lie
> Crushed by her tread, by her I die ;
> By her, by her—
> Beneath her blessed feet !' "

Mozart was thinking of the dear child, "It was—," and of his own life—its hopes, its strivings, its approaching end. And still there murmured in his heart:

> " Ah ! the poor violet !
> It was a darling violet."

CHAPTER IV.

THE UNKNOWN MESSENGER.

THERE was a feast to-day in the Mozart house--a festival which pleasantly broke up the somewhat straitened household life, and the incessant labor of the composer on his "Magic Flute." It was the christening-day of the new child, which had received its father's name, Wolfgang Amadeus.

Constanze was very happy. So many darlings had been taken away from her, that she pressed this precious gift to her heart with double love. Every one said·that the little world-citizen looked like his father; and that name had been given him, the dearest of all earthly names to her. The day before, too, Amadeus had exclaimed gleefully: "The boy will be a true Mozart, for he always cries in the very key in which I happen to be playing!" [1]

To-day, for the first time, she was again in the company of her friends, who had assembled at the christening-party. There was her sister Sophie, her brother-in-law Hofer, Abt Stadler, Schack,[2] Albrechtsberger, Görl, and Mozart's two favorite scholars, Süssmayer and Seyfried. They were all noble souls, and tried friends of the family. Süssmayer was afterward to be still closer bound to them by his marriage with Sophie Weber, to whom he already was fondly attached.

They had just finished a bountiful dinner, to which all had done full justice, and were now sipping their wine, and chatting, laughing, and making merry over the toasts which the occasion furnished, and over the improvised wit and poetry in which Mozart kept the lead. He was almost his old self to-day; and the look of weariness which of late had taken the place of his former animation, had been chased away by the genial society of his friends.

They talked long and pleasantly together, for there was no restraint in the little company; they knew each other and

---

[1] Historical.—Nissen, p. 587.
[2] Benedict Schack, first tenor at Schikaneder's theatre, for whom the *rôle* of *Tamino* in the "Zauberflöte," was written.

understood each other as one soul. They brought up bright scenes from the past, and enjoyed their happiness over again. Especially were all of Mozart's past works talked over, and the circumstances under which they were composed; and Amadeus related many a comical occurrence in connection with their history.

From the past they came to speak of Mozart's future, and the works which he would yet create. There was many a merry jest over the subjects which each of the company in turn suggested as themes for operas, and many a pleasant hope expressed for the future prosperity and honor of the great composer whom they all so loved.

But as the conversation drifted more and more into the unknown years that were before them, Mozart's face lost its gayety and brightness, and shadow after shadow deepened upon it. Constanze's faithful eyes had seen the change approaching long before it was thought of by the others, and had endeavored to lead the conversation back to lighter themes; but it was too late. Mozart's mind had left the present and its joyful surroundings, and was communing with that Infinite whose solemnity lay now habitually on his countenance.

"Friends!" he said, after a little silence, which had fallen on the company when they all noticed the hush that had crept over his own face and manner, "there may be little more for me to do of earthly work. It is little that I have done in all these years. I have never written the music that was in my heart to write. Perhaps I never shall with this brain and these fingers. But I know that hereafter it will be written;—when, instead of these few inlets of the senses through which we now receive impressions from without, there shall be a flood of impressions from all sides; and instead of these few tones of our little octave, there shall be an infinite scale of harmonies. For I feel it—I am sure of it!" and he rose from his seat, and paced slowly up and down the room; "this world of music, into whose borders even now I have entered, is a reality—is immortal. These musical ideas, which even now I bear within me, cannot be lost, cannot have been in vain."

"Dear Wolferl," said Constanze, with forced sprightliness, but with tears gathering in her eyes, "indeed they shall not! Haven't you already, insatiate worker that you are, nearly finished a new opera that is going to be splendid?"

Mozart shook his head thoughtfully, and said—
"That is not it!"

"And then, too," continued Constanze cheerily, bent on conquering the sombre mood of her husband, "there is Kaiser Leopold going to be crowned in Prague, and somebody has got to write a great festival opera for his Majesty. Who knows but they will—"

"That is not it!" repeated Mozart. "I cannot tell exactly what it is I am coming to."

At this moment the maid entered, and announced that a messenger was without, who wished to speak with the Herr Capellmeister Mozart.

"Where does he come from?" asked Constanze. But the girl could not inform her.

"He wishes to speak with the Herr Capellmeister himself."

"Let him come in then," said Mozart.

The door opened, and there entered an elderly man of pale countenance, whose tall and stately form was clad in a plain suit of sombre gray.

At another time there would, perhaps, have been nothing startling in the appearance of this man; but now, after what had just been said, and in the intense mood which held them all, it moved them painfully. Even Mozart was startled. But he recovered himself immediately, and going to the man, asked him in a friendly tone—

"Whom have I the pleasure of seeing before me?"

"I am but the messenger of another," was the laconic answer, "and I have this to deliver."

And he handed a note to Mozart. It was sealed in black. Mozart broke the seal and opened it.

"Without signature!" he exclaimed, in surprise, and read the contents. Suddenly he turned pale; then a deep red suffused his face; and, holding the note in his hand, with one arm behind him, he walked several times up and down the room. At last he stood still, and murmured softly to himself "Yes, this is it!"

The whole company had till now been following the master with their eyes in intense interest and sympathy. Now Constanze interrupted the oppressive silence:

"Well, Wolferl," said she, in as indifferent a tone as possible, "may we know what it is the messenger brings?"

"Certainly!" replied Mozart. "It is the question whether

I will undertake the composition of a requiem—a mass for the dead—and for what price, and by what time."

"A requiem?" repeated Constanze, and she knew not why the familiar word struck with such a shock upon her at that moment.

"Yes!" said Mozart. "I believe this is what I meant before. I have long desired to attempt the higher style of cathedral music." Then approaching the sombre messenger, he asked: "Who sends this order? From whom do you come, my good sir?"

But the man's pale and earnest face changed not, as he replied, coldly—

"That is of no consequence. ı ask only your answer."

Mozart made his decision at once. This mysterious message seemed to him like a voice from heaven, calling him to a work which he had long neglected. He sat down at his table, therefore, and wrote in reply, that he would undertake the composition of a requiem for a moderate price, but that he could not precisely fix the time of its completion, though he would like to know whither he should send the work when finished.

This reply was handed to the silent man in sombre gray, who took his leave with a deep and stately bow.[1]

Two weeks after this occurrence, Mozart received a commission to write the festival opera for the coronation of the new Emperor at Prague. There would be but eighteen days left to write the opera, if he should set out for Prague the next day, and the *Zauberflöte* was not yet completed. But he at once concluded to undertake it, and Constanze hastily packed up for the journey.

It was a bright summer morning when the carriage drove up before the door. All was ready for their departure, and Sophie Weber was to take care of the house and of little Karl during their absence. Mozart was in miserable health, but the excitement of the new commission and the idea of the journey had brightened his face and cheered his heart, so that he took leave of the friends who had assembled to see him off, with his old animation. As they left the house and descended the steps, the bright sunshine seemed to throw a halo of fairest hope over the laughing composer and his faithful wife, who leaned on his arm, while Sophie carried the little Wolfgang beside her.

---

[1] The whole account, here and afterward, is historical.

"In with you," said the smiling Sophie to her sister; "I will give you baby afterward."

But just then Constanze felt some one touch her on the arm. She started, looked round, and uttered a sharp cry of terror. Close by the carriage stood, silent and motionless as a spirit, the tall messenger in sombre gray, with his pale face turned toward Mozart.

"How goes it with the requiem?" he asked, fixing his eyes earnestly on the composer.

A slight shudder passed over Mozart's limbs, and it was as if he heard, in that solemn question, his own doom pronounced.

"I am called away to Prague," he answered. "Tell him from whom you come, that the requiem shall be my first work after I return. I know not whether he will wait so long."

"He will wait!" replied the messenger, who bowed low and disappeared. Mozart stepped in and took his seat beside Constanze, and the carriage rolled away.

Three weeks later there had been a little dinner-party, one evening, at Director Bondini's, in honor of the completion of that famous festival opera, "*La Clemenza di Tito*." The company had broken up early, for Mozart was too ill to remain. He had worked night and day on the opera, in spite of his constantly-failing health, and had not only finished it in season, but had written several airs for the "Zauberflöte" in the mean time. But to look at his wan face and hollow eyes, one would have said his earthly work was nearly done forever.

The guests had all departed, and Bondini had retired to his chamber, after bidding the last one good-night.

"So we have had Mozart here once more," said he to his charming little wife. "It was delightful to have him at our table again; though—"

But Bondini stopped, for his look fell on his wife, who was sitting with her face hidden in her handkerchief, quietly crying.

"My child, what is it?" said he tenderly, sitting down at her side. "It is a strange thing to see my little madcap in tears. What has grieved you so?"

"Can you ask?" she replied, sorrowfully. "Oh, I saw that it moved you as it did me, even while at table; but you would not let him see that you were thinking how changed he is"

"Yes," said Bondini sadly, as he rose and walked up and down the chamber, with his arms behind him. "I would gladly have concealed it even from myself. He is no longer the shadow of what he was four years ago."

"Ah!" exclaimed the little woman, and her bright eyes were full of tears, "how brimful of life and fun he was then! strong, too, in spite of his slender appearance, and a perfect giant in working; and now—"

"Yet," said Bondini, after pacing the room a few moments in silence, "it may not be so bad as it seems. He was very cheerful to-night at dinner."

"I know," she replied; "and it was that very cheerfulness which made me heart-sick. It was so quiet and sad. When he looked at me with his true eyes, so deep and mournful now, and when the pale tired face forced itself to smile, I could hardly keep the tears back. It seemed as if he would constantly say, 'I would so dearly love to live and be bright and happy, but—Death has laid his hand on my heart.'"

"He has worked his very life into his music, till his bodily frame is shattered."

"And his spirit is broken."

"Oh, no!" exclaimed Bondini. "It is wonderful what strength the man has spiritually. Think what he has lately done. He has written this coronation opera for us, and the "Zauberflöte" for Schikaneder, two works which are utterly different from each other, and both magnificent; and he is already thinking of a requiem, which is to be commenced as soon as he reaches home. But that is not all. In the last few weeks he has produced a cantata, a concerto for the clarionet, and another cantata for the Freemasons."[1]

"But," cried she, "cannot Constanze keep him from working so—cannot his friends?"

"We have done what we could," said Bondini, shrugging his shoulders. "You know how Duscheck and I have tried to keep him from his desk, and have tempted him to the only relaxation which he can be got to take, and that is billiards. But even with the cue in his hand he is busy with his music. Only day before yesterday we were all of us at the coffee-house around here, playing, when we noticed that Mozart was going 'hm, hm, hm,' all through the game. First Du-

---

[1] Historical.

scheck would make a shot, and Mozart would stand drumming on his cue-handle. Then Mozart would lean over the table,—'hm, hm, hm' he would sing with his lips shut, then strike his ball and fall to drumming again. At the end of the game he went into mine host's parlor, took out a sheet of music-paper and wrote for a few minutes. Then he called to us to come in, sat down at the piano, and played a quintette to us. It was for the first Act of the 'Zauberflöte,' he said; it begins with a humming song, where Papageno is to come in with a padlock on his mouth."

"Was it good?" asked his wife.

"Oh, I wish you could hear it!" replied Bondini. "It is delicate and airy as a moonlight dance of fairies; and the *Allegro* trips along in monosyllables, with all the free lightness of an instrumental *Scherzo:* 'Sil–ver—bells—and—mag–ic—flute—notes.' It is perfectly beautiful!"

"Bondini!" said his wife, "can it be they are so poor that he is killing himself with work, when we, who owe all our fortune to him, are so well and happy?" and the little wife hid her face again and wept bitterly.

"They are poor," replied her husband; "but there is something else. I would not have spoken of it to you, for it is a sad thought; but rather than have your dear heart feel that we are to blame, I must tell you. You have seen what a feverish restlessness possesses Mozart now-a-days?"

"Yes!"

"That unrest seems to me as though his body and soul felt already the near approach of dissolution, and sought to enjoy and to do as much as possible before it is too late! God grant that I am wrong; but I fear me I have seen correctly!"

There was a long pause: then said she, rising—

"If Mozart should go away so early—I cannot believe that he will—but if he should die now, what a tragic solemnity his history would wear! So great, so loved, so glorious, and yet so forgotten and unrewarded! departing without that unfading laurel-crown, which he above all other men has won! Bondini, it is a strange world in which such things happen—it must be a strange God who permits them!"

"Child!" said the Director, smiling as he looked into her earnest eyes, and smoothed the hair from her forehead—"remember that we do not see behind the scenes in these life tragedies. Perhaps when the play is done we shall!"

13*

CHAPTER V.

THE MAGIC FLUTE.

THE montl. of September, 1791, was nearly at an end. Mozart had returned from Prague more ill than when he left Vienna, and yet an enormous pile of work was awaiting him.

Schikaneder, to whom he had written beforehand what day he should arrive, met him at the carriage-door. The *Zauberflöte* was to be given for the first time on the last day of September; and there yet remained unwritten the Overture, and the Priest's March for the beginning of the second Act. Schikaneder was ready to despair; but Mozart laughingly reassured him, and two days before the performance both these masterpieces were ready.

When the time came, Vienna was in just such an excitement as Prague had been before the bringing out of "Don Giovanni."

Schikaneder had proved himself a master in the art of filling his purse by new operas. For weeks before the 30th of September, wherever he showed himself he went into raptures over the music of the "Magic Flute," and over Mozart.

"No!" he would exclaim with enthusiastic emphasis; "there never was such music heard before! The 'Don Juan,' 'Figaro,' 'Titus,' 'Entführung,' 'Cosa Rara,' 'Axur,' —all the new operas are nothing in comparison with it. It is the most popular, and at the same time the sublimest music that ever was dreamed of!"

Schikaneder was just the man, too, who could inoculate everybody he met with the same enthusiasm, and make every hearer rely implicitly on his words.

But Schikaneder was a diplomatist also. He knew that just as certainly as his rapturous speeches would excite a tremendous interest in the forthcoming opera among all classes of society, it would affect the enemies of Mozart as well. Salieri and his party could not have any more feared and hated thing than such an opera from the German composer. If they got the idea that it was to be what Schikaneder everywhere represented, they would turn the earth upside down to accomplish its ruin. By bribery, threats, intrigues, assassination—by every means which the devil could invent and an Italian execute, they would defeat it at the very outset.

So what does the shrewd Director of the Leopold Theatre? He calls in the aid of that sly fox, Signore Chigot, and instructs him to take every opportunity to confer with Salieri and his comrades, and under the seal of secrecy to confide to them that his master's enthusiasm was all a pretence, to which he was forced by his despair at the certain failure of the thing. Chigot undertook this *rôle* with delight, and played it to perfection. The music was—he could swear to it—the most miserable stuff; nothing but milk and water; a wretched attempt to gain popularity. It proved plainly enough that Mozart's strength was gone—his body and mind broken down. Chigot even studied his part so thoroughly as to go into minutiæ—making himself merry over different places in the libretto, and burlesquing the music, till the hostile party was lulled into complete inactivity, sure of victory. The members of the orchestra and the singers, meantime, were sworn to secrecy as to the whole matter.

Schikaneder was not satisfied with these strategic measures alone. He knew well enough that the fine music of the "Magic Flute" must eventually win its way by its own inherent excellence, without any strategy at all. But that was not sufficient. He wanted to make a great fortune out of it, and immediately. This could only happen by insuring to the new opera a "first night" such as had never been known in Vienna before.

And the Director knew his public to a hair-stroke! He set Chigot at work in all the *cafés*, and inns, and beer-gardens, dropping little scraps of information about the opera whose character had been kept so mysteriously hidden.

The wily and plausible rascal would take his seat and sip his coffee or his beer, letting fall, from time to time, some fresh wonder which was to appear in the *Zauberflöte.*

"What! a serpent?" cried one of the guests, with wide-open eyes.

"Yes! a gigantic serpent!" replied Chigot.

"Not alive though?"

Chigot shrugged his shoulders mysteriously.

"*Dear* Herr von Chigot! not *alive?*"

Chigot looked into his empty glass and said:

"As large as my arm!"

"Heavens!" cried several, pressing nearer to him. "Tell us what comes next?"

"I dare not; I should lose my place."

"Your place?" broke in the landlord, who had stood with open mouth behind Chigot's chair. "All Vienna knows that Herr Chigot is the Manager's right-hand man. He couldn't do without him."

Chigot simpered, as though greatly flattered; and the landlord beckoned to the maid to bring the guest another glass of beer.

"Tell us just a little!" he pleaded.

"Well—but you are not to tell a word of it!—then there comes out a troop of lions, bears, and apes."

"Lions?" exclaimed several voices. "Not real ones?"

"Lions from Nubia," said Chigot, behind his hand, lest the other guests should hear; "but tame ones, for they draw the triumphal chariot."

"Whose? Whose?"

"Hist!" said Chigot—"Hist! I have tattled too much already. This damned tattling! And then the Moors—oh! it is wonderful!"

"Moors, Chigot?—Herr *von* Chigot, I mean. Actual Moors? and many of them?"

"A chief Moor and twenty-four Moorish slaves. And if you could see how these Moors—," and Chigot began to laugh heartily—"how these Moors—," and he roared and shook with laughter, till they all laughed with him without knowing why.

"How they—?" asked the landlord, breathlessly.

"How they make up the infernalest faces, and dance at the sound of the magic bells—whether they want to or not, you see! Ha! ha! ha!"

"Magic *flutes*, you mean, don't you?" ventured one.

"Magic *bells*, I think I said!" answered Chigot, looking at the man severely.

"Magic flutes and magic bells, both? I must see that opera, if I take my pants to the pawnbroker's for it!"

"'Twill pay you!" exclaimed Chigot, shaking his head meaningly. "It cost us a monstrous sum!"

"Two thousand florins?" suggested one.

"Ho!" cried Chigot, disdainfully.

" Four thousand ?"

Chigot spread his hands apart, as if the real sum were not in the same arithmetic with that named.

" What! more than four thousand ?" asked the landlord.

Chigot motioned to him to put his head down, and whispered something in his ear.

" Great Peter! is it possible !"

" But no one must know it," said Chigot, holding his finger up.

" Not a soul," the landlord assured him; at the same time whispering softly to his neighbor—

" Eight thousand !"

" How much ?" whispered a second man, stretching his neck forward toward the first.

" Ten thousand !" was the reply.

" But, oh ! if I dared tell you !" said now Chigot, shutting his lips tight together and shaking his head, as if it fairly tottered with its weight of mystery.

" What—what is it ? We will be silent as the grave !"

" Upon honor ?"

" Upon honor !" cried all, though they could scarcely stand still with eagerness to rush off to the next alehouse and impart the news.

Chigot bent forward, that all might catch his whisper—

" The whole Freemasonry is to come out !"

" Impossible !   What! even the God-be-with-us ?"

" Hist ! Hist !" said Chigot. " Nobody must hear it. I say the whole Freemasonry, with all their unearthly secrets ! I tell you 'tis marvellous. But not a word more."

And Chigot paid his reckoning, and departed to repeat the same scene with some new assemblage.

At last, the day for the bringing out of the *Zauberflöte* arrived, and the excitement and curiosity concerning the opera were at their highest, not only among the lovers of music and admirers of Mozart, but among the theatre-goers and pleasure-seekers also, in the lower as well as the loftier ranks of people. Never had a performance been awaited with such feverish impatience and expectancy in Vienna, as was this. It seemed almost as if some event of transcendant importance to all the world were coming ; many a man was already so excited in the morning that he was not in a condition to do any work all day long.

The tickets had all been sold eight days before the per

formance. Schikaneder rubbed his hands with satisfaction.

But there was another man who rejoiced at the brilliant prospects of the new opera, and that was Lange, who now lived in Vienna, and had forced himself upward to an eminent position as an actor. He was nearly the same rollicking and reckless genius as of old, though the years were gradually giving him a little more earnestness and strength of purpose. He had not met Mozart face to face for years; but he had never forgotten the afternoon at the "Swan," in Neckarau, while at the same time he revered his old friend as the greatest living composer. It was no wonder, therefore, that Lange was on hand at the theatre long before the doors were opened that evening.

Besides his intense interest in the occasion, he thought it would be a fine opportunity to study from nature in the midst of all that swarm of human beings, and to catch varied expressions of face and action which might be turned to account on the stage. He was curious, also, to see to what heights of extravagance the popular rumors about the opera had reached, and to observe the different motives which brought people to hear it.

Lange took up a position just behind a group of laborers, who were among the crowd in front of the Leopold Theatre, and listened to their talk.

"How much do you say the opera cost?" asked one, in a tone of astonishment.

"Twenty thousand florins!"

"Twenty!" exclaimed a third. "It cost twenty-*five* thousand! I have it from a good source. A friend of mine keeps company with a niece of the man that lights the lamps in the theatre, and she told him."

"But," says the first, "that is a great deal of money!"

"Ho!" was the reply; "for all there is in this opera? I think it's very cheap. Four live lions from Nu—, Nu—, Numadia, I think it is, with two tigers, an elephant, and goodness knows how many apes and serpents!"

"Yes!" put in Lange, "and then the Moors—only think of the Moors!"

"Are they real Moors, then?" asked the twenty-five thousand man, with wide-open eyes.

"Of course," said Lange, seriously. "Herr von Schikaneder had them brought from Numadia with the lions."

"Ah! then they must have cost!—Is Numadia far?"

"I should think it was!" replied the twenty-thousand man, with a very learned look. "'Tis a good piece the other side of Africa."

"Yes," said Lange, "and you know the creatures eat raw meat, too, like the lions."

"Certainly," said a little smutty-faced man, who had been for some time eager to tell something; "my brother-in-law is a butcher, and supplies the meat for them."

Lange's mouth twitched at the corners, but he went on solemnly: "If only they don't get wild during the opera, instead of dancing!"

"What! the lions?"

"No, the Moors!"

"Yes," said the little man, looking scared; "at the sight of such a crowd! I'm glad we are going up into the gallery, anyhow!"

Just then a well-known voice fell on Lange's ear.

"That's Salieri!" he said to himself. "What in the world is the court Capellmeister doing among these plebeians?"

It was indeed the Italian, who was working his way slowly through the thickening crowd, arm in arm with an aristo-cratic-looking personage. For some unknown reason he was talking in an extraordinarily loud voice, as Lange noticed at once.

"H'm!" muttered the actor. "Either his companion must be deaf, or Salieri has some end to gain by this unusual exertion of his lungs." And he stationed himself where he could hear him without being seen.

"Yes, my dear Baron," exclaimed Salieri, so loud that every one turned toward him as he gradually drew nearer. "You can take my word for it: our poor friend Mozart is very much broken. Mind and body are failing him. I could weep to think of it, but it is a fact that the music of this *Zauberflöte* is utterly weak and unmeaning!"

"Is it possible!"

"That is the reason Schikaneder has spent so much on the externals of it. I confess to you that I go to it with the most painful anxiety lest it should be a perfect failure!"

"Too bad! And people are expecting so much!"

"They will be bitterly disappointed! and—"

But now the conversation was lost in the noise of the crowd.

"Scoundrel!" muttered Lange in disgust. But just then a hundred voices called out:

"Silence!—Silence!"

A stout fellow with a fresh face and red beard had raised himself on the shoulders of two muscular comrades, and now sung out:

"Don't you believe what they said! I don't know much about music—I'm only a carpenter; but I was at work in the theatre when the opera was rehearsed, and the devil may take me if it isn't the greatest music I ever heard in my life!"

A tremendous cheer greeted this speech as the orator jumped down, and a "Hurrah for Mozart!" spread through the crowd.

"Good!" thought Lange. "The heart of the people is always right. So the damned Italians are at their old tricks to ruin Mozart, are they? All right. As Hamlet says:[1]

> 'Let it work;
> For 'tis the sport, to have the engineer
> Hoist with his own petar: and it shall go hard
> But I will delve one yard below their mines,
> And blow them at the moon!' "

And he turned to go and seek Schikaneder, to warn him against plots that were probably brewing to break up the opera during its performance; but his way was blocked up by a troop of cobblers' apprentices. They came on whistling and singing, regardless of the public's ears, for their employers had given them the evening to go and see the apes, Moors, and lions of the *Zauberflöte*.

"By Apollo!" said Lange to himself, the instant he caught sight of them; "that's just the band of Trojans I need, to help me against my wily Ulysses!" and at once he stepped right in front of the advancing troop.

Their leader was a hard-looking youngster, with a bony face, and with shoulders and fists which suggested prize-fighting rather than cobbling. When he found Lange in his way he set up a vigorous whistling; and putting his fists in his pockets, and making sharp wedges of his elbows, he gave the obstacle a doughty shove, calculated to set him to one side. But the actor was prepared for it, and parried it as if it had been Laertes' rapier, without moving from his place.

---

[1] Hamlet was Lange's best *rôle*.

This excited the wrath of the young Trojan.

"Get out of the way, camel!" he cried.

But Lange seemed to possess the shield of Minerva with the Medusa's head; for suddenly the knob-nosed youth stood quiet and appeased. The actor had produced a twenty-kreutzer piece and held it up.

"Noble Trojan!" said he, "I will give you and each of your comrades such a twenty, and free entrance to the opera besides, if you will agree not to leave my side this evening, and to do everything which you see me do!"

"I'm a cobbler, and my name is Peter, and not Trojan; and you might have left your wit at home. We shall see apes and camels enough to-night besides you."

"But you shall see 'em without its costing you a kreutzer; and make a twenty into the bargain!"

"Strike the bargain, Peter!" cried the chorus behind him. "Strike the bargain—but the money first!"

"Here 'tis!" said Lange, giving each his piece. "I know you'll stick to the agreement."

"Yes, by the holy Crispin!" they all exclaimed.

"Now then, Trojans, follow me!" said Lange, pulling his cap down over his eyes so as not to be recognized; "only keep a few steps behind me. If I stand still, do you stop too: if I go ahead, push on also: if I clap my hands in the theatre—"

"We'll clap with you!" they cried.

"If I call 'Bravo!'—"

"You'll hear us shout till the walls shake!"

"And if I flog any one after the opera—"

"Hurrah! hurrah!" cried all; "we'll pitch into him!" and in joyous anticipation of the fulfilment of this hope, new cheers went up from the Trojan ranks.

This jubilation was not noticed, however, on account of the noise and jam of the crowd in front of the theatre. For the same reason, Salieri and his companion had not succeeded in advancing any further, so that Lange soon had him well surrounded by his cohort.

In vain sought the imperial Court Capellmeister to escape, but whichever way he turned, the accursed 'prentice lads confronted him, and they in turn were so pressed upon by the throng behind, that they could not have let him out if they would. Meantime they kept up such a din of whistling close at his ears that conversation was no longer to be thought of. So all in a heap, they shoved and were shoved along, and naturally toward that entrance which led to the galleries.

Salieri vainly called out that he wanted to go to the other entrance, which led to the boxes. Nobody paid any attention to him. It was one indiscriminate scramble, for the doors had been opened, and the whole crowd was filled with the single idea of getting a place in the theatre. There was no possibility even of turning round; and where a man here and there was unfortunate enough to be faced the wrong way, up the steps he went backward in spite of his struggles, and into the theatre.

Salieri was desperate. Miser though he was, he offered sum after sum of money—in vain! The noble Trojans could not have helped him if he had been made of gold, and given himself away piecemeal. The Fates had settled it, and before many minutes the Capellmeister and the Baron found themselves where they never had deigned to be before—in the gallery of the Leopold Theatre, in a crowd of mechanics and 'prentices, and so packed that they could not even get their snuff-boxes out of their pockets to brace up their fainting noses against that unwonted atmosphere.

Lange was in a state of the wildest delight over Salieri's predicament. He made some rare studies from the contortions of rage and despair on the clammy features of the little Italian, and quoted passage after passage from Shakspeare, as to villainy overreaching itself, for the somewhat obtuse appreciation of his Trojan neighbors.

So passed away something like two hours, when suddenly a universal excitement and a thundering cheer announced the entrance of Mozart and the beginning of the opera. Salieri gnawed his livid lips and cursed till he was hoarse, but the storm of cheers would not cease. At last, after ten minutes of uproar, the sharp rap of the conductor's baton hushed the house to silence. It was Mozart himself who wielded it.

It was an opera-night such as stands alone in the annals of Vienna.

From the first movement of the overture, the vast audience was breathlessly still, every ear bent to drink in that delicious harmony, that exuberant wealth of melody, that enchantment of fairy-like rhythm.

The throng which packed every corner of the immense theatre was made up of motley materials. Every class of society was fully represented, from the highest nobility and most cultured critics to the lowest laborers. Though the greater part had come for the sake of hearing Mozart's music, yet there were hundreds whose only idea had been to see the apes and lions and other scenic wonders. When the curtain rose, these latter were at first occupied mainly with what addressed their eyes, but before the conductor's baton had swept its rhythmic beat a score of times, the scenery was forgotten,—the beautiful music, so simple and so bewitching, so rare yet so intelligible to all, had captivated their hearts. Just as on the stage the silver tones of the magic flute led captive the wildest beasts and conquered every fierce and rugged thing, so now the great composer laid his mystic sceptre over all the hearts before him, from the most cultivated to the most uncouth, by the richness and magical sweetness of his melodies.

After each Act the storm of applause was so tremendous that the house shook with it; and every thunder-peal of plaudits within the theatre was caught up and re-echoed by the thousands who stood without in the street, unable to gain entrance to the crowded building.[1]

Mozart's face, grown so wan and wearied in these last times, had again for this evening renewed its old expression of animation and energy; his cheeks glowed, his blue eyes were sparkling, his heart beat stormily with enthusiasm and delight.

And Salieri—? Half dead with envy and conscious defeat, half deaf with the infernal uproar of hands and voices to which his Trojan bodyguard, led on by Lange, treated him, he suffered the torments of the damned. For in hell most truly he was, burning with envy, and rage, and self-contempt, and impotent hate. When the curtain fell, he sank more dead than alive against his companion.

As the multitude poured out of the theatre, cheering and shouting, it was evident how the "Zauberflöte" had taken hold of the popular heart. Down the different streets went the stream of men, women, and children, and every one of them was singing, humming, or whistling the melodies of the Magic Flute.

---

[1] Historical.

CHAPTER VI.

"AND THE DAY IS FAR SPENT."

HE had finished the "Zauberflöte," given it to the world, and saved Schikaneder from bankruptcy. Now there was time and opportunity for the Requiem; and disregarding Constanze's prayer that he would rest at least a few days, Mozart began its composition with a feverish haste that had something endlessly painful in it.

"I can no longer put off the unknown person who ordered it," said Amadeus; "and besides, it constantly reproaches me that I have not long ago done something in sacred music. I cannot help feeling that this work will bring me rest and peace."

So now, day and night, went on again his toil. To this composition he devoted far more care and painstaking than ever before. He seemed to seize upon it with a sort of sacred zeal. Not only was there within him a voice that urged him on to a higher and profounder music than he had yet attempted, but he felt that he must write something for the service of religion. He had written the music of happy hearts seeking more beauty and happiness on earth; now he must write the music of broken hearts seeking divine consolation—of homesick hearts that are seeking heaven.

For Mozart was a religious man. Outwardly he was a Catholic; but he often said, that for him the rites and ceremonies of the Church were a waste of time. He was in the truest sense a Christian. The life of the man Jesus was in his estimation the noblest human life the world has known, and only those who have traced the composer's steps in the minutest details of his existence, can appreciate with what childlike simple-heartedness and self-sacrifice he followed that ideal. If he failed of perfection, which of us shall cast the first stone?

The "Zauberflöte" continued to be a most brilliant success Night after night there was the same crowded house and rapturous applause as on its first performance. It rained gold into Schikaneder's coffers.

For the first few evenings Mozart himself conducted; but soon his work on the Requiem wearied him so much, that his fainting turns became more and more common, till he was obliged to keep his room for some time.

To-night the new opera was to be again given, but Mozart sat alone in his chamber. He had vainly attempted to work in the morning, and Constanze extorted a promise from him that he would rest for this one day. It had been a sorrowful day for him, but already it was drawing to a close, and the twilight was approaching. A raw November wind beat and howled at the windows, lashing the panes with angry gusts of cold rain.

Mozart was listening, leaning back in his chair, to the onset of the wind.

A cheerless autumn evening hung over the world and over his soul.

Near him on the table burned the little lamp, and on the shelf opposite ticked wearily the monotonous clock. Constanze was in the next room, hushing to sleep the little Wolfgang with a beautiful cradle-song which the father had written for his latest born.

Everything was still as death in the chamber. Mozart's eyes rested fixedly on the clock. His thoughts were with his opera, which now was being given for the twenty-sixth time: he was following the succession of the scenes in spirit.

"Now," said he softly, while an endlessly mournful smile played about his lips—"now the first Act is at an end."

And he hears the storm of applause, which will not cease; and he thinks how his labor has made so many rich and happy, and given more beautiful moments to their lives. He imagines how they look for him in the orchestra, where another is wielding the baton which his hand has held so royally. Forth streams the sweet music into those thousands of hearts, and he, the master, is sitting here alone and weary,— thrown aside like a worn-out tool—forgotten by the hearts for whose happiness he has toiled.

Long sat Mozart with his head sunken upon his breast. At last he said, as if he would comfort himself:

"Well, well! the soul remains, and it cannot cease to be glorious to have created, and to have made others happy Ah! so gladly would I create on and on, greater and greater things! It is so beautiful, this *doing*—it is so beautiful to live!"

And Mozart sighed deeply, and sank again in thought. Ever and anon he would raise his eyes to the clock.

"Now," he murmured to himself, "they are singing the 'Isis and Osiris!'" And as he heard the grand strains swell forth in all their pomp of mystic solemnity, heard them in his own creating imagination so as no orchestral instruments or human voices can give them, the master listened intently— more and more intently; for the strains are dying away now, —not as if moving into the distance, but as though he himself were being borne from them, farther and farther—borne swooning on invisible sweeping wings away from earth, away from life.

Again his eye falls on the clock, for its pendulum suddenly beats faster, as though driven by a demon's hand—quicker and shorter for a few faint strokes; then stands silent and still.

At that moment Constanze and Abt Stadler entered the room.

Mozart drew a long breath. It was as if a mountain load had been lifted off his breast.

But Abt Stadler seemed not in his usual spirits to-night. Usually a passionless calm, kindly and cheerful, but imperturbable, characterized the good Abbe. Now, however, after a curt greeting, he commenced to pace the room as though something irritated him beyond measure.

Mozart followed his friend with his eyes for a few minutes then inquired in a tone of surprise after the cause of his unusual restlessness.

Abt was silent a moment; then stopping in front of the composer, he said—

"Dear Mozart, there are some things in this world which will upset the calmest of men. I can't stand it to see such outrageous rascality!"

"Such as what?" asked Mozart, quietly.

"Tell me," said Stadler, "did you make any contract with Schikaneder in relation to the 'Zauberflöte?'"

"No," replied Mozart. "Why?"

"Nothing whatever in writing?"

"What need of anything written between honorable men?"

"Just as I thought!" exclaimed the Abbe, and his forehead contracted in angry folds. "Always this unlucky confidence! Friend, when will you learn to be prudent? Because you are a man of your word, you think everybody else is."

"What!" said Constanze, turning pale; "Schikaneder will not—"

"What was your agreement?"

"I gave him the score of the 'Zauberflöte,'" answered Mozart, "for nothing; only I stipulated that he should not sell it to other theatres, so that in case it was successful, I could myself dispose of it in the other German cities."

"And he agreed to it?"

"Why certainly! He was delighted with my willingness to help him out of his difficulties, and agreed that I should have the whole disposal of the opera."

"And has Schikaneder, who has made a fortune already from it, paid you anything as yet?"

"Oh no!" replied Mozart; "I give it to him freely. Now, if I can sell it to one or two other theatres—"

"'*Give* it!'" exclaimed Constanze, with troubled heart; "but, dear Wolferl, think how much we need money. What we received for the 'Titus' is all gone for the old debts."

"Never mind, good heart," said Mozart, forcing a sad smile, "you mustn't be so troubled. The 'Zauberflöte' has had a success beyond all my other operas. If I can only sell it at Munich, Stuttgart, Dresden, and Berlin—"

Here Abt Stadler stamped his feet in anger on the floor, an unprecedented action with him.

"Oh yes—*if!*" he cried, and his eyes blazed with righteous indignation—"*if* Schikaneder were not a knave and a robber, and had not already sold the score to all the other theatres!"

After a long pause Mozart said quietly: "I don't believe it."

"But I know it!" replied Abt. "You sent Süssmayer to offer it to the aforesaid theatres."

"Yes!"

"Well, this is their answer. Süssmayer hadn't the courage to tell you, and I do it only to help the matter, if it can be helped. The Directors reply that they are obliged to you, but they already have the score from Schikaneder."

"It can't be!" said Constanze, overcome by this new blow. "Schikaneder is his friend, and has spent so many hours in our house, and so often expressed his friendship and gratitude, and—," but the words died on her lips; she was speechless with astonishment and grief.

Stadler paced back and forth with compressed lips and silent wrath. But Mozart only said, once for all:

" The whelp !"[1]

" Why not enter proceedings against him ?" asked Stadler.
" I will agree to manage everything."

Mozart shook his head. Then said he, turning to his wife
and his friend :

"If you love me, say no more to me about the matter.
Schikaneder is a man, as we all are. The bad is not in him,
but on him ; it is the foul garment of an originally pure soul.
The poor devils of humans are mostly good, if one only looks
at them right. All these discords and jangles in them re-
solve at last into the eternal divine harmony."

Mozart, in whose tone there had been a wonderful gentleness, was silent. Constanze rose and left the chamber un-
noticed. She must go and fling herself down by the cradle
of her sleeping darling, and weep out her trouble unseen by
any eye save His who alone could save them from the thick
darkness which seemed to her to shroud the future. Abt
Stadler was full of astonishment. What a noble soul was
this, which could receive the announcement of a friend's
treachery and villainy without its casting one shadow of
anger over him! He could have knelt at the composer's
feet and kissed his hand in reverence. A false friend had
stabbed him in the back, stabbed him mortally it almost
seemed, and he only spoke a single monosyllable of contempt,
and forgave !

And as Abt Stadler thought of this, he was himself calm
again, and forgetting all the meanness of smaller souls, he
saw before him only the nobleness of this friend, whose very
heart seemed to beat only in music—the music of endless
human love.

[1] Historical.

.

CHAPTER VII.

THE REQUIEM.

SLOWLY and solemnly died away into the deep night the bell-strokes of St. Stephen's Cathedral. It was twelve o'clock. Over the ground swept a cold and desolate autumn wind. And the wind wailed in the trees till they shuddered off the last dry leaves, which had clung but faintly and dreamily to the branches, and which flew far away to seek a grave somewhere in a corner of the distance. Through the streets of the city it went whistling and howling, so that the few whom it found there fled before it to seek shelter within protecting houses.

And once more the glittering stars stood high overhead; but their splendor was a cold and lonely one. As the wind, sweeping through the trees and along the streets, so the breath of thousands and thousands of years had swept away beneath them; and as now the autumn-blast was stripping off the withered leaves and whirling them away, no one knows whither, so the Time-storm had swept away the worlds before their eyes, and buried them like atoms in the unfathomable All. Upon these coming and vanishing worlds they had seen myriads on myriads of mortals appear and disappear, with their weal and woe, with their swiftly-fleeting pleasure and their long-consuming pain, with their being that flashed up for an instant and suddenly flashed away. Now once more they looked down, and beheld death and destruction swinging their pitiless sickle; but calmly they glittered and lightened on, for they knew that this too was but an appearance, and that there was no death and no destruction, but an eternal and inseparable life. Yet between their knowledge and that of mortals lay a sombre cloud, and even now unnumbered eyes were weeping in sick-chambers and over death-beds.

Like a vast, immeasurable churchyard lay now the world. Even Vienna,—bright, busy, luxurious Vienna, lying now in the stillness of the midnight,—seemed but some silent corner of that immeasurable churchyard, so empty and solitary were its streets; so dumb, stern, and sombre rose the houses, like towering monuments to those who but yesterday had inhabited them.

Only at rare intervals glimmered here and there from a window the twinkle of a light.

Before one such house now stood, shrinking among the shadows, a dark form. It was a woman, but so thickly veiled that no one could have recognized her, even if there had been any living being near. A heavy black cloak completely enveloped her in its ample folds, which fell quite to the ground, and even covered the head with a kind of cowl.

The night-wind swept harshly about her: she heeded it not. Persistently it plucked at her mantle: she only drew closer its heavy folds.

In this way that dark form had stood since ten o'clock. It had struck eleven—then twelve; she remained motionless in the same spot. It was an extraordinary enchantment which held her so chained. From an upper room of the house swelled forth strains of wonderful music—music that breathed an awed, unspeakable grief; music that was woven of love and sorrow and sacred tears.

There were but few instruments and few voices; but what they uttered was of unearthly sweetness.

Softly, softly—as with nameless eternal sadness and self-renunciation—it breathed forth upon the night:

"*Requiem æternam dona eis Domine! et lux perpetua luceat eis.*" *Rest everlasting grant to them, O Lord!—and light forever shine upon them.*

"*Te decet hymnus Deus in Sion, et tibi reddetur votum in Jerusalem.*

"*Exaudi orationem meam, ad te omnis caro veniet.*

"*Requiem æternam dona eis Domine! et lux perpetua luceat eis.*"

The veiled form breathlessly drank in every tone. Many a Mass for the Dead she had heard before, but never such a one as this. She listened and listened; and it seemed as if before her eyes the world were builded to a vast cathedral, and the night hung its immeasurable walls in black, and the stars were the light thereof. Then before her, out of the earth, uprose a catafalque, draped in black and surrounded with torches, and on it stood a coffin, and in the coffin lay a quiet slumberer. And all about it hundreds were kneeling, praying to God with streaming eyes and broken hearts, and from their lips arose the music—

"*Requiem æternam dona eis Domine!*"

But what is this? Is it not an angel's voice, that sweet, clear tone, shrilling out above the others, not by its strength, but by its very sweetness? Is it not St. Cecilia herself, accompanying the silver flute-note of her voice with the golden flood of the organ? Ah, no, no! That can be music of no mortal creation! Whoever wrote this, he must already have looked into the eyes of death; to him must the Almighty have granted a vision of the plains of Eternity.

The close-mantled form bends shudderingly before these thoughts. She sees the lid of the coffin on the catafalque spring open. She sees—Mozart's corpse! A cry escapes her breast: it is the bitter anguish of a woman's broken heart.

But the cry has recalled her to herself. Fearfully she looks about her. It is silent as the grave. No one has seen her—no one was there to hear. And he—? Oh, he dreams not who is standing here before the house,—who was summoned from afar by mournful intelligence, arrived but to-day, and this very night, in defiance of darkness and storm, has hastened hither, only to be once again near him in faithful love; but once again, before his light should be—who could tell how suddenly?—extinguished forever.

The music has died away, and all is still. The veiled one listens intently. Now a slight rustling sound is heard: they are going.

Quickly the form draws the cowl low over her face, gathers the cloak closer about her, and hastens toward the next street. There, giving a sign to the waiting attendant to follow, she vanishes like a shadow.

A few minutes afterward the door of Mozart's house is opened, and there come forth Abt Stadler, Süssmayer, Seyfried, Schack, Albrechtsberger, and Sophie Weber. But not laughing and jesting, as so many a time before; a deep seriousness pervades them, and their tone and manner reveal that they have been taking part in some solemnity. At Mozart's repeated and urgent request, they have rehearsed the beginning of the Requiem.

With smothered sighs they press each other's hands; and they too disappear in the darkness of the night.

—The next day was bright and beautiful. The wind

which had been so tempestuous through the night, had toward morning, gone down, and the sun rose in a pure, deep blue sky.

Who does not know those delicious autumn days, which tempt us irresistibly into the open air? The sun, already low in the north, but bright and warm, throws its last summer kisses to the earth, and the atmosphere is balmy with all spicy odors. It is the season of endless farewell—the dying-scene of Nature; and therefore for every sensitive spirit the autumn has something inexpressibly tender and sad,—except that we can look beyond the grave in which winter is burying the world, and can perceive the certainty of spring, which *must* come, and already comforts us in anticipation.

The rehearsal of the Requiem the night before had greatly shaken Mozart, in his weak condition, and Doctor Clossel, family physician, expressed strong disapprobation of it; and now he advised Constanze to take advantage of the fine weather for a short ride with her husband. The good physician felt in his heart that it might be the last time.

Constanze went immediately to send the maid after a carriage. When she returned to the chamber, she found Amadeus leaning at the window, through which the sun shone in, mild and warm. He was drumming on the panes in his old way. Turning slowly to her, he asked, almost dreamily—

"Stanzerl, why have we not been more happy, now for this long time?"

But Constanze could not answer: her grief pressed too closely on her heart. Could her husband have seen his wasted form in the mirror, all other answer would have been unnecessary.

"You are silent?" said Amadeus. "Dear heart, you have had many a trouble, I know;—trouble about money, and anxiety for this troublesome sick fellow, and then—the Requiem!"

"I don't know why *that* should trouble me," said Constanze as cheerily as she could; "except that you work too hard on it. I think we shall both be all the better off for that, if only my dear husband will have a little bit of patience, and give himself more play-spells."

Mozart shook his head, while a little smile of incredulity played about his mouth.

"Next summer," continued Constanze, putting her arm

over his shoulder, and lightly kissing his cheek and brow. "we will take a famous journey, for our health, together You shall see how the fresh air and the fun we will have wil make new folks of us. I shall get so plump, Wolferl, you've no idea!"

Mozart looked at her with such a strange, mournful tenderness in his true eyes, as he stroked the hair from her forehead, that she could scarcely fight the tears down with the smile which she must, she *would* maintain.

"It is a long way off to summer, Stanzerl!" said he. "'Tis autumn now. What a strange effect these last bright days have on one! They remind one so of the perpetual coming and going—blooming and withering—illusions and disillusions."

"Yes; but of spring also!" said Constanze, in the brightest tone which she could command; "and of all the beauty and song that it brings with it."

"But they come only for the new blossoms—the old and withered ones no longer see and hear."

"Yes, Wolferl," said his wife eagerly; "but we are not talking about blossoms. Every spring scatters the new flowers over the earth by millions. But man outlives them, season after season, if only he keeps his heart fresh and full of sunshine. I don't know," she went on, cheerfully, "somehow this changing in nature doesn't seem sad to me. Certainly everything in the world is subject to it; but isn't this very change for our greater happiness? What would the earth be without its shadow and light? In these changes I find my education. What would your little wife have been good for if she had not gone to the great school of changeful life? That is where we get all our character and energy. I think, too, that my husband has sufficiently proved that in all this change there is something enduring and immortal."

"How do you mean?"

"Are not your musical creations proofs of it?"

"Do you suppose they are to be immortal?" asked Mozart, smiling.

"No," replied Constanze, "not in the fullest sense of the word, of course. But the spirit which is in them is immortal. The beauty, the truth of them, are immortal. Your music, Wolferl, is true music—coming out of the heart, and penetrating to the heart. You have pointed out the true path of music, and given the death-blow to the cling-clang of the false Italian school. You have created a German music, and your name must endure so long as that does. Dear Wolfeil, isn't that a pleasant thought?—And then a little bird has told me that you will have some fine appointment pretty soon, with ever so much salary; and next summer you shall put all our beautiful journey into music!"

"But the Requiem must be finished first!" said Mozart, smiling mournfully.

"Why let that trouble you so?" urged Constanze. "That will soon be done, and then—"

"Stanzerl!" answered Mozart, looking down on her loving face with endless tenderness and pity, "I am writing the Requiem for myself!"[1]

CHAPTER VIII

THE ANGEL OF DEATH.

IT was the morning of the 5th of December, 1791. Over all the country the snow lay sparkling beneath a flood of bright sunshine, but through the close-drawn curtains of Mozart's chamber fell only a faint glimmer of the broad daylight without. In the stove the fire was snapping: except for this, there was perfect silence in the room, for Mozart lay sick. Yet Mozart was at work,—there could be no rest for him till the Requiem should be finished.

More and more had the conviction fastened upon him that it was for himself it must be written;—the grave over which these melodious tears are required of him, is his own. There is no longer room for doubt, for hope.

Every moment this thought has become more defined and familiar in the mind of the sick master; but the inspiration of this thought lends him supernatural strength. He writes, —and every thing else is forgotten. From now on, the night may follow the day, and the day follow the night, but for him there is only a brief remnant of time in which to finish his earthly work.

The dawn-light which again arises without bringing hope

[1] Mozart's own words

to him,—the darkness which wraps the world without giving him repose, leave him and find him always writing in the same position. There is but one idea before him—to hasten, to hasten: there is so much to be done; there is so little time.

The sheets of the Requiem have gradually been completed. It is done now as far as the *Sanctus*. But the hand of the master can no longer wield the pen. Süssmayer, his beloved scholar, sits by the bedside at his table, and writes.

Only the fire snaps in the dim, silent chamber. Mozart is lying quiet, but not asleep. His eyes are looking upward, and their changeful expression betrays that the mind is at work. Every passage of his music had to be first completed there before it was put upon paper. Still as it is about him he is hearing wonderful tones, and harmonies of immortal greatness.

Now he turns weariedly his head toward his scholar, who has been noiselessly but rapidly writing, and has just laid down his pen.

"Süssmayer," asks the soft, clear voice, "have you finished the *Quam olim* as I told you?"

"Yes, Maestro!"

"Did you put in the trumpets at the commencement?"

"Yes, just as you said."

"Let me see."

Mozart took the extended sheets and looked over them. Here and there as he read he nodded his head, and a little smile of satisfaction played on his face.

Süssmayer's looks rested lovingly, and with endless sadness, on the features of his friend. No one knew so well as he what the world was soon to lose; no one had like him had the opportunity of entering into the plans and wishes of the master. He had watched him in all these last times, and seen him holding death off with one hand while he composed with the other,—pressing on in defiance of his failing strength to complete his last great work. The score of the sublime fugue, *Quam olim*, had been just finished according to the directions and the pencilled hints of the master, and he well knew that, even while he was rapidly completing it, Mozart's tireless spirit was already busy with the *Sanctus* which should follow.

Amadeus handed the sheets of music back.

"Thank you, dear Süssmayer," said he, affectionately

"You have understood me perfectly. It is a great blessing
that I have you. If I should die before it is done, you must
finish it. You know my plan, and there in the upper drawer
are the scraps on which are sketched out the ideas for the
Benedictus and *Agnus.*"

"Speak not so, dear Maestro!" said Süssmayer. "You
shall finish it all yourself, and many another great work besides."

Mozart shook his head: "He comes too swiftly! We have
no time to lose. Hand me that sheet of music-paper,—I have
an idea for the *Dona eis.*"

Süssmayer reached him the paper and pencil.

"See here!" said Mozart; "this is the movement of the
accompaniment; it must express the majesty of death.
Then—this is for the quartette; and—you see the succession
—the angels bearing it up to God—"

But the composer's momentary animation was gone, and
he was exhausted. Motioning to his scholar to continue
writing, his head sank back and he closed his eyes.

When he awaked after half an hour's slumber, Constanze
and Sophie Weber were sitting by his bedside, as well as
Süssmayer, Stadler, and Schack.

Mozart smiled as his eyes fell upon the little group:
"You true souls!" said he. "Thank God there are some
friends who hold fast even in bad times."

"And many a one," said Constanze, "besides the few who
are here. You know that, dear Wolferl!"

"Yes, Stanzerl, I believe it!" said Mozart, looking from
one to another of the group, and holding out his hand to
each in turn. Ah, how thin and white the hand now was
which had always been so beautiful! Schack turned pale as
he took it lightly in his own: it seemed as if Death had already claimed it.

Just then there was a little knock at the door, and there
entered Seyfried and the maid. The former brought a bright
face, full of some good news: the latter brought three letters
for Mozart.

Sophie handed them to him, and he broke the seals with
tremulous fingers. As he read one after the other, his face
expressed a joyful surprise: his eyes lit up with pleasure,—
but it was only for a moment. Then he passed the small
wasted hand over his forehead, and murmured, scarcely
audibly and with unspeakable sadness—"It is too late!"

The letters slid from his relaxed grasp, and closing his eyes he sank back in Constanze's arms.

The little group of friends leaned anxiously forward, in error lest this might be the end; but no, the pendulum was not yet motionless, the hour not reached. Opening his eyes, and looking tenderly into Constanze's face, Mozart whispered to her to read the letters. The first one offered him the position of musical director of one of the first Capelles of Germany; the other two were from Pressburg and Amsterdam, giving orders for the composition of several works at a large price.

Then said Seyfried: "I too had something to tell you. The city of Vienna has elected you as Capellmeister of St. Stephen's Cathedral. Here is the decree." And Seyfried reached the paper to Mozart. The master opened it, glanced over its contents. Then the momentary joy left his eyes and they filled with tears. Shaking his head, he murmured:

"It is too late!"

A little after noon of the same day, a number of Mozart's friends were assembled in the room next to his sick-chamber. There was but little speech among them, and that was in hushed tones. There was that solemn awe upon their hearts which always pervades a house where death is awaited.

Mozart lay patient and still. No one but Constanze knew that he was suffering, in body as well as spirit: no one but himself knew what invisible comfort and support he had in those last hard hours. By-and-by he asked—

"Are some of them there?"

"Yes," answered Constanze, and she named those of his friends who were in the other room.

"Let them come in, Stanzerl," said he; "I want to hear the Requiem once."

Constanze looked inquiringly at the physician, and when Dr. Clossel nodded his consent, she left the room to call in the friends. Then she returned and took out the parts of that wonderful death-song. Süssmayer sat down at the piano, Schack sang the soprano, Hofer the tenor, Gorl the bass, and Mozart—the dying Mozart—the alto.[1]

The good physician had led Constanze into the other room, for the scene was more than she could bear. Here, weeping and sobbing, she hid her face in the pillows of the sofa

---

[1] Historical.

Then softly, softly, swelled forth that ineffable music from
the dying-room: and it was to her as if she heard far-off
angel choirs imploring at the throne of God for her darling,
her dying beloved. And bowing down her awe-stricken, desolate heart, she mingled with their prevailing voices her in-
articulate prayer.

Still went on the sweet, sorrowful, sacred death-song;—now
swelling up in its solemn pomp, as if it ushered in the very
presence of majestic Death; now breathing out the childlike
supplications of imploring hearts.

And the waves of music swept softly outward from the
dimly-lighted chamber, across the sunshine of the silent
street, and in a cold, still room they touched and thrilled
another broken heart. The window was open, notwithstanding the frosty air, that those sounds might freely enter; and
on the floor before a crucifix lay a woman's form. She had
been kneeling there till her limbs had failed from exhaustion,
and now her eyes were closed, and her wan face was pillowed
on her arm amid a wealth of dusky hair. She was clothed
all in white, but not for bridal. These were vestal robes—no
whiteness of marriage blossoms, but the snowy purity of
everlasting maidenhood. And as the sacred sorrow of the
master's death-song came fainter to her heart, she heard it
not as it thrilled that icy air,—her spirit had fled away to
Italy to take its last farewell of earth.

When the night came, it found Constanze kneeling by
Mozart's bedside; Sophie Weber stood near her, and Süssmayer sat watching the apparently sleeping face of his revered master. The chamber was silent as the grave. Only
the clock ticked softly on the shelf, as it marked the weary
hours of the passing night.

Suddenly Mozart moved one hand, as if he would find that
of Constanze, which lay near his breast. "What is it?" said
she, terrified at the look which overspread his face.

"Death!" whispered Mozart.

"Wolferl—oh, Wolferl!" cried she. "Oh leave me not!
O God—my God—let him not go from me!"

But he whispered:

"Courage, darling!—I told you—I wrote it for myself—
'tis almost done. God bless you, true wife—He has kept us
kindly, and will—'Slumbers not nor sleeps.' Forgive me the
many times—little Stanzerl—for I always loved you—my
whole heart—farewell!"

For a moment his eyes closed, and he seemed to fall away into sleep again. Presently he murmured once more:

"Constanze—keep my death secret till Albrechtsberger—can get my place."

Even in his last hour his thoughts were not for himself, but for his friends! He whom fate and men had repulsed and forgotten through his whole life, on his very death-bed was planning that his friend might receive the only gift he could leave him—his own position, which he had but that morning received.

At this moment the door opened, and Dr. Clossel entered the room. He found Mozart with a burning head, and ordered cold applications. Their effect was altogether unfavorable. The dying man seemed to lose the power of speech and motion.

Then his eyes fell once more on Süssmayer with such a meaning look, that the scholar, as if by inspiration, understood the silent glance. Bringing the score of the Requiem, he held it up before the master.

Mozart looked earnestly at it, as Süssmayer slowly turned over the leaves. When he came to the *Sanctus*, Mozart, who could no longer speak, tried to imitate the sound of the drums with his lips.

"The drums!" said Süssmayer; "I will not forget them."

Then he was restful again and closed his eyes. Slower and fainter grew the muffled drum-beats of his own heart, over which Süssmayer had laid the Requiem.

It was just midnight;—one deep, deep sigh, one stretching of the body, as for more perfect rest—the new day came, and Wolfgang Amadeus Mozart was no more.

Requiem eternam dona eis Domine! et lux perpetua luceat eis.

FINIS.

www.ingramcontent.com/pod-product-compliance
Lightning Source LLC
Chambersburg PA
CBHW021211270326
41929CB00010B/1086